A JOURNAL OF CONTEMPORARY WRITING

IRISH PAGES

IRISH PAGES is a biannual journal (Spring-Summer, Autumn-Winter), edited in Belfast and publishing, in equal measure, writing from Ireland and overseas.

Its policy is to publish poetry, short fiction, essays, creative non-fiction, memoir, essay reviews, nature-writing, translated work, literary journalism, and other autobiographical, historical, religious and scientific writing of literary distinction. There are no standard reviews or narrowly academic articles. Irish language and Ulster Scots writing are published in the original, with English translations or glosses.

IRISH PAGES is a non-partisan, non-sectarian, culturally ecumenical, and wholly independent journal. It endorses no political outlook or cultural tradition, and has no editorial position on the constitutional question. Its title refers to the island of Ireland in a purely apolitical and geographic sense, in the same manner of The Church of Ireland or the Irish Sea.

The sole criteria for inclusion in the journal is the distinction of the writing and the integrity of the individual voice. Equal editorial attention will be given to established, emergent and new writers.

The views expressed in IRISH PAGES are not necessarily those of the Editors. The magazine has no editorial or financial connection to the Linen Hall Library or its Directors.

Submissions are welcome but must be accompanied by a stamped addressed envelope or an international reply coupon. Reporting time is six months. If work is accepted, a copy on disk may be requested.

Your subscription is essential to the independence and survival of the journal. Subscription rates are £16stg/€26/$24 for one year, or £24/€39/$36 for two years. For postage outside Ireland and Britain, add £4/€6/$5 per year for Europe, or £6/€9/$8 per year for the rest of the world. A subscription form is at the end of the magazine. Credit cards are welcome.

IRISH PAGES
The Linen Hall Library
17 Donegall Square North
Belfast BT1 5GB

IRISH PAGES is designed by Tonic and set in 11.5/12.5 Monotype Perpetua. It is printed in Belfast by Nicholson & Bass.

This issue has been generously funded by the Arts Council of Northern Ireland.

ISBN 0-9544257-3-1

A JOURNAL OF CONTEMPORARY WRITING

IRISH PAGES

CHRIS AGEE, *Editor*

CATHAL Ó SEARCAIGH, *Irish Language Editor*

SEÁN MAC AINDREASA, *Managing Editor*

EDITED AT THE LINEN HALL LIBRARY IN BELFAST

SPRING / SUMMER 2003

IRISH PAGES

—

VOLUME 2, NUMBER 1, SPRING / SUMMER 2003

CONTENTS

Camp Boundary, by Paul Seawright

THE VIEW FROM THE LINEN HALL

In the midst of Boston's financial district stands the Old State House, once the headquarters of British rule in North America. Overshadowed by skyscrapers, this edifice of pitched roof and sashed window seems small for a centre of power, even in the 18th century. Still empanelled in the brickwork of the seaward gable is the gold regalia of the Lion and the Unicorn – of the sort one sees within the walls of Edinburgh Castle, or the grounds of the Tower of London – as well as an Anglican-style clock swagged with a wreath. A ways below is the narrow balcony from which The Declaration of Independence was first read to the populace of Boston. The distinctly European air of the building is an apt metaphor for the New World's severed umbilicus to the Old.

Nor has the surrounding palimpsest of Colonial Boston been wholly effaced. A stone's throw from the Old State House (admittedly, a long one) is Old South Meeting House, where Sam Adams, patriot and rabble-rouser, mustered, in 1775, a crowd of 5,000 – in modern Boston terms, hundreds of thousands – to rail against the mounting indignities of the colonial regime. Nearby streets bear the names *Milk*, *Water*, *East India Wharf*. Over the rise of the original hill lies the Boston Common, where the first witch in North America, an Irishwoman, was hung; and where, on the crest of the same hill, the gold dome of the Massachusetts Capitol now surveys the pleasant scene. Facing the Legislature, in turn, at one corner of the park, is St Gaudens' nineteenth-century bronze bas-relief, the Shaw Memorial, commemorating a Massachusetts Negro regiment in the Civil War, whose iconography was made famous by Robert Lowell in his mid-sixties state-of-the-nation poem, "For the Union Dead".

As this imagery suggests, the basic political and cultural landscape of America, both daily and symbolic, remains resolutely rooted in the town, the city and the State. In comparison, the federal – or the "federal-imperial", as it may now need to be called – constitutes a more remote, less lived-in landscape of power and meaning. Outside the great federal swathes of Washington and Virginia, its constitutional branches and bureaucratic manifestations, its monuments and necropolises, the actual physical presence of the national government in American daily life is more episodic and centripetal: a Lilliputian weave of federal buildings, courts, banks, bases and so on binding together the great continental Gulliver that is the United States. Inhabiting no one place fully, the federal cynosure is, necessarily, most intensely present in that epitome of placelessness, the national media. As with other federations – historical or contemporary; imperial, communist or democratic – the power of the centre may irradiate all, but it cannot attain to the foundational quality of the units that comprise its *raison d'etat*.

After a century and a half at the periphery of Empire, Americans like Sam Adams grew sick of the bad marriage between a distinctly evolved continental identity and the imperial highhandedness of a remote capital. For much of the élite and probably most of the European population – a population the size of contemporary Ireland, or Shakespeare's England – it became seasonable to ask if a form of independent government could not be devised to reflect the growing confidence of a long-established society in its cultural distinctiveness. Thus was born (though, forever, over-egged by the rhetoric of American politics) not only a first and truly revolutionary template for modern republican government, soon impacting on France and Ireland, but also the beginnings (not much egged, at all, these days) of what would evolve into a no less revolutionary principle, "the right of national self-determination".

Out of imperial succession came republican federation; out of the victory of a then-small people over European empire, the rise to global superpower. To the Irish eye especially, the intimate scale of the American Revolution, long obscured by the Brobdingnagian expansion of the United States, will have a certain atmospheric familiarity. The plaques in Dublin commemorating the fallen of the Easter Rising are not so far-removed from those in Boston telling passers-by of the events of the Revolutionary period, or marking the walls of graveyards where patriot leaders are buried. Much of the Declaration of Independence, penned by Jefferson, is a cleverly personalized diatribe against the abuses of the King, whereas the colonial élite's real grievance was against the "Crown in Parliament," the untrammelled sovereignty of Westminster. In cognate fashion a section of the Anglo-Irish élite turned its back on Empire in the decades preceding Irish independence. Pearse was no Jefferson, but he too penned a Proclamation and had it read under the nose of British rule.

In the final republican arrangements that emerged from American independence, the twin constitutional pillars of the new system can be seen as the quintessential expression of the colonists' long struggle with the overweening power of an imperial Parliament. *The separation of powers* sets up a series of "checks and balances" by which power is dispersed between the legislative, executive and judicial branches, thereby ending the single all-powerful "Crown in Parliament"; while *the division of powers*, or federalism, specifies the respective powers given to the federal government and the States, reserving all unspecified powers to the people. Whereas the first might be said to constitute the foreground workings of the American Republic, the second, the deep background architecture, has been the fulcrum for its moments of greatest internal and constitutional struggle: the Civil War, the New Deal era, and the Civil Rights Movement. However submerged by the power of the federal centre, the role of the States remains central to the system's genius for equilibrium, which is, of course, the symbolic meaning of the national flag. In the matter of federalism especially, the Constitution reflects the indelible anti-colonial bias of the American Republic.

But what happens if, in the phrase of one contributor to this issue, "the New Imperial Symphony" (Askold Melnyczuk) becomes the controlling variable in the federal algebra? How will the constitutional equilibrium fare if the federal power has indeed reached a Rubicon moment, embracing explicitly the oxymoron of an imperial republic? If the United States is now at "a radical, a very radical, turning point — possibly the moment when the Republic may have ended, and the Empire begun" (Susan Sontag)?

Even five years ago, the idea that the troubled history of the North of Ireland might have some political lessons for the vastness of the United States would have seemed far-fetched indeed. True, like the rest of the island, Northern Ireland at its best could offer some salutary correctives about the comparative strengths of smaller cultures and polities, especially in the matter of community, democracy and national distinctiveness. But, in truth, the political traffic was all in the other direction. From its zone of multicultural and metropolitan stability, seemingly insulated against the religio-national conflicts dogging the Old World, the Clinton Administration was the presiding international genius that helped usher the Good Friday Agreement into being. If the North communicated, in the opposite direction, any widely-received messages, these were mainly a litany of negatives. *Here be dragons ... The mix of sectarianism, nationalism, provincialism, terror and counter-terror is truly incendiary ... It took decades to escape ... Do not go down our road ...* And so on.

How the mighty are fallen. Now even the dogs in the streets of Belfast could give a political lesson or two to President Bush concerning his War on Terror. Anyone who has intellectually bought into the new Northern dispensation will recognize the tenor of its commonsense mantras.

That terrorism can never be defeated, fully, by purely military means. That extremist politicians of all hues can insert their pre-existing agendas by piggybacking on "the politics of the latest atrocity". That a common foe unites the strangest of violent bedfellows. That democratic authoritarians will be glad to curb the liberties in which secretly they never much believed. That the cycle of terror and counter-violence is, in own terms (often deeply personalized), a machine of perpetual motion. That the control of language through the media is decisive in such conflicts and cannot be granted, *carte-blanche*, to the major political and military actors. That "seeing like a state" – the perspectives of politicians-turned-state-functionaries, simplifying the political algebra – should never be confused with reality. That reality itself, to echo Yeats, can express itself in contradiction, as in the simultaneity of *liberation from* and *occupation by*. That, from the standpoint of the innocent dead, there is no difference between terrorist intention and collateral acceptance. And so on – and on.

In a famous formulation, the German sociologist Max Weber defined the state as "the *legitimate* monopoly of violence". That adjective is crucial and, of course, it flows in the modern period from democracy. Let us consider, then, where Weber's definition leads us in the new theatre of American imperial ambition, the aftermath of the Second Gulf War.

Is the Iraqi Occupation legitimate? Hardly. Legally speaking, of course, it is completely outside the UN system of international law, and belongs, even within American law, to the constitutional penumbra of "inherent" presidential powers. The justification flows, rather, from the internal dynamic of American exceptionalism described brilliantly by Michael Foley in his contribution, "America and the World". Thus it can be persuasively argued that the American Occupation and, for that matter, the Iraqi insurgency, have no clear democratic legitimacy.

What is now emerging in Iraq is a Hobbesian freefall, wrapped up in abstract homilies about freedom and democracy. The insurgency clearly has substantial passive support, and probably includes major tribal and nationalist dimensions well beyond the Baathist remnants and foreign Islamacists. Moreover, even the Bush Adminstration acknowledges the principle of Iraqi sovereignty, inseparable by definition from the right of national self-determination. To accept the separation of sovereignty from the reality of self-determination, which is the actual Occupation strategy – the Devil in the detail – amounts to a quintessential piece of imperial thinking. For one thing cannot be gainsaid, from the democratic point of view: the exercise of sovereignty and self-determination must belong to the polity or people in question, and no one else. For the classic expression of this idea we have no less an authority than Thomas Jefferson in the opening paragraph of The Declaration of Independence.

More than the pre-emptive invasion itself, the Occupation of Iraq is now a real war: Vietnam Redux, a well-calculated mixture of IRA tactics and Viet Cong insurgency. Probably, in the near term, the only question is whether the violence will settle into a sort of Arab Northern Ireland, a low-intensity conflict with "acceptable levels" of violence; a brutal Israeli-style occupation of Arab lands involving an escalating cycle of terror and counter-terror; or an American replay of Soviet Afghanistan, in which erstwhile Islamicist freedom-fighters once worthy of Western support are re-designated mindless terrorists to whom no sanctuary could ever be given. Quite conceivably, all three scenarios might pan out: Northern Ireland for the Arab-Kurdish North; Palestine for the Shia South; Afghanistan for the Sunni Triangle. This descent into further chaos might, in turn, be the antechamber to the mother of all dénouements, a Mesopotamian Yugoslavia. (Not so improbable as it might seem, when one recalls that both states were created at the same time, out of the wreckage of the two ends of the Ottoman Empire.) The blowback from any of these unravellings would strengthen the dangerous idea of "a clash of civilizations" between the West and the Muslim world, to say nothing of the potential havoc an endless war on terror could wreak on global civil liberties. Exactly, of course, what the Islamicist Frankenstein seeks: understanding all too well the asymmetrical advantages of small groups acting against Great Powers.

The Occupation of Iraq is also a highly decisive war, perhaps more so even than Vietnam, a single chapter in the long Cold War saga. It may determine the immediate fate of the neo-conservative project for an aggressively imperial Republic. The current Administration is best understood not as a conservative faction in any historical sense, but as right-wing world-transformers deploying "revolutionary power" in an almost Napoleonic manner. Clyde Prestowitz, a writer of impeccable conservative credentials, has described its theorists thus: "The imperial project of the so-called neo-conservatives is not conservatism at all but radicalism, egotism and adventurism articulated in the stirring rhetoric of traditional patriotism...Real conservatives have never been messianic or doctrinal." Perhaps it is this element of evangelical, world-transforming mission that accounts for Tony Blair's enthusiastic participation. Still more puzzling is the impression he gives of having failed to assimilate, in regard to Iraq, despite its long history of anti-colonial nationalism, the lessons of his own Irish statecraft.

The siren-song of an emboldened Pax America has also enchanted some unlikely intellectual fellow-travellers. Writers of real repute, like Christopher Hitchens and Michael Ignatieff, have been in the forefront of endorsing the beneficent outcomes of American superpower. Now that the UN has been disregarded, and the threat of weapons of mass destruction proved chimerical, their case rests wholly on the state-building argument. It has, undeniably, the compelling logic of noble outcomes. Apart from the crucial issue of illegitimacy, what makes one balk, then, at their paper scenario of *war + reconstruction = human rights & democracy*?

For one thing, if politics is a sequence of calculated equations – motives, means, effects – then we are entitled to study the variables, in order to factor out those which are peripheral to the real dynamic. That is why parallels with other times and places are so telling, and not just a counsel of perfection. We can see, for instance, that Bosnia's overwhelming claim to a human rights intervention was cancelled out for years by the lack of Great Power strategic interests; or that UN resolutions, when it comes to Israel, simply vanish in a puff of American politics. War, in this light, reminds one of Hannah Arendt's quip that the hypocrite's crime is to bear false witness against himself.

For another, "seeing like a state" in the Iraqi context is high-octane danger. It seems that the lessons of Orwell in Burma, or Forster in India, must be learnt afresh. Empire-building is not merely the bureaucratic execution of the high-modernist belief in the re-ordering of society by the state, which caused so many revolutionary and ecological calamities in the last century. It is also an actual interface with the intractable stuff of humanity: lives, kinships, traditions, cultures, histories, worldviews. That is one reason why home-grown revolutions are to be preferred. In this sense, the arrival of Pentagon office-think amongst an ancient people has already precipitated a complete disaster.

Finally, not only is war an addiction, it defaults, inescapably, to inertial ambitions. Power abhors a vacuum and the power, in this case, is the American military and economy. In short, Saddam was *then*, but the Americans are *now*.

Even if the case for humanitarian intervention argued by neo-liberal intellectuals were valid on its own terms, defence of the Republic would be justification enough to demur on the grounds that the imperial project threatens the Constitution's long-term health. Every democratic polity has the right to defend its constitutional bases. Indeed, empires have often been undermined from within, from Ireland, to Austria-Hungary, to the Soviet Union, despite the siren song of their apologists. Even now, despite all the planning exercises, global Pentagon power depends, ultimately, and quite imponderably, on the political quiescence of the homeland. Will the federal power get this, if the imperial project stretches on decade after violent decade?

The emerging struggle between the new empire-builders (neo-con, neo-liberal, whatever) and the conservers of the inherited American Republic may prove as titanic in scale and duration as the Slavery Question (slavery being a kind of internal empire), which relentlessly overwhelmed the country in the first half of the nineteenth century. Not that the great taboo of American politics, secession, is at all in question; but the thing it expressed, a long-term crisis between the centre and the States, is entirely conceivable in the light of the upheavals of American history.

PERFORMANCES

(from a new play)

—

Brian Friel

The work's the thing. Or is it?

The composer Leos Janacek's work-room in Brno, Moravia. The décor, furnishings, curtains, etc are all in the style of the twenties. A functional, bachelor's room. A wood-burning stove, unlit. A piano, work-table and chairs.

It becomes evident very early in the play that Janacek is long dead. Anezka is an eager young woman who is doing her PhD on the later work of Janacek — and Janacek is the elusive interviewee.

Janacek wrote his String Quartet No. 2 — Intimate Letters *as he called it — over a period of three weeks in January/February, 1928. He was then in his seventy-fourth year. He died on 12 August, 1928.*

Time — the present.

A few minutes into the play:

ANEZKA	Because there must be a connection between the private life and the public work, Mr. Janácek.
JANAEK	Must there?
ANEZKA	Oh yes. Don't you think so? And I believe a full appreciation of the quartet isn't possible unless all the circumstances of its composition are considered — and that must include an analysis of your emotional state at that time — and these letters provide significant evidence about that.
JANACEK	Mightn't this kind of naïve scrutiny have frightened off your little statistician? — *(Instant regret)* — apologies.
ANEZKA	In fact that is really the core of my thesis, Mr. Janacek: the relationship between the writing of that piece and those passionate letters from a 74-year old man to a woman almost 40 years younger than him — a married woman with two young sons — and what I hope to suggest — of course with your approval — is my belief that your passion for Kamila Stösslova certainly had a determining effect on that composition and indeed on that whole remarkable burst of

creative energy at the very end of your life – probably caused it for heaven's sake – because it was a most astonishing blossoming – you must agree it was, Mr. Janacek? – and only six months away from your death.

JANACEK   Known by the rabble as the condemned man's final erection as he mounts the scaffold. And this "only six months away" – is this mischievous count-down necessary?

ANEZKA   And I will try to show that when you wrote this quartet – *Intimate Letters* – you call it that yourself when you were head-over-heels in love with her – that's the word you use to her – my thesis will demonstrate that the second string quartet is a text-book example of a great passion inspiring a great work of art and it will prove that work of art to be the triumphant apotheosis of your entire creative life.

JANACEK   Gracious me.

ANEZKA   And I intend to draw parallels between your story and the story of the other classical passions – Dante and Beatrice – Petrarch and Laura – and I must confess to you, Mr. Janacek – and I have lived with this material for over two years – I have got to tell you it is a story that breaks my heart into tiny fragments and at the same time sends it soaring exultantly.

JANACEK   Poor abused heart.

ANEZKA   (*Delving into the letters*) Bear with me for another second, Mr. Janacek, please. "I have just finished the adagio" – that's the second movement –

JANACEK   Really?

ANEZKA   Exactly. "And it is all about you, my sun, my galaxy of stars, and how our very first meeting set my soul ablaze with the most exquisite melodies" – And then he goes into that stuff about being enslaved – I quoted it to Ruth – nonsense about being her slave forever – "And this will be our composition because it will be quick with our passion, and our mutual love will bear it in glory up into the heavens".

JANACEK   Along with your abused heart.

ANEZKA   Then when you begin the third movement –

JANACEK   The moderato.

ANEZKA   Exactly, Mr. Janacek – you write to tell her about the lullaby you are weaving into it – Ruth just played it – a haunting filigree theme repeated twice – "because I want to hint at the idea of motherhood" – that's something you keep coming back to – motherhood – Kamila pregnant with the child of your passion – "so that the work will be seen as the consummation of all our desires". Freudian crap – pardon me – but deeply, deeply moving.

JANACEK   That at least. Now take a deep breath and listen to this, Anezka.

ANEZKA   Then when you come to the final movement –

JANACEK   The allegro.

ANEZKA   Exactly, Mr. Janacek – then you wrote to Kamila: "The last movement is charged with energy and defiance" – interesting word that, "defiance" – suggestion of opposition around, maybe even hostility – but from whom? Zdenka Janackova? – Mr Stossel? – you give me no hint – tantalizing – "But it is a movement without fear; just a great longing and something like a fulfillment of that longing". Don't quite understand that.

JANACEK   (*Quietly*) Listen.

ANEZKA   "I am calling the piece *Intimate Letters*. And as I wrote it I trembled with such joy, such happiness, that every bar is a proclamation of my desire for you" – you're doing rewrites at this point, February 20, 1928 – "because my whole creative life takes its heart-beat from you".

JANACEK   May I, Anezka?

ANEZKA   "Because you, Kamila, Kamila my love, you are my very essence and without you I cannot exist". The work and the life. Inextricable. Indistinguishable. Identical. (*Softly*) I'm sorry, Mr. Janacek. I get a little bit…. I just find it all so…

JANACEK   Listen to this.

ANEZKA   Sorry.

JANACEK   This is the last thing I ever wrote.

ANEZKA   (*Excited again*) In your holiday house. In Hukvaldy.

JANACEK   In Hukvaldy.

He begins playing I'll Wait for You.

ANEZKA   You and Kamila were along there – at last.

JANACEK   (*Quietly*) We were. Yes. A time of frenzy. Violence even. Despair too. And then when all that ferment was about to overwhelm me – a few minutes of sudden peace – no longer – an amnesty sent from above maybe; and this fragment came to me, a little melodic tendril. Trivial, I know. But I remember placing those limpid notes on the page with such care, so delicately, as if they were fragile. And I remember thinking: simplicity like this, innocence like this, that's closer to the heart of it, isn't it? – that's what you should have listened for all your life and not now at the frantic end. It stops in mid-sentence. Listen. (*He illustrates*) Almost with expectation, as if it were holding its breath for a conclusion to be offered. And I remember thinking: if he could sing, maybe Adam sang something like this to Eve. (*Laughs*) Or maybe, Anezka, maybe it wasn't simplicity at all. Maybe at that point the old composer was finally threadbare. And he called it *I'll Wait For You*. Silly title: his time had run out by then.

ANEZKA   No, no, you're wrong. You didn't die for another –

JANACEK   Being grisly again? You're right of course: he did love her.

ANEZKA   Over seven hundred letters, Mr. Janacek. I know so well.

JANACEK   Adored her – so he told himself.

ANEZKA   Such a pity she insisted you destroy most of her letters to you.

He jumps to his feet. He is suddenly brisk again.

JANACEK   Forever vigilant of her good name. A slave to small-town tyrannies. Anyhow, writing letters – for God's sake writing a grocery-list – sent her into a panic. (*Whispers*) Between ourselves – practically illiterate. (*Aloud*) As for my music, what I was reaching for – altogether beyond her sympathies. What you must understand is that Mrs. Stosslova was a woman of resolute ... ordinariness. Wasn't he a real pig.

ANEZKA   I just know you did love her.

JANACEK   But that's what you're thinking, isn't it? Aren't all artists users. If I sit too long I get a pain in this leg. Artery trouble. That's where it all began. (*Heart*) Have some lettuce. I live on lettuce and water ever since that bout of shingles. Miraculous stuff. What's keeping these people?

Ireland's foremost playwright, Brian Friel was born in Omagh, Co Tyrone in 1929 and now lives in Greencastle, Co Donegal. Performances, his 27th play, was first staged on 30 September, 2003 at the Gate Theatre, Dublin. He is also the author of three volumes of short stories. This extract is published courtesy of the author and The Gallery Press.

DESCRIPTIVE FOUNDATIONS

Maxine Sheets-Johnstone

Darwinian bodies – and the languaging of experience.

I

"No foundation all the way down the line. "These words are uttered several times over in the course of William Saroyan's play *The Time of Your Life* by an otherwise near-mute character. The words could be uttered with equal conviction by a social constructionist to a foundationalist or by a foundationalist to a social constructionist, the charge of the social constructionist being a denial of anything foundational, the charge of the foundationalist being a denial of anything foundational about the social constructionist's denial. From an evolutionary perspective, I believe the truth of the matter lies in the acknowledgment that what is evolutionarily given is culturally reworked in multiple and intricate ways, and in the corollary acknowledgment that our task as educators and as academic explorers is to inquire into both the foundations of our humanness and their cultural translations. I described this inquiry several years ago in the following way:

> [T]he difficult task that lies before us, perhaps particularly now, at the tag-end of a fractious and fractionating twentieth century, is to delineate the ways in which cultures differentially rework the heritage that is our common evolutionary heritage. The rewards of this difficult and patient work will be to understand in the most fundamental senses what is pan-cultural and what is idiosyncratically cultural, not in order to have the differences between the two identified as some abstract bits of knowledge to add to our lore, but to appreciate in our bones and behaviors what it is to be the particular animate form and gendered bodies that we are. *(The Roots of Power: Animate Form and Gendered Bodies*, Open Court Publishing, 1994)

Let me begin by pinpointing a few foundational aspects of our pan-cultural human nature. Animation is foundational; bipedality is foundational; concepts deriving from the body – hunger, sleepiness, itchiness, hotness, coldness, thirst, pain, for example – are foundational; kinetic qualia – qualities of movement such as expansive, constricted, forceful, weak, straight, curved, diagonal, slow, fast, attenuated, abrupt, collapsing – are foundational; movement patterns developing in the course of infancy and childhood – both individual movements such as reaching, babbling, crying, and walking, and socio-relational movements such as joint attention, imitation, smiling, and turn-taking – are foundational. Foundational aspects of human nature derive from what is evolutionarily given. They testify to the fact that we are first and foremost Darwinian bodies, bodies that are at once the source of corporeal concepts and of an intercorporeal semantics.

Nonhuman animals are no less Darwinian bodies than we human ones. Darwin described these bodies far more extensively than he described human bodies. He described them not in ways that diminished them, but as the living individuals they are, that is, as morphologically and behaviorally distinct creatures – what might be called *animate forms*. His painstaking, worldwide observations of nonhuman animals led him to conclude that mental powers and emotions evolved no less than morphologies. He thus described how nonhuman animals are attentive to things in their environment; how some are curious; how some have the capacity for language; how some imitate other members of their species; how some remember past happenings and modify their future behavior accordingly; how many of them imagine, as is evident from movements and sounds made while sleeping, i.e., while dreaming; how some reason; how some are more intelligent than others within the same species; how some use weapons and tools. Darwin's writings are in fact studded with remarks about the acuity and feelings of nonhuman animals. His many detailed accounts include the following observations, the first paradigmatic of emotions, the second paradigmatic of reasoning:

> The fact that the lower animals are excited by the same emotions as ourselves [he observes] is so well established, that it will not be necessary to weary the reader by many details. Terror acts in the same manner on them as on us, causing the muscles to tremble, the heart to palpitate, the sphincters to be relaxed, and the hair to stand on end.

> Animals may constantly be seen to pause, deliberate, and resolve. (*The Descent of Man and Selection in Relation to Sex,* 1871)

Moreover his detailed studies include reference to the whole of the animal kingdom, observations of invertebrates as well as vertebrates. Speaking in a section on the development of mental faculties with respect to increasing brain size, he draws an analogy between the extraordinary size of the cerebral ganglia of ants and the extraordinary size of the human brain. "It is certain," he states,

> that there may be extraordinary mental activity with an extremely small absolute mass of nervous matter: thus the wonderfully diversified instincts, mental powers, and affections of ants are generally known, yet their cerebral ganglia are not so large as the quarter of a small pin's head. . . . [T]he brain of an ant is one of the most marvellous atoms of matter in the world, perhaps more marvellous than the brain of man. (*The Descent of Man and Selection in Relation to Sex*, 1871)

He furthermore observes what Swiss biologist Adolph Portmann terms "inwardness." Speaking of how dogs in general like to go walking and describing antithetical postures and feelings of his own dog depending upon the path chosen for a walk, he recounts how initially the dog "showed his pleasure by trotting gravely before me with high steps, head much raised, moderately erected ears, and a tail carried aloft but not stiffly," and then how, at a possible turning point in the walk, the dog's initial posture and feelings might change. "Not far from my house," he writes,

> a path branches off to the right, leading to the hothouse, which I used often to visit for a few moments, to look at my experimental plants. This was always a great disappointment to the dog, as he did not know whether I should continue my walk; and the instantaneous and complete change of expression which came over him as soon as my body swerved in the least towards the path . . . was laughable. His look of dejection was known to every member of the family, and was called his *hothouse face*. This consisted in the head drooping much, the whole body sinking a little and remaining motionless; the ears and tail falling suddenly down, but the tail was by no means wagged. With the falling of the ears and of his great chaps, the eyes became much changed in appearance, and I fancied that they looked less bright. His aspect was that of piteous, hopeless dejection. . . . Every detail in his attitude was in complete opposition to his former joyful yet dignified bearing. (*The Expression of Emotions in Man and Animals*, 1872)

These various descriptive accounts of nonhuman animals leave no doubt but that Darwinian bodies are no mere automatons. Further, they leave no doubt but that Darwin was a keen observer of nature – actually, of plants as well as animals. Further still, it is clear from these various descriptive accounts that Darwin's *experience* of nature was neither anthropocentrically biased nor anthropomorphically inclined. His experience was objective in the best and even proper sense: it was unsullied by pretensions; it was unfettered by theory, most specifically, theory in advance of evidence; it was genuinely inquisitive; it was motivated by a genuine respect for all forms of life.

Now while it is common to speak laudingly of the keenness and scope of Darwin's observations, it is not commonly recognized, certainly not explicitly, that his observations, as written, *describe his experiences*. His observations are in fact equivalent to his experiences in the sense that they detail what he saw, felt, heard, smelled, and even tasted. Though focal attention is consistently – one might even say, exclusively – riveted on his theory of natural selection, Darwin's *descriptive* writings are of fundamental significance, for it is these descriptive writings that ground his theory, that are its foundation. More broadly, all evolutionary understandings and explanations of Nature are in the end tethered to this experientially-derived descriptive literature. In other words, Nature is explained – the basic theory of natural selection arises – only in light of observable evidence, evidence that Darwin lays out in detailed *descriptive* terms for the reader. Reading this literature, we learn a good deal about nonhuman animals. We learn that they are perceptive, thoughtful, and affectively moved by creatures and things in their environment, and we learn further, that their perceptive, affective, and thoughtful ways are intimately related to our own.

In sum, Darwin's descriptive accounts of the natural living world reveal something about the lives of others and in turn reflect something about our own lives.

I highlight the *descriptive* foundations of evolutionary theory in part because these descriptive foundations have fallen by the wayside, particularly in the highly visible present-day writings on evolution by sociobiologists and cognitive scientists. When I noted earlier that Darwinian bodies are not automatons, I could have added "as per Descartes," and gone on to point out that neither are Darwinian bodies robots lumbering about on behalf of selfish genes, as per latter-day scientists wedded to sociobiological theory, nor are they head-end neurological mechanisms, as per cognitivists of all stripe who collapse bodies into brains. Darwinian bodies are out there in the world for all to see. We have only to open our eyes. Opening our eyes, we experience them and the whole of nature, the natural world. I am highlighting the descriptive foundations of evolutionary theory to call attention equally to experience, specifically to the fact that descriptive foundations are themselves grounded in experience. Descriptive foundations do not come by way of reducing the living world to genes, collapsing it into brains, or modeling it along the lines of a computer. Descriptive foundations are laid by way of direct experience of the living world. Only by hewing to experiences of that world have we the possibility of arriving at veridical descriptive accounts of nature, and in turn, arriving at explanations of nature, theoretical constructs, and the like.

In what follows, I would like to clarify and amplify these thoughts along two distinct lines. The first line concerns phenomenology and Darwinian evolutionary biology. I turn to phenomenology for three inter-related reasons: like Darwinian evolutionary biology, it too is tethered to experience and is basically a descriptive project; it is methodologically essential to understandings of human nature; and again, like evolutionary biology, it too is concerned with origins. I will very briefly characterize these aspects of phenomenology in preface to sketching focal concerns of an evolutionary semantics and to specifying how an evolutionary semantics exemplifies basic accords between Darwinian evolutionary biology and phenomenology. In this context I will also pinpoint more explicitly – by way of acknowledging the critical importance of descriptive foundations – how certain present-day versions of evolutionary theory compromise Darwin's original insights. I will then follow up on the second line of thought, elaborating the claim that ecocritical literature is basically of a piece with Darwin's writings, not just in terms of an obvious mutual focus on Nature, but more deeply in terms of offering descriptions of nature, and in so doing, answering to the challenge of languaging experience, a challenge that is common to both literatures but distinctive in each case. In essence, what I hope to do by pursuing these two lines of thought is show how there are indeed foundations, all the way down the line, and that these foundations undergird what we otherwise think of and in fact separate academically as disparate fields of knowledge.

II

Phenomenological analyses are descriptive analyses of experience. It is presumably for this reason that phenomenology has of late been accorded a foot in the cognitivist's door. Formerly, all one found behind the door was a cerebral mall displaying a variety of offerings: nervous systems or parts thereof – frontal lobes, for example, or selected neurons; algorithmic formulae; brain imaging programs of various kinds; hypothetical brain modules; hypothetical brains in vats; hypothetical entities like cognitive maps, feature analyzers, and autonomous response planners; and of course that perdurable hard-core item, the computer. Experience was nowhere around. To be more precise, the *behavior* of the cognitivist's hardware and software was investigated, fantasied, postulated, or programmed behind the door, but whatever the behavior, it was not equivalent to experience. Behavior is in fact a category of experience and in that conceptual sense is parasitic on experience, first-person experience.

Now in order to do justice to the complexity of first-person experience, phenomenology requires that a certain methodology be followed, a methodology that in the first place requires bracketing, or putting out of gear everyday assumptions, beliefs, and the like that epistemically color and shape what is actually there, sensuously present in experience. The first step is thus something of a cleansing procedure, akin perhaps to washing one's hands and putting on special gloves prior to surgery. The purpose is to de-contaminate oneself of bugs – doxic in the phenomenological case, toxic in the surgical case – that have taken up home in or on us and that we easily transfer to any objects with which we interact. The result for the phenomenologist is to make the familiar strange, to greet it as for the first time, in order retrospectively to understand how what was once strange came to be familiar, that is, meaningful in the ways it now is. Phenomenological analyses and descriptions thus take us back to origins; we come to understand how, in Husserl's words, things come to have the meaning and value they do. Analyses disclose processes of sense-making at the core of experience. Descriptions of how we make sense of the world – how we put it together – elucidate a process of constitution: we do not *create* the world; we *constitute* it in the course of our experiences of it. In the most fundamental sense, we constitute it via our bodies. Our bodies are semantic templates. Hence it is not surprising that fundamental human concepts are corporeal concepts, and that concepts in the nonhuman animal world are equally corporeal concepts.

However different their methodologies, phenomenology and Darwinian evolutionary biology are both concerned with origins. I documented the convergent concern initially in *The Roots of Thinking* by presenting eight paleoanthropological case studies ranging from an analysis of the origin of stone tool-making and the origin of counting, to the origin of hominid sexual signalling behavior, the origin of language, the origin of the concept of death, and the origin of paleolithic cave art, showing in each instance how the body was the source of concepts central to each invention, discovery, or practice. Understandings of origins are crucial to understandings of human nature, to human self-understandings. On the one hand, however much attention is given to answering two of the three basic questions of biology — *how does it work?* and *what is its survival value?*—it cannot make up for a failure to address the third question, the question of origins: how did such and such come to be? On the other hand, however many socio-historical specifics are amassed, they can never make up for an ignorance of origins, and thus can never illuminate the foundations of human nature. Socio-historical specifics indeed take for granted the very things to be explained as fundamental to humankind: language, counting, and drawing, for instance, unless, of course, one takes these human capacities not as hominid inventions or discoveries but as *deus ex machina* creations.

A neglect of origins is particularly telling with respect to the invention of verbal language. Consider, for example, that one of the conditions of possibility of verbal language rests on an awareness of oneself as a sound-maker. Corresponding to this awareness, and hence condition, are certain lingual powers, both tactile and articulatory. Short of the awareness and of the corresponding powers, an articulated verbal language could hardly have been invented. In other words, a voice must be discovered and with it, a world of possible lingual and sublingual movements and positions that create a world of possible sonances of varying pitches, textures, amplitudes, and so on. Clearly, ancestral hominids would have had to have made such tactile/aural discoveries before a verbal language could be invented. Moreover their invention was necessarily contingent on tactile-kinesthetic invariants. If verbal language was to have a fixed place in an individual's world and if it was in fact part of a shared world, a *social* phenomenon, then a common body of experience was requisite, a common body of movement possibilities and capacities, precisely in the form of species-specific tactile-kinesthetic invariants.

Phenomenological findings such as these about the origin of language are properly part of an evolutionary semantics, a semantics that, in elucidating how meanings are corporeally created and generated across the whole of the animal kingdom, takes into account an extraordinarily diverse range of phenomena. An evolutionary semantics includes form values (morphological patternings, colorations, and so on) and animate values (postural, gestural, or otherwise kinetic patterns that articulate particular kinds of social relationships such as invitations, threats, and reassurances, or which are affectively expressive of feelings such as fright, sadness, surprise, and so on); it includes signalling behaviors (sexual and otherwise) and what ethologists commonly call "displays"; it includes the symbolic structure of primordial verbal language, the symbolic structure of gestural languages, the relationship between speech perception and production, and more. (I initially outlined an evolutionary semantics in *The Roots of Thinking*, 1990, and subsequently fleshed it out along further lines in *The Roots of Power*, 1994, and *The Primacy of Movement*, 1999). In effect, an evolutionary semantics exemplifies how, in addition to being mutually concerned with origins, phenomenology and Darwinian evolutionary biology can be mutually concerned with producing descriptions of how meaning is corporeally represented across the animal kingdom. It exemplifies furthermore how, being concerned with descriptions of life as it is lived, both phenomenology and Darwinian evolutionary biology are necessarily rooted in experience, in highly distinctive ways, quite obviously, but rooted in experience all the same. In sum, insofar as meaning is integral to experience and a constant across the whole of animate nature, an evolutionary semantics is an open field calling for interdisciplinary investigations into forms of meaning as they are corporeally created and sensed by animate forms of life.

The points of convergence between phenomenology and Darwinian evolutionary biology testify to the foundational significance of attending to Darwinian bodies, what the eminent biologist J. S. Haldane referred to as "manifestations of persistent wholes," that is, intact living creatures in the throes and pleasures of their everyday lives. Only by attending to such bodies do we come to veritable understandings of Nature, understandings that are truly ecological, that spell out for us in living terms the singular integrity and interconnectedness of all living forms. From this perspective, one can readily appreciate why selfish genes are not ecologically meaningful: they are divorced from the living bodies they purportedly inhabit. Indeed, selfish genes do not, properly speaking, have environments or bodies. They have only an aim: to be passed on and thus represented in the next generation. Brain modules and their kin are similarly ecologically meaningless because they too are divorced from the living bodies they purportedly inhabit and from the living world as well. In short, entities such as selfish genes and brain modules have no descriptive foundations because they are nowhere to be found in experience. They are pre-eminently explanatory constructs, hypothetical conjurations of life rather than the real thing. It is important to note that because they have no factual existence, they cannot be refuted by science through standard experimental procedures, i.e., through bona fide scientific methodology. It is perhaps hazardous but relevant in this context to point out a parallel state of affairs with respect to postmodernism and phenomenology. As briefly shown earlier, the foundations of phenomenology are descriptive. Description is fundamental both methodologically and substantively. In neither respect is description fundamental to postmodernism; language is not commonly a descriptive power for postmodernism but a rhetorical one. Hence, the distance of postmodern thought and methodology from Darwinian evolutionary biology and from an acknowledgment of nature to begin with.

In sum, a fine and diligent attention to experience leads us to the possibility of fine and diligent descriptions of experience. Descriptive elucidations of experience, in turn, lead us to the possibility of elucidating origins. We can thus appreciate why descriptive foundations are the bedrock of both Darwinian evolutionary biology and phenomenology. In turn, given the grounding import of descriptive foundations, we can readily begin to appreciate the quintessential place of languaging experience in the formulation and production of knowledge and the quintessential challenge it presents.

III

The task now is to show how ecocritical writings and Darwin's writings are of a piece, being grounded in descriptions of nature that answer to the challenge of languaging experience.

Theoretical issues aside, ecocritical writings are either writings of nature directly or writings about the writings of nature by others. The writing may focus on a place, a journey, an interaction with an animal, or it may flesh out a character's relationship to a garden or landscape, or it may examine certain cultural practices with respect to nature, but whatever the particular focus and whatever the particular form – an essay, for example, or a poem – the writing is pre-eminently descriptive or pre-eminently concerned with description. It is because the writing is at heart descriptively tethered that the challenge exists to language experience and that, correlatively, the impact of the piece is affective, stirring feelings, images, reflections.

To highlight the centrality of description to ecocritical literature, it might be instructive to distinguish briefly between describing nature and representing nature. The not uncommon idea that nature is *represented* – that what writers do is *represent* places, journeys, interactions with animals, relationships with the environment, and so on – belies the descriptive foundations of ecocriticism. What is descriptive hews to the *whole* of experience, that is, to the conjunction of subject and object, or, in phenomenological terms, to the conjunction of meaning-giver and object as meant. What is representative condenses experience solely to what-is-out-there. It leaves out the experiencer, measuring itself against certain objective, what-is-out-there features of experience, judging whether to render them more exactingly, for example, or in greater detail. It would be nice to say in this context that biological writings represent nature and that ecocritical writings describe nature, but unfortunately, the joints are not there to carve. We can straightaway acknowledge the lack of fit by recalling the earlier citations from Darwin's writings. It would be nice too to say that the difference between nature described and nature represented is nothing more than a matter of perspective; writing may be viewed as the labor of a subject, for example, or as an already accomplished act and may thus be said to describe nature from the writer's perspective and to represent it from the reader's perspective. Conceptually, however, the difference runs far deeper than these declared categorial distinctions, and the reason I believe it does is that the challenge facing an ecocritical writer is precisely not to *represent* nature – to portray it, depict it, or even symbolize it, and in so doing to linguistify what-is-out-there – but to language experience, and in justly languaging the experience of nature, to do justice to nature.

This experiential conceptualization of the ecocritical task coincides with a certain conceptualization of the value and purpose of ecocritical writings. Whether one is writing of one's own experiences of nature or, for example, analyzing and glossing the experiences of a character in a novel, inquiring into cultural attitudes toward nature, examining discourses of environmental degradation or of environmental transformations of human consciousness, reflecting on scientific texts as literary productions, exploring the complex meanings of environmental change, what is wanted is not an objective veridicality but a resonating experiential veridicality. The ecocritical task, then, is clearly one of languaging experience since the only way one attains to a resonating experiential veridicality is by meeting the challenge of languaging experience.

I pointed up a basic distinction between nature represented and nature described, and in turn am distinguishing between an objective and a resonating experiential veridicality, in order to accentuate the fact that the foundations of ecocritical literature, like the foundations of Darwinian evolutionary biology – and phenomenology – are descriptive. What, then, is the descriptive difference between Darwin's writings and ecocritical writings – or do Darwin's writings also resonate with an experiential veridicality? We might note to begin with that just as Darwin's descriptive accounts of the natural living world reveal something about the lives of others and in turn reflect something about our own lives, so also do ecocritical writings. One might thus justifiably be led to answer that the descriptive difference between the two writings is a difference in degree rather than in kind. I say "justifiably" because the difference in degree can in fact be spelled out more exactly, and precisely by way of language and the challenge of languaging experience. By justifying the answer in this way, I will hope to clarify my insistent claim that ecocritical literature is fundamentally a matter of languaging the experience of nature.

To begin with, language is not experience and experience is not language. Language comes not only after in a phylogenetic and ontogenetic sense; it comes after experience in the more specific sense that we move, see, hear, feel, imagine, hope, think, cry, smile, understand, judge, and so on, quite without language. We experience ourselves, other animate beings, inanimate things, and spatio-temporal happenings in meaningful everyday ways that are wordless. Words not only often but regularly come afterwards. We language what we have heard, seen, felt, and so on. We relate – verbally or in writing – what happened at a meeting, for example, or how a slight cold turned into the flu. And not only do we read stories, articles, messages, and so on, that tell us of the experience of others, but we relate what we have read: verbally or in writing, we share with others our excitement over a new book or our dismay in reading new assaults on English by our new President. In brief, experience is what we talk about, write about, read about. The trick, then, is to have – or to imagine – the experience.

Realizing the trick in the course of everyday Western life is itself a trick, and this because everyday Western life is crammed with television, answering machines, cell phones, the internet, e-mail, books, newspapers, magazines, postal messages, friendly conversations, tête-a-têtes, family gatherings, and so on. The unceasing din of our techno-cultural paraphernalia and the ever-present hum of our social communications can readily lead us to think that language is an omnipresent condition, even a fated incessancy of being human, and as such, is *constitutive of experience to the core*. When we closely examine experience, however, we find that we are sensuously present to something – the smell of an orange, the sound of a voice, the feel of a breeze – and at the same time that we go beyond that sensuous presence toward meaning. Humans are not alone in this respect. All living beings find the world portentous in some way: inviting, threatening, reassuring, pleasant, noxious, and so on. A complex of judgments, expectations, and feelings enters into meaning, and while for humans the complex may include verbal snatches or litanies of thought, just as it may include fleeting or recurrent images, it is not constituted by them. When we are immersed in experience, we are immersed affectively, reflectively, sensuously, cognitively in meaning, not language. Language from this perspective is an *ex post facto* phenomenon, and is thus far less something to be taken for granted as constitutive of experience than as a challenge to one's experiential acuity and one's imagination.

The *place* of language in everyday Western human life in fact presents an interesting perspective on, and extension of, ecocritical concerns with *place* at the same time that it provides a compelling example of how we are deflected from realizing the *ex post facto* nature of language with respect to experience. Consider, for example, the extent to which urban and suburban landscapes are linguistically cluttered places: grocery stores, banks, shopping malls, bars, restaurants, government offices – all are overrun with language, saturated with it: words are written and said everywhere, though we should perhaps note that, in comparative terms, in no place are they written and said more than in academia. Consider in contrast how wilderness is singularly pristine. It is fresh, untainted by language, untouched by human tongues. It is simply there, complete in itself; it has no need of linguistification. Its contrast with the everyday human world is stark, striking. One is reminded of Paul Claudel's *théâtre du silence*. Experience resonates in a silence replete with meaning. The trick is indeed to have the experience.

The trick, however, should not blind us to the formidable powers of language. The power to construct a reality, to retell a life, to detail an encounter, to flesh out an intimation, a suspicion, or an anticipation, all these powers testify to the complexities and subtleties that language can engender. To approximate to these powers, one must delve into language; one must explore, invert, transpose, even sound out to find *les mots justes*, words that not just adequately, but quintessentially capture a reality, a life, an encounter, and so on. At the same time, one must attend to experience, listen to it, return to it, reflect on it. Only then can one judge whether what one is saying resonates experientially, and with an essential veridicality. In effect, the power of language to capture experience is not a ready-made power but a cultivated one, cultivated not in the sense of being something *recherché* but in the sense of requiring painstaking, diligent effort. Ecocritical writings are distinctive in this respect. A ready-made language is not there to appropriate. In contrast, a ready-made language *was* there for Darwin to appropriate, just as it is there to appropriate by any present-day biologist. A ready-made language conforms to the central descriptive task of a biologist: namely, to be in the service of observation. Yet, as we have seen from citations of Darwin's writings, a biologist's observations *can* resonate experientially. When they do, they readily evoke an experientially-resonant response – an appreciation, for example, as of the marvelous cerebral ganglia of ants, or an empathic recognition, as of the bodily feel of terror, or simple laughter, as at the piteous, hopeless dejection of a disappointed dog. An otherwise objective veridicality can thus pass over into a resonating experiential veridicality. Hence, while language is a ready-made for a biologist, it is not thereby of necessity devoid of experiential resonance. When present-day writings in ethology strike experiential chords, they testify precisely to a difference in degree: everyday language is not just in the service of observation, giving us the facts, but is descriptive of life as it is lived from the inside out.

If I were to characterize more finely the realization of a resonating experiential veridicality, I would say that it stems from writing that is qualitatively alive, that aims at evoking the dynamic livingness of nature, that implicitly senses a full-bodied reader at the other end, and that throughout, heeds the tacit injunction to be true to the truths of experience. Hewing to experience leads to a vast terrain that present-day scientists customarily banish, all the while, however, taking it for granted and utilizing it naively in their own observations and clandestinely in what they call "verbal reports." If ecocriticism emulates the spirit of scientific methodology, as Glen Love urges, then it emulates it not directly but by wrestling with the challenge of languaging experience and of being true to the truths of experience. In this respect, methodology is important, and a phenomenological perspective in particular becomes significant. Phenomenology *completes* science by grounding its assumptions, presuppositions, and most crucially, its basic concepts – concepts such as space, world, culture – in experience. Toward the very end of his *Cartesian Meditations*, Husserl writes of phenomenology as "*the beginning of a radical clarification of the sense and origin* (or of the sense in consequence of the origin) *of the concepts: world, Nature, space, time, psychophysical being, man, psyche, animate organism, social community, culture*, and so forth." Clearly, in banishing experience, scientists cut themselves off from the foundations of their knowledge. In contrast, however diverse their perspectives, and whether explicitly or implicitly, phenomenology, Darwinian evolutionary biology, and ecocriticism all insistently refuse a world without experience. They thereby insistently authenticate a world of living subjects – a world of Darwinian bodies.

Their joint anchorage in experience is suggestive; that is, their common foundation in experience suggests that in fundamental ways, everything academic is interconnected. The common foundation thus adumbrates an ecological academy, an academy that would ultimately flesh out those interdisciplinary ties that bind us in a common pursuit of knowledge, in a common humanity, in a common creaturehood, and in a common natural world, and that would indeed, through such fleshing out, illuminate foundations all the way down the line. The encompassing ecological perspective would not only recognize but celebrate differences in all their richness and complexity, yet as variations upon the common themes they embody, not as themselves foundational truths. An ecological academy might thus come to redefine human nature and in ways that resonate with D. H. Lawrence's apocalyptic vision: "We ought to dance with rapture that we should be alive and in the flesh, and part of the living, incarnate cosmos. I am part of the sun as my eye is part of me. That I am part of the earth my feet know perfectly, and my blood is part of the sea"*(Apocalypse*, Viking Press, 1932).

This essay is a revised version of an address delivered to the biennial conference of the Association for The Study of Literature and the Environment in June 2001 in Flagstaff, Arizona.

A former dancer, Maxine Sheets-Johnstone is an independent scholar living in Oregon. In addition to the volumes mentioned above, she is the author of two books on dance, The Phenomenolgy of Dance *(University of Wisconsin Press, 1966) and* Illuminating Dance: Philosophical Explorations *(Bucknell University Press, 1984). She is currently completing the third volume of a trilogy,* The Roots of Morality.

PROSE AND TWO POEMS

Michael Donhauser

Our eternal homeland.

(UNTITLED)

Low season, some pneumatic hammering from
the sea wall, the ocean, cloudbanks, and sunny
with sand the question of whether to stay, as
we gaze far out over the shoes on the duckboard

barefoot and breathing the wind, on the beach
a dog barking blue murder at a distant ship that
pushes on to harbour unimpressed, and we laugh
under the rims of our hats, as if under trees

where I sat all morning, the pavement asphalt
with cracks, and a fest it was to rest in the
cup of a plastic chair and look: the leaves at
play with the light about the hopping sparrows

Park, a park, cares abandoned of what tomorrow
may bring, the coming autumn, at the pond edge
a shrub grown tall: a cool breeze, the promise of
leaves, depth in the crowns of trees, garden paths

that bend over backwards rerouting to a well, a
tree thick with chirruping, high-pitched cheeping
till late in the evening, like now, when the waves
and their rims reflect, shimmering on the underside

of the bamboo leaf, and on late afternoons, hence
the mixed-up times, and the southern glow to
the mud, shingle, moss: vines grew curling from
the mouths of beasts facing the end of the night

Coastal landscape with tyres on tarred tarpaulins, the
bays, the railway embankment overgrown with whins
and bracken, brambles rank under the vast blueness
and pale clouds banked over the sea, then pines, the

sweet chestnuts heavy with fruit between serrated
leaves: Naiva, Otur, pavements, vertical rain streaks
the panes, trickling sideways, and hedges, bindweed
entangling the corn, the platform freshly painted, red

as oxblood the concrete paving, yellow its edges: to
stand here until it's night and guess at the glim of the
farms, hydrangeas, and muck in rows of heaps, the
slopes, in the scattered light, the barking, those dogs

Autumn crocus on the grass slope, there again and
just glimpsed, its pale violet, one October's day
on the route to Santander, and hence abandoned
the succession of numbers on the tipper wagons

on the suspension railway, black and yellow, rusty
and dented, directed the length of these tracks daily
clattering along, then turning off into the distance
with pylons, we drank mead and the autumn was off

to a start, the dust of the summer days rising from
dried puddles, avenues of trees lining the roads, with
the nut leaves yellow, a soft rattling, and ringing
laughter as far, so they said, as the eye can see

Morning mist on the land, fields draped, and the
sun pale over crowns of leaves, bare treetops
alders, moon-white in the dawn, radiant and
rising, the day showing its face with a blue sky

at the sand, the gravel, maize, and a cartload
heaped and covered with tarpaulins, a loading

space, brickwork, grey, and again more veiled
horses grazing near the river, with fences, then

hens, where a motorway crosses a parking zone
on stilts, and mistletoe denser in the light, which
late now, still pale in patches in the mornings, is
clear, stone by stone enwreathed with red vines

Is it, it is, it's a twig that's beating against the
glass sty door, the converted pigsty, the cottage
as you called it, where I lie listening to the wind
from afar, and nearer, and slightly throaty, the

whistle of a train, its two tones before the bridge a
warning called into the night below timbers that
darkly bear this darkness, and the train itself might
have been mine, to Nantes, but the evening went

well, anger resting after the day, was a blackbird
its call a new beginning, we talked, we drank, the
twig dreaming, beating, the sea wave by wave, the
throaty wind, and into the timbers darkly, the night

Streaks of a storm in a distance grown of fields
with clouds, untroubled, and a rainbow going up
over multiple rows of poplars, diaphanous and filigree
leafless tender and close trunks, entwined with ivy

willow tops with rods, eternal homecoming, in doubt
of where ourselves, and staying, chewing, as if you saw in
this vastness meadows crushing meadows with farms
the villages at the hill foot, and out where the ways cross

roads in the wind, so that I followed the hedges, tousled
swaying, the swirling of leaves, now cast like jetsam
on the edges of puddles: a shovel was there, leaning
the shovel was all leaning, hands and peace and sleep

INTO THE MOUNTAINS

It was summer, and here and there a linden, its first winged seeds twirling to the ground, still exuded its fragrance. It had been hot for several weeks, and the days were cooler now in the shade of the ivy, above which a hoverfly briefly lingered, then started away. Darting from one moment of trembling suspension to the next, it seemed to be seeking an early blossom, but there were only dry petals, lodged between the newer shoots. Whatever needed doing had already been done; the season had passed its zenith, but had not yet begun to turn. A breath of wind, a through draught, stirred the leaves, and I might have been sitting in some monastic refectory under this overcast sky, living in a stillness where things were but copies of themselves, ornamental – the creeper, the fly, a nearby hydrangea flowering lilac and pink, but not yet in bloom, its clusters barely full. Now and then a dove flew from roof to roof, perching on a gable, and further away, a blackbird, darker, sleeker, sat on a more pointed roof, while another chattered in the garden. Then, later on, it grew brighter, but not warmer, as the clouds parted and a radiance filled the sky. There were voices, but I hardly heard them, as I breathed in the scent that rose from the paved ground, where leaves lay green on the reddish flags, which were wet and dark and edged with moss. The boxed plants, the geraniums, the oleander, the parsley, kept watch; as if the earth slept. Dust and sand lay on the ledges and in the cracks and corners, and the shrivelled stalks and heads of faded blossoms had collected at the foot of the wall, and in the saucers under the flowerpots.

One afternoon, sitting near the garden door, I gazed at the wooden threshold, at the red raffia carpet crossing the room to where the porch could be seen through the glass wall. Shadows shifted on the raffia herringbone, overlapping and paling, playing with the dancing light-beams that tumbled through the leaves and reeled across the floor. Sunflowers in a vase stood on a small side-table at the end of the mat, and I thought of the fields I should soon be seeing on the way to the mountains. In the window the flowers stood out in dim silhouette against the brightly lit wall on the other side of the road, opposite the open door. One flower alone shone out almost bright yellow against the heavy, drawn-back curtain in the entrance hall, where the lamp on the ceiling glowed like an amber ball. It would all stay, waiting for my return; only the sunflowers would wilt, their petals drooping, their stalks bent, their stamens spilling golden pollen in a pool on the table-top, until the vase was taken away and the surface wiped. These were my thoughts; and I pondered too on the splendour, the exuberance of which these flowers were practically the emblem; it was their colour, something they would lose, as, parched and withering in their vase, their ability to feed slowly diminished. The heat would return; I looked forward, with patience, to my departure.

The train journey took me through a long glen that lay deserted under the sun, with meadows full of dry hay, patches of wasteland, fields of wheat. I had bid my adieux, spending the evening over a last glass of wine with Asma, and Leda. A birch-tree shimmered next to a car park; a field of thistles bloomed pale violet; the backrests of chairs leant against the edges of the tables in a garden restaurant. Thus the landscape was the course of a river; it was the allotments, the sewage plant, and the way the glen narrowed or spread. I saw the willows, and the way they followed the line of the river, how narrow their leaves were, how translucent their foliage. Then the mountains: I had anticipated the way their sheer presence would make me draw back, the sense of peace they would instil. The easiest to envisage was the Falknis, whose bright, granite peak hovered high above the forests that clothed its feet and climbed to the cliffs and the slopes of grass that hung on its breast like the folds of a shawl. This was the Falknis I would see again, and Maienfeld, and the way the vineyards lay in its shadow in the morning and were caressed by the evening light that touched the mountain's flanks and suffused the slopes with its glow. At last I arrived at Sargans station, which seemed to lie at the very heart of the country, surrounded by a wreath of mountains. Inwardly I greeted the scene, and its familiar features returned my greeting: the bicycle stands, the kerbstones, the projecting roof of the bus shelter, the post-trailer with its veneered sides, metal fittings and, whenever it stood here, empty loading space.

By the following day I was already making my way up the Sevelerberg, driving up through the woods on its lower slopes, until the trees suddenly cleared, leaving only the heights, the views, and the air. Cowbells jingled, and in a steeply sloping meadow a cherry tree lifted its topmost branches to the sky. A yellow post-box had been fixed to the wall of a grey, wooden byre, and a single black cable stretched from pole to pole along the road. Here stood a couple of houses, and lower down a second cowshed, this one paired with a silo, and a muck-heap covered with tarpaulin and bounded on two sides by freshly-built concrete dykes. Nettles swayed by a shed at the edge of the meadow where the wind ruffled the dockens and chervil. Pop songs and the voice of a local disk jockey issued from the bar of the inn, while I sat alone on the terrace, remote now from the dream I had dreamed of the mountains. Then, listening to the water gushing and splashing into the trough of a wellspring at the back, I let the dream seep back into my thoughts. The wind that buffeted the well at the back of the inn was stronger, streaming from a storm in a neighbouring weather zone, and the cool air it brought mingled with the scent of brushed grass. I stood on the inn car park, and there was no legend to transfigure the place, nothing to help one figure out how it came to be there at all, with its three dogs – one lying in the open boot of a car, the second tied up near the well, while the third, after settling down in the grass, kept its eye on me; or how I went over to the well, took of its water and drank, while the tarmac behind me was wide enough to turn a bus, and on the bank a rowan stood, delicate, with its plumy leaves troubled, extolling the icy water that flowed in its shade.

Then, one evening, it started: heavy drops at first, soon growing louder and harder, lit white by flashes of lightening, accompanied by distant thunder, finally pelting it down on the paths and embankment. Fragrance filled the air; a great cleansing was underway, a fiesta! I saw the forks of lightening, the landscape bright through streaming rain. Thunder rumbled, echoing from the high hills: great masses of air colliding with one another like boulders in a rockfall, yet keeping their distance. It rained that night without interruption, a constant, drumming downpour, and I lay in bed surrounded by trickling and bubbling and the gurgling of drains. I lay there and listened, and fell asleep. The morning after was full of stillness of a different sort: collected in puddles, in the sodden weight of the leaves and fruit, hanging in the blackberries and quinces. Everything felt wet and close, dripping still, stirring now and then in the breeze, though the rain itself had ceased. The tops of the trees were motionless; clouds draped the peaks: pale shreds, or denser banks that frayed at the edges. Only in the afternoon did the lightening return, and thunder butted against the windowpanes. It meant snow, they said, when lightening struck the wet earth; and I saw the damp blossoms of the geraniums, and the way single petals lay strewn on the cement-coloured ground. Their pigment would run, staining the ground red; but not for long, I knew, and stayed.

No dust rose from the gravel; it was too heavy; and stretching away from the track climbing gently up the flank of the hill the meadows were waterlogged. A burn, audible through the firs, rushed along the bottom of the glen, while scattered gangs of cattle grazed on the slopes, their bells a-jangle as they stretched their necks and nuzzled and tore at the grass. Everywhere I looked the blossom was nigh to fading, or had already faded and now was beginning to wither. The glen was so lovely, so big with seeing, mournful eyes, eyes blessed and blessing, that I fairly slung along, as they say of a determined gait, when thoughts will dissolve in the raptness of looking. My gaze shifted from the sky to a thistle, from the rowan to the lip of the burn, back to the berries from the gravel on the track; or I suddenly caught sight of the hill farm further up, looming out of the distance, as if it were approaching me. The front yard there, next to the byre, had been surfaced with concrete, and cleanly swept, with brown sharny streaks left here and there; but there was great shame here too, mere beginnings, and emptiness. The stable doors were open, a broom leant against the wall, a hosepipe left on the ground; and the milk was a white exhalation rising from the concrete, and from the grooves across its surface. Milk was the emptiness, and milk was the stillness, resounding in vats and churns. The scent of it was white, and I stood in the yard, amidst all the purity and germs. The summer was milk, the clouds and grass were turned to milk. The steading was silent, would stay silent too, until the evening saw the cattle, driven off their pastures, lag for a moment in the yard, before thronging to the byre.

September was on its way, and I took a room, Room 2, in an inn situated in a small pass called the Steig. The inn, together with the byre, formed a steading that faced onto the road and was open to a walled enclosure. The yard enjoyed the shade of two sycamores, beneath which the rows of tables and chairs stood a little forlorn. For Tuesday, the day I had arrived, was closing day, and the only sounds I could hear, lying on my bed upstairs, were those of the animals: the hens and cows, together with the well, whose gentle spring seemed less to flow freely than murmur. I gazed at the dark beams supporting the white ceiling of my room. The evening light capered in between the curtains at one side of the room; and there was such an immaculate odour about the whole place, a sensation at once warm and cool, that the nearby border, with its military post and village at the foot of the meadows on one side of the pass, seemed far away. On the opposite side of the pass, beneath its sloping vineyards, lay Maienfeld, whose bells, equally, were a little too distant to hear on the Steig. Here was a constant breeze; and one night as I lingered in the scattered lamplight at the entrance, its soft rumour grew to a loud rushing in the branches of the sycamores. The elders by the wayside had already carried dark clusters; but here the grapes on the vines were still only pale blue. The following morning I was woken by the scratching of a broom on the asphalt, and going to the window that looked over the yard I saw dry sycamore leaves on the ground. A cat was playing with a leaf, pushing it along, jabbing at it with one paw; and it was if I had recovered eternity.

Golden then was the word for the yellow sycamore leaves; and I sat in the sun, whose rays, pouring a milder sheen over everything around me, streamed to the distant, snow-crowned peaks, gleaming heights that floated above the forests and crags that carried them. But on the earth, beside the roads, the crow-toe bloomed and the haws were red; while walnuts, fresh enough to peal the damp little husks from their covered halves with ease, lay in great numbers in the thinning shadows of the nut-tree tops. Dahlias stood in dying splendour beside the garden fences, and anemones swayed to the softest of breezes, which, only days before, had carried the scent of early snow: the earliest to fall in the high hills for several decades. But now the grapes hung dark and full or in glowing yellow hues in the warmth of the afternoon sun. The beech woods at the foot of the mountain still were green, and only a pear-tree here, a poplar there – more silver now, more trembling – had turned. I looked at the dandelion leaves and saw the way they played about the base of the stakes that propped the rows of vines, touching the wood and the brownish tar. I had left the mountains. And I saw them again. I saw the berries, the snow and the meadows, the cows recumbent and chewing with dignity in the sun, as if these last rays of sunlight belonged to them. I sat and looked; and my eyes were hands, my roaming gaze a caress, and words – were almost intact. Not until evening, at my friend's, did I come to collect the nuts that lay strewn in the yard, bending down, the leaves rustling, my friend preparing the meal inside; and the glen, an inhabited place, over towards Sargans, lit the sky above.

THE LARCH WOODS

To be,
Like you, familiar with all the divine ones
Of this world, is never too much.

Friedrich Hölderlin

Airy shadows
a light rippling
of door curtains
(plastic strips)
an afternoon
a space for language
faint stirrings

The larches

A translation
of the poetic

into the factual
(the conceivable)
airy, lucid:
on a dry slope
remote from the Alpine meadow
the well-watered meadow
(by a spring further up)
that is rich in flora

The fragrance
densely suffused
with gold-brown-red
at their trunks' feet:
the fragrance making ground
of the lightest kind
where
columns, though
with garlands,
interstices
grow:
Apollo, Dionysus

Sheep, stillness
cones
tufts of needles
(like in old
men's ears)

the movement of a veil
though veil-less
clarity: here
feeling through space
a probing ripple
faint, airy

The larch woods

Airy shadows: a light rippling.
Of door curtains (: plastic strips).

Plush cords: stillness of an afternoon.
Lifted: now faintly stirred.

The larches

A translation: of pines.
More southerly ones: to the tree line.
Of their long hair: into eyelashes.
Eyelashes: though barely curled.
(Into the eyelashes of Pausanias.
When he lowers his eyelids.
To take a breath: to keep silent.
To be fully conscious of the spoken line.
Of the next line: before he speaks it.
Or the line he has already begun to speak.
As if reading in his heart of hearts.)

On a dry slope.
Remote from the well-watered meadow.
From the Alpine flora: the names of flowers.
(The names of flowers as tokens of love.
"No love: only tokens of love."
Hundreds of blossoming memorials.
Motherly ones: kept in my heart.
The meadow is thus an encyclopaedia of epic.)
So our talks too were remote: there.
Here: the larches do not form a grove.
More a piece of woodland: no temple.
Even if the scent of needles does rise.
If not in the form of incense: though from bowls.
From the bowl-shaped hoof-prints of cows.
(Between tufts of grass, moss-covered stones).
Induced to rise by the warmth of the sun.
Thus the larches recall the erstwhile halls.
Forests further south, redder hair.
But they do form (stay) an eyelash forest.
With an eyelash forest floor.
(At their trunks' feet).
Yet not as a carpet, more as patches.

The lashes of millions of batted eyelids, seconds falling.
Collected in bowls, as if by nymphs.
Yet barely housed, so fugitive.
Rippled.

Frothy, thinning, shady.
(No black or German forest).
As if supported by what is lightest.
By the scent of needles: thus the stature of larches.
(Though deep-rooted: resistant).
Columnar (their trunks tall): draped (messily).
With loosely hanging pendants: drooping twigs.
(On boughs bent stiff: decked with lichen).
Studded with nubs: at regular intervals.
Sprouting bright needles: in virginal green.
(In bunches: like the tufts in old men's ears).
On which sit cones: like the bowls of pipes.
Spiralling skywards on the drooping twigs.
Which are moved like a veil: by the wind.
In that rippled, lucid space.
(Remote from the Alpine meadow, so rich in flowers).
In this space for language: though veil-less.
The movement of the veil still bears a similarity.
Outwardly: viewed from the distance (of the meadow).
Outwardly, gauged by the fragrance of its stillness.
Or else: gauged by the length of its eyelashes.
By the hush as they fall.
And fallen, lie, and fragrant, rise.
For unlike other conifers:
their needles shine bright yellow, and fall.
They do not hold to a density.
They translate the woods into trickling.
No word holds.

Translated, from the German, by Iain Galbraith.

Michael Donhauser was born in 1956 in Valduz, Lichtenstein and since 1976 has lived in Vienna. The author of several acclaimed volumes of poetry and prose, his most recent work is Vom Schnee *(About the Snow, Urs Engeler, 2003).*

POEM

———

Moya Cannon

CARRYING THE SONGS

for Tríona and Mairéad Ní Dhomhnaill

It was always those with almost nothing else to carry
who carried the songs
to Babylon, to the Mississippi —
hard places, both, in which to sing.
Some of these last owned less than nothing
did not own their own bodies
yet, three centuries later,
deep rhythms carried from Africa, in their hearts, their bones
pervade the world's songs.

And for those who left my own country,
girls from Downings and the Rosses
who followed herring boats up to Shetland
gutting the sea's silver as they went
or boys from Ranafast and Horn Head who took the Derry boat,
who slept over a rope in a bothy,
songs were their souls' currency,
the pure metal of their hearts,
to be exchanged for other gold,
other songs which rang out true and bright when flung down
upon the deal boards of their days.

Moya Cannon lives in Dunfanaghy, Co Donegal. Her third book of poems, The Parchment Boat *(The Gallery Press), was published 1997.*

THE SEANCHAÍ AND THE DATABASE

—

Tim Robinson

Epiphanies of the Earth.

Muing na Fola is a small area in Cill, which is one of the three ancient
subdivisions called cartrons of Inis Ní, which is one of the sixty townlands of
Roundstone Parish, which is one of the four parishes comprising the Barony
of Ballynahinch, which is one of the three baronies in Connemara. To find
Muing na Fola, take the coast road to Roundstone, turn left across the
causeway to Inis Ní, follow the sideroad south to the village of Troscaí, go up
the boreen past the ruined chapel or *cill* from which the area is named, until
you see a damp reedy hollow – it is called Loch Bheag, little lake – on the left;
the *muing* lies just beyond it to the west. When I first heard the name of this
place, from a farmer whose land lies nearby, I was reminded of another Muing
na Fola I had come across in Connemara, out on the bog east of Cashel Hill.
Why *na Fola*, which means "of the blood"? Was it for the same reason a certain
place in the townland of Leitir Móir na Coille near Ros Muc is called Cnocán
na Fola, being formerly the traditional venue for faction fights? But if a *cnocán*
or hillock is a good place for boastful shouting and swinging blackthorn sticks,
a *muing* is the opposite, being a particularly wet and soft and overgrown part
of a bog. Fortunately my Inis Ní farmer had heard the reason for the name
from his parents. In the past, he told me, it was the practice to bleed cattle, by
cutting them on the tongue or the tail, as a supposed cure for various diseases;
the poor creatures naturally objected to this, and the easiest way to catch and
hold them for the operation was to "bog" them, by driving them into a *muing*
where they would sink up to their bellies. "The place used to be red with
blood," he added.

    That conversation was one of thousands, through which I have been able
to access something of the communal memory of Connemara. And not before
time, since that memory is being scattered like ashes in the winds of economic
and social change. The old folk who remember hearing of such obsolete
practices are thinned out by death; their sons and daughters often do not care
to be reminded of the hard old times, and the youngsters' minds are on city

matters. Nevertheless placenames come into my possession, or my care, from local inhabitants all the time. A car pulls to a stop beside me in Roundstone and a neighbour shouts, "I've got another one for you; Poulacholla, the hole of the sleep, somewhere up on Errisbeg Hill." "Poll an Chodladh?" I say to myself; "That wouldn't be the best of grammar, and it probably doesn't mean the hole of the sleep; I'll have to get other sheep farmers to pronounce its name for me and pinpoint its position among the hundreds of holes and corners of the hillside." The information I've gathered in such enquiries would overwhelm a map and would not be adequately represented by a printed text; it calls for a mode of expression that shares the web-like structure of interrelations between place and place, and the superimposed web of relationships between placename and placename too. For this reason I am now working on a database, to be published as a CDROM, of all the placelore I have accumulated about the Parish of Roundstone over the last two decades. (By "placelore" I mean not just placenames and their interpretations but any information – geographical, historical, cultural – that can usefully be correlated with places and filed under placenames.)

Much may have been lost of this information, but enough remains to remind one that *dinnseanchas* or placelore was central to Celtic culture once, and by putting many fragments together one can reconstruct a sketch map of the mentality of the *seanchaí*, the treasurer of the community's oral arts and genealogies, and more particularly of the *dinnseanchaí*, the one learned in topography, the local micro-geography. The placename is a key concept in this reconstruction. A bit of the Earth's surface will have a name only if it is or was of some unitary significance in human life-patterns. The giving or using or remembering of a placename stands for the primary act of attention – a discrimination, an appreciation of uniqueness – that turns a bare location into a place. Thus a placename is a creative force, a word of power; it allocates value and, ideally, directs our care.

A placename is a particularly complex mental object. It sits at the centre of many webs simultaneously, a hyper-spider. (Any academic worth a pinch of salt could get us bogged in a *muing* of theory here, so I will be brief and concrete.) Most obviously, through the place it names, and by virtue of that place's geographical position, a given placename will occur in lists and hierarchies with others, the place it names being part of a more extensive place or having smaller places within it, sharing or disputing boundaries with other places, belonging to a sequence of places lying along a river, road or coastline, and so on, as I have already illustrated by the case of Muing na Fola. One place will relate visually to certain other places: a hillside may overlook a plain, a lake reflect a village. Arising out of such spatial relationships are those of physical and cultural geography. The mountain's separation of watersheds, the river's channelling of history, are inscribed through placenames in legal documents, songs, stories, sayings, the whole library of the spoken and written word.

But most placenames do not just denote a place; they also specify it, by description, ascription of ownership, historical allusion and other devices. Many placenames are in themselves condensed descriptions or images. Among the Beanna Beola, the central mountain range of Connemara, the one lumpy-topped mountain among the sharp-pointed "bens" or *beanna* is called Meacanacht, which according to the late Professor Tomás Ó Máille derives from *meacan,* an obsolete term for a thick lump. Among the Mám Tuirc mountains is one called Mioscán, another "lump" or mass. The highest mountain in Connemara – strangely enough, its name is unrecorded by the Ordnance Survey – is Binn Idir an Dá Log, peak between the two hollows; you could hardly get a more explicit topographical name, for this sharp summit, which has a deep corrie on either side. Another mountain just beyond Leenaun is called, amazingly, Magairlí an Deamhain. I was recently shown a 16th-century map on which this name is correctly translated as The Devil's Ballocks. The OS in the 1830s euphemistically recorded it as The Devil's Mother, and attached the name to the wrong mountain. Fortunately the late, the irrepressible, Bina O'Loughlen, Queen of Connemara, was able to give me the right name for the right mountain, when I was making my Connemara map some fifteen years ago. (Actually that 16th-century map identifies Magairlí an Deamhain with the whole range of the Twelve Pins, which gives one an even more impressive idea of the potency of the Father of Evil.)

A large proportion of placenames take the form of a noun plus a qualifier: An Goibín Géar, the sharp little point; Fó na gColm, the creek of the rock doves; Aill an Dréimire, a cliff with ladder-like clefts in it; Aill na Caillí, the cliff of the hag. Through such particularising elements, the cliff of the hag exchanges echoes with and sets itself off from other cliffs – the cliff of the ladder, the cliff of the churns, the cliff of the curses, the cliff of the birds, all of these in Roundstone Parish. The noun in such names identifies the place as having a landform of a certain type; thus it enters into a series of landform terms characteristic of the area. In Connemara: *clochar*, a stony place, a patch of scree on a mountainside, and more often a mass of boulders out on the bog, a pile of glacial erratics; in this usage it is a word for which there is no single English equivalent; *fonsa*, a rim – this occurs in the names of two or three spectacular ridges between peaks of the Twelve Bens; *leitir*, a rough hillside;

seanadh, which appears to mean a smooth hillside – Professor Ó Máille suggested to me that it is or was a hillside suitable for the holding of an assembly, a *seanadh*; *tamhnach*, an arable patch in otherwise uncultivated land; *fiodán*, a narrow waterway in a bog; *criathrach*, a bog with many bogholes; *lathach*, a muddy place... Some of these landform terms are of great interest in themselves. *Imleach* is used in Connemara for the sort of rounded hill of glacial deposits geographers call a drumlin, but this sense of the word is not to be found in any dictionary of the Irish language. The meaning of other placename elements has been lost: *trosc*, for instance; P. W. Joyce's famous old book *Irish Names of Places* associates it with codfish, or alternatively with *troscadh*, fasting, but according to Professor Ó Máille both these interpretations are unlikely. In fact he thinks the word seems to have signified some feature of boggy land, perhaps an elevated and relatively dry part (hence the *tr-*, from *tur*, the rest of the word being perhaps from *easc*, a hollow), but if this is the derivation, nobody remembers the word's exact meaning and various scholars have debated it inconclusively. (Tomás Ó Máille was my guru on such questions, in my mapping days, but I also used to consult the late Professor Tomás de Bhaldraithe, and of course they rarely concurred in the advice they gave me so generously. I remember one Tomás saying of the other, with a touch of irony, "Tomás's derivations are always so *learned!*")

No local cultural study can afford to be deaf to the quiet testimony of placenames, for they preserve the trace of the past, the footmarks of bygone lifestyles. Half-forgotten under the recent spread of Roundstone's suburban girth we have Bólard, and further out in the bog, Loch Bólard, from *an buaile ard*, the high "booley", a hillside pasture to which cattle used to be brought for the summer season of milking and butter-making, to be tended by the womenfolk living there in temporary dwellings while their men were engaged in fishing and kelp-making along the shore. A little village near Roundstone is Coogla, from *Cúige Uladh*, the Province of Ulster, where refugees from anti-Catholic pogroms in Armagh were settled by the landlord, Humanity Dick Martin, in the 1790s; they brought the name of their homeland with them, as did the unfortunate outcasts from Connemara who were charitably transplanted to the prairies of Minnesota in 1880, the "Conamaras" as they were called, and who eventually settled in what became known as the Connemara Patch, in Minneapolis.

Something of this multiplicity of actual and conceptual interconnections is present in the mind of anyone aware of a placename and its application. In a given neighbourhood, even today, the enquirer will soon be directed to the man or woman in whom this network inheres most fully. But such people are becoming rare, and soon there will be none. So, other forms of communal memory are called for: the map, the book, the computerised database. There are interesting ways in which a database such as the one I've assembled for Roundstone Parish shares some of the features of the knowledgeable local inhabitant's mental gazetteer, rivalling it in flexibility of association, transcending it in powers of recall and logical organisation – but falling far short of it as a memorandum of lifelong habitation.

The parish *dinnseanchaí's* outlook is highly perspectival; tiny fields and nooks and corners in the foreground of his or her life will be known by name, while distant objects must tower mountain-high to overtop the horizon of indifference. I treasure these fond little names when they come into my keeping. From the shores of An Cheathrú Rua, I remember a creek a few feet wide called An Ing Mhór, the big notch, and close by it, an Ing Chaol, the narrow notch, with between them a pinch or two of sand called, believe it or not, An Tráighín Idir Dhá Ing, the little beach between two notches. Would I even have noticed these places on strolling by, if they had not been named to me? Out on the bog east of Scríb there is a *fiodán* or streamlet that passes under the track via Droichidín na Circe Fraoigh, the little bridge of the grouse. I'm told that before the bridge was built the water was channelled under the road through a pipe, called Gulletín na Circe Fraoigh. Micro-history, embedded in micro-topography. At the other extreme of this perspective effect, I find that even the best-informed old sheep-farmers of Roundstone cannot name the individual mountains of the Twelve Pins, Na Beanna Beola, which form the backdrop to their lives.

However there is an effect that complicates this perspectivism, if it does not reverse it. The village sage may not consider the familiar and homely little placenames worthy of record; after all, *dinnseanchas* originally meant the lore of mountains, forts and suchlike eminent places. Ideally, the database, compiling information from a wide variety of sources, can avoid both the egocentric outlook and the suppression of awkward matters. In my computer archive of Roundstone Parish lore there is a record for Letterdyfe House, which is where the landlord's agent lived; the name would have been connected in the local mind with rent demands, evictions, gunboats in the bay, the Land War, as well as with much-needed charity and employment; all important matters. And just a hundred yards from the gate of Letterdyfe House is a bend in the road nicknamed Flaggers Hotel; this was (perhaps still is) a courting place, where couples in search of privacy in the bare and generally treeless landscape of Connemara, so unfriendly to lovers, could scramble over the wall into the grounds of Letterdyfe House and hide themselves in a grove of New Zeeland Flax, which is known locally as "flaggers". Which of the two is the more important placename, Letterdyfe House or Flaggers Hotel? The village sage, who may have been the most unflagging client of Flaggers Hotel, who may in fact have been conceived there, would probably not regard its name as worth mentioning, or even suitable for mention, to the enquirer from outside the village. What does the database say on that question? In terms of content, of course there is more history to record of Letterdyfe House. But in terms of form, the database is exactly as accommodating to one place as to the other; structurally, the database makes no judgements.

Seanchas, being the creation of an oral community, is rarely confronted with written records, whereas the database meshes technologically with library catalogues, book indices, web sites – and if this mesh is not perfect its failings are immediately apparent; discrepancies are like squeaky bearings in a machine. A database that draws on both traditional lore and written records will also show up inconsistencies, and in a clash between the official and the vernacular it is well to remember that error can be ingrained on either side or both. Thus for generations the well-read visitor to Roundstone has trotted out the received idea that "Dog's Bay" is an ignorant corruption of the Irish *Port na Feadóige*, the bay of the plover – but this assertion is in fact incorrect. It arose from an ambiguously placed name on a map drawn by John O'Donovan for the Ordnance Survey in the 1830s, and was made generally known by Robert Lloyd Praeger in his book *The Way that I Went*. But in reality Dog's Bay and Port na Feadóige are different places, as those locals who were not overawed by the prestige of the printed word could always have told us, had anyone asked them. Nobody did, and the mistake was copied from map to map and from book to book for a century and a half.

Unlike the database, traditional lore is very tolerant of internal contradictions and does not suffer from what Keats called the "irritable searching after fact and reason" – but this "negative capability", while conducive to romantic poetry, is frustrating for the researcher. I remember getting unreasonably cross with a man I depended on for placename lore in An Cheathrú Rua who could tell me that a nearby stream was called Sruthán an Mhuilinn because there used to be a mill on it, and had wondered all his life exactly where that mill had stood, but had never bothered to go a few hundred yards out of his way to walk along the stream and look for its ruins. A small gap in his knowledge was no problem to him; but for me, the compiler of a database, it was an annoyance, a scandal. In such respects the database is quite intolerant; its searchability and powers of cross-correlation depend on consistent and methodical compilation, and in the face of ambiguous and doubtful data it simply sits down and refuses to cooperate. The database's very format, in which each record consists of a number of "fields" or spaces each to be filled with information of a particular sort, prompts a drive towards full coverage and uniformity of treatment. Thus in the forthcoming *Placelore of Roundstone Parish*, there is a record for each place, and in each record are a number of spaces to be filled in with the history of the place, its archaeology, the meaning of the placename, the location, the associated oral lore, etc. And if I lack the information to fill in all of these "fields" there is an obvious blank. The database is, visibly, a mosaic in which the holes where bits are missing are objectionably apparent. The computer is insatiable, it hungers and thirsts for data. I know this as the master of a computer, or the slave of a computer; sometimes I feel as driven by it as a blackbird feeding a nestful of chicks.

This demanding nature of the database also gives it the intriguing and even addictive qualities of a game, a crossword puzzle, that one cannot relinquish until it is completed. And having covered one area, one parish, there is no reason not to go on to the neighbouring one. So the task will never be completed; it stretches to the horizon and beyond. As a game of patience, it will not come out this side of eternity. Therefore, looking at it positively, it is a resource for life. Nothing is more satisfactory than solving one of its constituent problems; one becomes absurdly proud of little triumphs. It is a pleasure to realise the aptness of a name or to discover its meaning through an observation of the place. Ellustrum or Ellistrin is the name of a small coastal area between Roundstone and Dog's Bay; not named on the OS maps but noted on Alexander Nimmo's chart of 1823; how satisfactory to go down there and find the marshy land along the shore ablaze with Yellow Iris or Flag, the *eileastron* or *feileastram*. There is a spot on the east shoreline of Derryclare Lake in Connemara for which I was given the name Sindile, an old word meaning a paddle for beating washing. The place is too remote from habitation to have been associated with washing, so I was puzzled by the name, until I went out there and found that the place was a small squarish peninsula with a narrow neck joining it to the shore, i.e. it was just the shape of a *sindile*. How gratifying it was when having noted down the local name for a little lake out in Roundstone Bog as Loch Reddington, first to be told the story of Reddington, a man on the run, who called in at a house in the now deserted village of Aircíní, suspected he was about to be betrayed by his host there, went off into the bog and escaped the tracker hounds by swimming out to an island in this lake; further, then to hear a scrap of an old song: "As I sat down in Camden Town / I heard the ferocious voice of hounds" – Camden Town being a nickname for the village of Aircíní, near the lake in question; and finally, in a report of the Commissioners of Public Instruction dating from the 1830s, to come across the name Patrick Reddington, who kept a hedge school near Aircíní. A whole historical novel emerges from the ashes. Then doubts arise as to its coherence: would Camden Town have been as familiar to Connemara men in the 1830s as it is today? The past rises like a loaf in the baking, and then crumbles when one tries to slice it too thinly.

Apart from the fervours and frustrations of compiling them, what is the use of placename collections, whether computerised or not? Nowadays many little community groups, schools and development committees are assembling lists of local placenames; some of these progress to the point of publication in some form, on computer disc or paper; others rest unseen when the grant money runs out or the principal mover in the project loses interest or leaves the area. I try to ensure that copies of as many of these lists as possible from Connemara and Aran and the Burren come into my hands, and are added to my archive, which will eventually go to NUI Galway. Now, it may be that some minor historical puzzles can be resolved through consulting such lists, or a scholar may use them to buttress a thesis about land-use or emigration or plant distribution. That is, the placenames become grist to the academic mill. Artists and writers may pick and choose among them for their own creative purposes. But they are not out in the mouths and minds of the people. The act of collecting them does give them a brief flicker of life; I know that a lot of people have made enquiries on my behalf and resurrected many half-forgotten names; but that soon dies down. What is the life-expectancy of a placename once it is severed from its place?

And the obverse question in no less pressing. What is the future of a place if no one remembers its name – which is a sign that the place has lost its distinctiveness or usefulness, its role in human life? In the west of Ireland in particular a vast topographical loss impends. Extensive tracts of countryside, such as the South Connemara coastal plain from Bearna to Slyne Head, and the whole of the three Aran Islands, are divided into minute fields by stone walls. These are cultural landscapes of the highest interest and beauty, filigree webs of place, densely set with placenames. They are the historical result of ingenious and frugal accommodations between hard-pressed generations of humankind and a harsh stony terrain. In their way they are as remarkable as, say, the rice-terraces of Bali I have admired in photographs, or the great avenues of shade trees along the old roads and canals of France. And they are being lost to hazel scrub and to gorse. No Rural Environment Protection Scheme is going to keep people going through the motions of 19th- and 20th-century small farming, cutting the briar arched across the boreen, replacing the stone that falls off a wall. The landscape becomes impenetrable, its lore forgotten. Tóin an Naigín, bottom of the noggin, a tiny field by the shore near Carna; Straidhp an Tae, a strip of bog in Ros Muc noted for the amount of tea the turf-cutters drank there; Lathach na gCapall, the muddy place of the horses, once a ford, long built over by the road to Scríb – all fading from the community's mental map. Let me insert a footnote here on the rhythms of these names, their graceful phonic balance. Baile na hInse, Aill na Caillí, Gleann na nDeor, Sruthar na Míoltóg, Cuan an Fhir Mhóir – they all hop lightly from bank to bank on the stepping stone of that unstressed article, *an* or *na*, in the middle of the phrase. Contrast them with the many British placenames put together on the lines of a goods train: Manchester, Birmingham, Sandringham, Edinburgh – in which only the first syllable has motive power and the rest come dragging and clanking behind. Because of the neat feature of the Irish language, that phrases like Baile na hInse using the genitive case do not need an article at the beginning of them, they cannot be translated into English without inserting two dud syllables: Sruthar na Míoltóg, the current of the midges. So in my files I can look up innumerable concentrated particles of poetry. Caorán na gCearc, the moor of the grouse, Aill na Graí, the cliff of the stud, Mám na Gaoithe, the pass of the wind, Cnocán na Tine Chnámh, the hillock of the bone-fire, Móinín an Damhsa, the little meadow of the dancing (it was the fairies who danced there) – these names are so many isolated lines from a lost epic of everyday life, saved from oblivion perhaps by my noting of them, but desiccating in my record-files.

However, perhaps – and this is sheer fantasy – after a period of sleep and forgottenness these names might emerge to a higher form of life, like butterflies from their chrysalises. Imagine that in a few hundred years time humanity has put aside all its misguided supernatural beliefs and turned its religious instincts to the Earth, the true author of our being. Then a rite will be called for to celebrate this thoroughly realist and romantic-materialist cult of the Earth. This rite will be the Visiting of Places, to contemplate them in all their particularity. By then the thousands of fields of Cois Fharraige and Aran and all such highly individuated tracts of the Atlantic seaboard will have been carefully conserved and their placelore compiled. We will walk through the boreens and observe the quirks of the field walls with due attention (for, according to the Cartesian philosopher Malebranche, I read somewhere, attentiveness is the natural prayer of the soul). Or we will wander through the labyrinth of lakes in Leitir Seanadh near Roundstone and revel in their quiddity; here is Loch Clochar an tSionnaigh, named from a heap of boulders a fox has its lair in nearby, and Loch Coscéim an tSionnaigh, the lake of the fox's step, with a narrow part a fox can jump across; here is Loch an Ghé to which the white-fronted Greenland goose used come from Iceland in winter; here is Loch na mBreac Caoch, so called from its blind or spent trout; Loch na bhFraochóg, with a little island on which the *fraochóg* or bilberry grows. And the language of this rite will obviously be Irish – which by then will be as remote and arcane as all those other secret languages of Ireland R.S. Macalister wrote about: Ogham, Hisperic, Shelta, Bearlagair na Saer. The celebration and interpretation of place through this mysterious jargon will be in the hands of a new learned class, a computerised clerisy, a cross between the seanchaí and the database…

… A fantasy, as I said; also a parody of my own procedures. When I first had the honour of addressing Cumann Merriman, eleven years ago, I coined the word "geophany", meaning a showing-forth, an epiphany, of the Earth, and I claimed that Irish was the geophanic language of the Irish landscape. Since then, in the intervals of other work, I have continued to collect Connemara placelore, and have begun the task of ensuring the safety and accessibility of my records by computerisation. A difficulty arises in that the task of compilation can become compulsive, obsessional. If an individual has rashly undertaken a database of a topic of such density and plenitude as placelore in a countryside as fine-featured as Connemara, the only way to escape its demands is to walk away from it, admitting that it cannot be satisfied by the labours of one person …

… Which I intend to do. *The Placelore of Roundstone Parish* is a partial and faulty record, an indication of what could be done, and a template for similar local studies. It is also a thank-you gift to life for having given me so many years of pleasurable walking, inquiring, photography, rummaging in libraries and poking around graveyards, an expression of gratitude to the hundreds of people who have contributed their local knowledge to the making not just of this archive but of all my books and maps of the region. In it you will find: Loch na Brocaí, the lake of the badger's den; The Dugout, where the IRA men hid out on Errisbeg Hill during the Black-and-Tan raid on Roundstone; Gáirdín na bPáistí, the garden of the children, a children's burial ground; Gleann na gCoileach, the glen of the woodcock; Cnocán na gCorp, the hillock of the corpses, where coffins were rested when being carried over the hills to the churchyard; Bóthar na Scrathóg, a relief-work road that used to have a strip of sods or *scrathóga* down the middle for barefoot people to walk on; Binn an tSaighdiúra, the peak of the soldier, one of the Twelve Pins, where during the primary triangulation of Ireland in 1828 the soldiers of the

Ordnance Survey waited through seven misty weeks for a clear day to receive a heliograph signal from Mount Brandon, and one of them died in a cliff fall ... These are a few of the triangulation points in the web of observations spun across both space and time by the placenames of one small locality, a tissue of care and remembrance. I offer them as a hint of a wealth we hardly know we have.

This essay was adapted from a talk given at the Cumann Merriman Summer School, Co Clare, in August 2003.

Tim Robinson, cartographer, naturalist and writer, lives in Roundstone, Co Galway. His two-volume Stones of Aran *(The Lilliput Press) appeared in 1986 and 1995. His most recent book is a collection of fictions,* Tales and Imaginings *(The Lilliput Press, 2002).*

ACROSS THE FIELDS

(a poem sequence)

———

Hans van de Waarsenburg

Into Aran's dream.

GALWAY

We smelled the smoke in the pubs, gazed
At the peat fires, as if everything would
Last and nothing had changed. Words
Unspoken, suppressed, left in the dunes,

On beaches. Perhaps, you said,
There are journeys one should go alone,
If we lived without time or need.
But wherever the roads went, ships arrived

And I looked for your face in every port.
Horizons are but a perspective, in an ever-
Changing light. Your voice is parched, you said.
Come here and put your lips to glass or verse.

ARAN ISLANDS 1

The ferry to the islands cleft the waves.
The holy water swept in from the Atlantic
Across the edges of the bay. A gale
Intertwined our hair and grains of salt

Filled the lines of years. A hand
Covered a hand. Stacks of peat rose
In our heads. Like a pig being
Stuck or crumbling black pudding on

Our plates, steaming amidst apples and
Autumn. But surely it's spring, you said and
Hummed an old tune in my ear. We stared
At the empty waters of the luminescent sea.

ARAN ISLANDS 2

Sailor's legs felt for the quay. A duck
Waddled from the ship. There was
A man lying on the cobblestones. Drunk, dropped
Out of the picture, his tongue still grey with whiskey,

Erosion of porter on his lips. Today this is
Our island, you said and pulled me away
From him. Salt rain corroded the houses.
And not a tree to carve your name in.

Grey the skies, grey the water. No hangover
Lurking here. We gazed across the forgotten
Islands, where stone rules over the dead
Unintelligibly, and the day drew in.

ARAN ISLANDS 3

Shivering we huddled in blankets.
The horse's hoofs thudded steadily,
As if the roads were soft paths, every
Step reversible. Seals were swimming

Towards the horizon. Potatoes lay like
Eggs in the scanty peat. On your lips
I tasted the salt that encrusts stone.
And then you looked at me, looked back

Through my eyes. This is the end of a world
You said, where old can never age. Where
Time is silence, paper-thin. Aran,
Dream with the smell of horse blankets.

ACROSS THE FIELDS

Across the fields, well past the midst
Of life, the shadows of the paths.
The changing of the harsh afternoon light.
A feather in his throat and watching

Things tumbling slowly. Across the fields
The word strides, so slowly that sound
Is lost, dissolving in the mist over the
Stubble fields. And the walker? He

Peers across the fields at the fading
Horizon. Tries to step out of his
Shadow, while dusk falls around
His head. The dead rustle among

The autumn leaves or rest on the branches
Of the past. If there should be a farewell,
Let it wait a while and bring same "wood
To the forest and peat to the moors".

Translated, from the Dutch, by Peter Boreas.

Across the Fields will be published by In de Bonnefant (Banholt, Netherlands: with screen prints by Jan Hendrix) in November 2003, in a limited edition of 60 copies.

Hans van de Waarsenburg, poet, essayist and critic, was born in 1943 and is chairman of Dutch PEN. His most recent book of poems is Wherever the Roads Went (Wereldbibliotheek, 2003). He lives in Maastricht.

THREE POEMS

Gary Allen

BEING

The German shepherd sleeping in the sun
is a stone dog

in my memory:

and I was always awed
by the shafts of light

falling across the disciples
and a serving of simple fare

like the table filling the kitchen,
the tin bath hanging behind the door,

the smell of broth and linseed oil.

For there is meaning in all these things,
or was,

to a lonely child seeking permanence
outside the absence of parents:

a grandfather's roosters,
the withered hand of the old woman in the next yard

reaching through the wire,
caked with excrement.

Then everything changes,
and the moment becomes unsustainable:

on still days
the clack clack of bicycle chain

and the sough of plane over wood
helped me to understand the holding of time,

and the exact perspective of everything.

ON THE FIRST DAY

Those were the days of hunger
long hours stretching like an empty belly

to the tune of the rent-man, clubman, debt-collector.

All my blood were broken to labour,
when labour they could find,

grateful for fifty years of sweat.

And sometimes there was nothing
to chew on, to distract, to hold out for,

each laying blame to the one above.

I took my turn on the wheel:
those eyes old with tiredness,

she gave me the last two cigarettes

and a white breast
that was neither infantile nor sexual

hung useless from the nightdress.

My youth was angry, impotent like the white frost
on the council greens

or the knowledge that my seal was set:

the lorry engines warming-up in the depots
seemed to tell me with a sigh,

This is the twenty-eighth word –
and the Lord answered, The desert among my earths.

ONE SUMMER EVENING

This woman here
wanted the sun
to make her new,

went out the back
children's ragged clothes
left on the boil,

a husband hammering chairs together
in the front room,

but got no farther
than the line of telegraph-poles
stretching like a chain

between peat-bogs

and returned disconcerted
to a house where no one knew she had left

and a kitchen steamed
with the loss of light.

Gary Allen was born in 1959 in Ballymena, Co Antrim and lived for many years on the Continent. His first book of poems, Languages *(Flambard / Black Mountain) appeared in 2000.*

POEM

—

Frances Thompson

LOUGH NEAGH II

In a bedlam of birds and breezes
I found a flat stone by the Lough.

My hands went in, refracted,
paling, and my arms to the elbow.

The hospital windows flashed,
but the Lough was blind, and gathered,

thick-flecked, on me,
building a causeway to the sky,

to yet more Ireland. My hands
were fins, working, as if a creature

could outwit water, as if will
could reorder the world.

A child of the manse, Frances Thompson was born in Belfast in 1944. She attended The Queen's University of Belfast and taught in North Africa and London, before settling in Devon. She is currently working on her first collection of poems, Feather in the Ground.

SAFETY IN NUMBERS

Chris Arthur

In the wilderness of strangers.

I

Every now and then, for no convincing reason I can summon to explain it, the question *"What happened to Darlene?"* surfaces in my consciousness. It prompts speculation about a range of possibilities – most of them unhappy – and remembrance of the little girl in question. Ours was an accidental and slight acquaintance. If you added up all the times I'd said "Hello, Darlene, how are you today?" (or, as commonly, "Go away, Darlene!"), together with her glumly monosyllabic responses, we'd not have exchanged more than a few hundred words at most, no more than would fit on this single page. That was the sum total of our communication. Picturing it clumped together now, I regret its pathetic meagreness and the fact that I didn't make more effort with her.

She lived in the cottage next door to mine. I was just passing through, spending six months struggling with a piece of writing in the cheapest accommodation I could find. Darlene was rooted to the spot. She'd been born and brought up there, lived all her years within the narrow ambit imposed by this locale. For her, that row of damp, cramped cottages was home. Some were boarded up and empty, some let out on a temporary basis to short-term tenants like me, a few – like the one she and her parents lived in – were occupied by families who had been there for years. There were a dozen cottages, built in a line in clumps of three. A narrow lane between each trio led to an alleyway that ran behind them all, separating the houses from a jumble of sheds and back gardens. A few of the gardens were well tended, but most were unkempt and scarcely distinguishable from the rough pasture of the surrounding fields. At the front, the cottages were separated from the main road by a row of white-painted kerbstones dotted along the edge of a narrow gravelled strip just wide enough to park a car.

My brief acquaintance with Darlene dates from thirty years ago. I haven't seen her since, or re-visited Mullaghcartin Cottages. Perhaps they and their inhabitants have gone, for even at the time there were rumours of eviction, demolition, relocation. And yet, despite the time that separates our meeting, and despite the slight and superficial nature of what passed between us, *"I wonder what happened to Darlene"* remains a not infrequent musing of the mind. To my surprise, I can picture her today with a clarity that eludes the recall of many more fondly remembered faces, with whom my relationship was chosen, longer, and more intimate.

I'm not sure exactly when this happened, or why, but Darlene became for me a kind of symbol of the precarious vulnerability of individual existence, of our fragile aloneness in the world and the way in which any claim of meaning we may make for our lives can so easily be reduced to the seemingly absurd once the scale of our momentary being is honestly confronted. The process of symbolisation she underwent seems to have made Darlene lodge in my mind with the persistence of a splinter that won't come out. That this awkward, damaged child would leave a dark speck permanently embedded in the flesh of remembrance was certainly not something I expected at the time. The criteria employed by the mind to sift experience, making it hoard some things and jettison others, are often opaque and inscrutable to any rational attempt at calculating memory's likely harvest. This is a case in point. If you'd asked me then what cargo of memories I would carry away with me from that time and place, I would have nominated the novel I was attempting. In fact I remember almost nothing about it now beyond the relief that accompanied my eventual decision to abandon it. It was a piece of unsalvageably mediocre writing yet, for a while, it possessed sufficient pretensions of importance to dictate how I spent my days. Quite eclipsing its dismal plot and characters, and constituting by far the strongest images remaining from this brief period of my life, are my memories of Darlene and the mingled smell of sandalwood and mould – the cottage was damp and I lit joss sticks to try to combat the dank fungal reek that gave the place the odour of a crypt.

Mullaghcartin Cottages were owned by a great estate nearby and had been built to house its labourers. When I lived there, only two of the cottages were still occupied by estate workers. The rest held a mixture of the elderly, the unemployed, those who worked in a new synthetic fabrics factory only a few miles away, Darlene's family, and myself. Her father worked for the Electricity Board, her (much) older brother, who still lived at home, was a postman, her mother looked after the house and took on occasional cleaning jobs in Antrim or Randalstown. Darlene also had a sister, who visited occasionally. She lived in Ballymena, about twenty miles away, worked as a dental nurse and, so her mother often told me, had married a "lovely man" who "spoiled her rotten" – descriptions that certainly couldn't be applied to the household separated only by a wall from where I sat writing my miserable, soon to be aborted, opus. Judging by what was audible through the blessedly muting stone, Darlene's parents lived in a state of more or less perpetual animosity.

The cottages were on the main road between Antrim and Randalstown. They were separated from Lough Neagh, Northern Ireland's giant freshwater lake (whose size almost makes it a kind of inland sea), by only half a mile or so of fields and woodland. But this geographical proximity was deceptive when it came to actually getting there. Going straight across the fields meant battling with barbed wire, tightly planted hawthorn, sheughs, nettles, and brambles which seemed to increase in density the closer you approached the Lough. Going by track or road meant an elaborate winding route that took so long it gave the impression that Lough Neagh was miles away, its waters somehow stealthily receding as you tried to reach them.

Renting was cheap. The estate preferred to have the cottages occupied, even if they only got a pittance, knowing that, once seen to be empty, deterioration happened very rapidly. Vandalism, even in so rural a setting, was hard to stop. It seemed an almost automatic process. Once a property went vacant for more than the briefest period, it attracted window-breakers, graffiti writers, shadowy vagrants who left fugitive traces of their passing in a litter of beer cans, cigarette ends, old newspapers and excrement. My cottage was let unfurnished, had no bathroom or indoor toilet, and the wall in one room was so damp that you could scarcely see the stone beneath the slimes and moulds and fungi that had grown together into a grotesque organic tapestry, flourishing in ugly profusion. The smoke from the joss sticks gave a perfumed overlay that was preferable to the raw stench otherwise instantly evident, but it masked rather than cured and has left me with a lasting aversion to sandalwood. Anytime I smell it now, it seems like a disguise, its sweetness merely a façade beneath which something rotten lurks, waiting to overwhelm.

II

I disliked the name Darlene and, if I'm honest, the child who bore it. That made me feel guilty, for Darlene had enough to contend with without adding people's dislike to her burdens. I tried to be kind, or at least to be patient, with a strained artificiality that would have hurt a more sensitive child. Whether or not Darlene noticed, I don't know. She gave away few signs of what moved her. Beyond rapturous grunts of animal delight if she had ice cream, crying if she fell and cut a knee, or shrieking with rage if the little band of children she went about with needled her beyond the threshold of dumb placidity that seemed to absorb without complaint a cruel level of torment, Darlene's mood was hard to gauge. She was nine years old, named after her sister's favourite Country and Western singer, and an "accident", as her mother confided on our first meeting. No, not "confided", that sounds the wrong note. Darlene's mother was loud, brash, indiscreet, and often angry. If people can be the embodiment of words, she seemed like the very incarnation of "blowsy", as if the definition had risen up from the pages of a dictionary and taken fleshy form in her. She described Darlene bluntly, in the child's hearing, as "simple", "not right in the head", "with a bit missing" or "a screw loose". One afternoon when Darlene had caused her particular annoyance and when, I suspect, she'd drunk more than her usual intake of gin, she raged to me – and anyone else in earshot – as she dragged Darlene after her, "I don't know what we'll do with her", "I'm at my wits' end", and, a terrible parting shot just before she slammed the door of their cottage, "Christ, I wish I'd got rid of her!"

I'm not sure what the technically correct vocabulary would be for Darlene's disabilities, but they rendered her what my parents' generation, untroubled by thoughts of political correctness, would simply, if brutally, have labelled "sub-normal". Darlene seldom spoke, and when she did her answers tended to be "yes", "no", "dunno", or "ask mum". It was hard to tell how much she understood. In appearance she was unprepossessing, close to ugly. Her wispy hair, a pale anaemic brown, seemed to cling flatly to her skull. Her cheeks were fat and perpetually red with a brightness too extreme ever to be described as "rosy", with all that word's cosy connotations of healthy cuteness. She moved awkwardly, with a kind of shuffling gait, and her hands and feet seemed too big for the rest of her body. What was most immediately striking about her, though, was the expression – or rather lack of expression – in her eyes. They were possessed of a dullness that suggested the tragic absence of life's sparkle, that lovely brightness that normally shines out in children's faces. Accentuated by the thick glasses she wore, the blankness of her eyes, combined with her customary open-mouth, gave Darlene a distinctly moronic mien.

To begin with I was, of course, an object of interest to all the children of Mullaghcartin Cottages and (though they displayed it less openly) to the adults too. Normally if a cottage was let it was to someone they knew, or at least knew of. But here was a complete stranger, someone from outside their network of reference and association, suddenly turning up unannounced, uninvited, to live in their midst. And, instead of working on the estate or at the synthetics factory, or just being unemployed, I was someone who was there not to engage in any of the repertoire of roles they recognised, but to pursue an activity that most of them had abandoned with relief after whatever schooling they'd received. Their interest in this unexpected alien manifested itself on various levels of subtlety. Marking the pole of complete, open, wholly undisguised curiosity, was Darlene's habit of climbing up on the low windowsill of my cottage's only serviceable downstairs room and standing there, just staring in. The first time she took up this position, I thought she'd soon tire of it and go away. After all, there's nothing very interesting to see when someone's sitting writing at a rickety card table. But ten minutes passed and she was still there, like some inquisitive inward-facing gargoyle. It was hard to concentrate knowing I was the subject of such scrutiny. When I went out to talk to her, she climbed down and scuttled off in her ungainly fashion, only to reappear as soon as I went back inside. In fact, in between my excursions to chase her away and the momentary absences these engendered, she stood there most of the first afternoon I was there, just gazing in, her expression blank, equally oblivious to being ignored, smiled at, waved to, scowled at. The next day too she was there, face sometimes pressed so close against the glass that it misted over with her breath and she had to wipe it before she could see through clearly. Even after a week had passed, her interest had only waned very slightly. Repeatedly, she'd break off from whatever games she was playing with the other children to come and stand on the windowsill and stare in at me. I tried writing with my back to the window, but then she would tap the glass softly but persistently until I turned. Eventually, I cycled into Antrim and bought a cheap net curtain to screen out her intrusion. Met with its opaqueness, the window seemed to lose most of its appeal, though every now and then she'd still clamber on the sill and stand there, trying, I suppose, to see through the barrier I'd interposed between us. It made me feel almost guilty to see her shadowy form behind the curtain, straining to penetrate the gauze, knowing that I'd created a further layer of difficulty in her already too difficult world.

III

Though Darlene irritated and spooked me, though I often wished she'd go away, I worried about her too. I wondered why she wasn't at some special school where whatever abilities she had might have been nurtured and brought on. Most days she ran about outside with a little band of children from the other cottages. They were all pre-school age and, for the most part, seemed to tolerate Darlene's presence in their midst, like some outsized cuckoo chick they'd grown used to but didn't much like. She joined in their games in a half-hearted sort of way, standing at the margins rather than being fully involved, being ordered about rather than dominating. Sometimes, though, her junior companions became tormentors, taunting her until she gave them the satisfaction of shrieking with rage and blundering after them, fists flailing ineffectually. Their games ranged all round the cottages and in the immediately adjoining fields. Often they played on the narrow gravel strip that ran between the cottages and the main road, where traffic went by at speed en route between Antrim and Randalstown. If I'd been a parent I'd have been concerned at what seemed like the not inconsiderable risk of their getting run over. Somewhere at the back of the mind there was also the realisation that, given an unlucky combination of chances, one of the hundreds of anonymous drivers going past might be someone who would stop, seize an opportunity and lure a child away. Perhaps the children had been well-drilled about the dangers of accident or abduction. Perhaps Darlene's mother kept a closer eye on her than appearances suggested. But my suspicion was that, even had she been keeping watch from her window, by mid-morning her eye would be fairly dimmed by the drink whose faint, sweet aroma almost always clung to her. Nor was I entirely sure how far her concern for Darlene extended. Given some of her comments, might she have almost been relieved if her little accident had stepped over the row of white-painted kerbstones and met with a swift dispatch?

One afternoon when we were talking, she must have sensed my unease about the children's safety. She called round every now and then with something she'd baked, or to cadge a cigarette, or to ask if I'd heard the news if some terrorist atrocity had happened. Since this was Ulster in the mid-1970s, such incidents were far from rare. As so often, Seamus Heaney's words fit with a precision so deft it's as if he was standing there, an invisible presence, rhyming at our shoulder. When I first read "Whatever You Say Say Nothing" in *North*, I immediately felt some of its lines fall around the neck of many of the exchanges I had with Darlene's mother, noosing their quality with startling aptness:

> Expertly civil tongued with civil neighbours
> On the high wires of first wireless reports,
> Sucking the fake taste, the stony flavours
> Of those sanctioned, old, elaborate retorts:
>
> 'Oh, it's disgusting, surely, I agree',
> 'Where's it going to end?' 'It's getting worse,'
> 'They're murderers', 'Internment, understandably...'
> The 'voice of sanity' is getting hoarse.

We were well used to those fake tastes and stony flavours, though Darlene's mother's tongue didn't operate within the niceties of poetic diction. Her expressions of disgust were seasoned with gross obscenities, as if she wished to visit on the heads of the terrorists some kind of verbal payback for the shocking violence they were visiting on the community. Sometimes Darlene's mother would stand at my door chatting for an hour or more. But she would never come in. I suppose she feared what gossips might make of that, and how her husband would react to reports of his wife being closeted with a stranger. To begin with, I resented these interruptions. I'd come here to focus on my writing, I thought loftily, with the smug and stupid arrogance of youth, not to listen to her prattle. But then the possibility dawned of using her as a template for a character, and I became deliberately interested in her appearance, body language, speech patterns, in that part predatory, part parasitic way that (bad) writing can engender. On that particular day as we stood there talking (or rather, as she stood talking and I stood listening and watching), Darlene and the other children were running up and down the gravelled parking strip at the front of the cottages. Indicating her daughter with a casual wag of her head, she said, "I never worry about her, you know. There's safety in numbers."

IV

That there's safety in numbers was a piece of folk wisdom I'd heard repeated often enough by adults in the course of my own childhood for it to have the plausibility of the familiar. We enjoyed a freedom then that's usually denied to children now. It's hard to say whether there really are more threats to them today, or if it's more a case of increased awareness of possible peril and the apprehension such awareness sparks. We ranged freely over our small territory in an unruly band of friends, siblings, and cousins that provided us with a sense of safety that was, I now suspect, more imagined than offering any real protection against marauders, had we been unlucky enough for any to cross our path. Darlene seemed to enjoy a similarly untrammelled existence, largely independent of adult supervision, though her younger playmates did look after her, so far as this considerable responsibility lay within their capabilities.

I think one of the reasons that Darlene became my totem of individual frailty had to do with the precariousness of her position within that finite calculus of number which allows the psyche to compute its sense of security. The ties that still, just, kept her bound within that little noisy tribe who roamed the territory around Mullaghcartin Cottages, would soon erode and snap. When the younger children, already more advanced than she was, matured and grew beyond her, Darlene would be left behind. As they went to school, forged new relationships, grew in confidence and knowledge, struck out on their own, so, incrementally, she would be abandoned. Our sense of self is tightly bound to our sense of community, the way we're fixed within whatever group provides our ground and anchor – parents, siblings, neighbours, colleagues, friends. Darlene's place in the network of relationships we all depend on was tenuous at best. Unwanted by parents, awkward with friends, siblings who shared and reflected familial unconcern. She was, even when I knew her, already on the edge, poised on the icy periphery of exposure. When the strained social bonds that so loosely cradled her parted and let her go, when her friends tired of this perpetual ungainly child in their midst, when her parents split up (as seemed inevitable judging by the frequency and violence of their rows), when her postman brother moved away and her sister's visits – which already excluded her – stopped, what would be left to cradle Darlene in that familiarity in which we know and are known? What would prevent her from plummeting into the anonymity of the unnamed, unloved multitude of strangers that crowds in on the boundaries of every human group?

So far as I could judge, this small unlovely accident was regretted, and regarded with so little evidence of esteem or love that I doubted their existence. It was easy to see a future unfolding where her essential foundation of familiarity would be altogether destroyed, that territory where we recognise the landmarks of known others and are ourselves recognised by them, a territory from which we can advance with confidence into the unknown. What then? Institutionalisation? Exploitation, neglect, abuse? Or, whether through luck, or love I'd failed to notice, would Darlene somehow manage to find some niche of belonging in the world? Sometimes when I think about her likely destiny, Darlene's situation seems like being in a foreign city where no one knows you and where you know no one. That feeling can be exhilarating. But if it was paired with an only rudimentary grasp of language, a virtual inability to forge new relationships, an almost total dependency on others, an incapacity to engage in gainful work, I imagine such exhilaration would quickly change to fearful apprehension or outright terror. It's one thing to be temporarily alone, momentarily an outsider, a stranger for a while. It would be quite something else for this to be your enduring status without hope of alteration.

Sometimes, looking from the cottage's tiny skylight window on a fine summer's evening, you could see what appeared to be a dense smoke rising from the trees that edged the far end of the fields on the other side of the main road. The fist time I saw this, I thought a huge swathe of woodland must have caught fire. Soon I realised it was clouds of Lough Neagh flies, an insect only found within the orbit of the Lough, whose mysterious watery gravity creates a unique ecosystem with its own small constellation of species. When there's a hatch, the Lough Neagh flies swarm in incredible numbers. Fortunately they're harmless; if they stung or bit, it would render the whole area virtually uninhabitable at certain times of year. Sometimes, when a cloud of them strays down to road level, you can see vehicles going past at a snail's pace, their wipers on, a sludge of insect bodies streaked across the windscreens. It's like driving through heavy rain or fog. Walking or cycling under such conditions means squinting, your eyes reduced to fly-defying slits. The insects get in your hair, up your nose, into your mouth. Long after you reach the sanctuary of indoors, you'll find those that lodged in the folds of clothing crawling free and fluttering weakly towards the nearest light. The flies provide an obvious – but effective – image of multitude and individual insignificance. Within the human swarm, whose density and number, considered in global terms, far surpasses these billows of insect-smoke, we stake out our known territories, forge our links and ties. Cut them, and we plummet into the gargantuan anonymity that surrounds us, but is unnoticed and unthreatening so long as we're safe in the huddle of the tribe. I wondered when Darlene's fall into the wilderness of strangers would happen. It seemed to be a case of when, not whether, and the obvious precariousness of her position acted as a prompt, reminding me that everyone exists surrounded by an abyss of chilling numbers that threaten each individual's little calculations of present safety and position.

V

Going higher than the Lough Neagh flies could ever manage and looking down, has become almost commonplace in this era of routine flight. Aerial views can be breathtakingly beautiful, but gazing at our world arrayed below, in the deceptive neatness and clarity of line that distance imposes, can also be unnerving. It can emphasise the frailty of our moorings, our essential lostness in the crowd however much we may enwrap ourselves in relationships. At one point in *Rings of Saturn*, reminiscing about a flight to Holland, W.G. Sebald observed that:

> If we view ourselves from a great height, it is frightening to realise how little we know about our species, our purpose and our end.

For me, part of this sense of knowing frighteningly little stems from the way in which seeing from the air tends to spark a sense of scale that re-calibrates all our mundane measures. Darlene's mother was right, there *is* safety in numbers – but there can be terror in them too when the small-scale tribal co-ordinates that ground us in family, place and history, that mark out who we are, multiply and swell beyond any comforting containment. Fly over Antrim town with its thousands of inhabitants and sense can still be made of it. Here are known landmarks – the 10th Century Round Tower (one of the best examples in Ireland), the Castle with its Anglo-Dutch water gardens, the railway station, the arts centre, streets we have walked down – recognisable co-ordinates, the possibility of familiarity. Even County Antrim, with its hundreds of thousands of souls, can seem almost containable within our ordinary categories, graspable in language, intelligible within the small compass of our understanding, when it's seen spread out below you in all its complex patterns of sub-divided greens and urban grey-brown smudges. But when you consider Northern Ireland as a whole, with its population of 1,685,287, or fly over a megalopolis like Sao Paulo, with its 18 million, or Tokyo with its 28 million, or when you consider the UK's 58 million inhabitants, the waters of incomprehension start to rise and threaten to overwhelm any sense of individual significance. How can Darlene, how can any of us, find safety amidst the sheer scale of number needed to encompass the human swarm? Six billion people inhabit the world today, and that is a mere 10% of all the people who have ever lived. Does the multitudinous nature of our species not undermine the security of any one life? How can we feel safe when confronted by the dreadful sums our numbers yield (13 million children under five die each year as a result of malnutrition; 800 million people still suffer from hunger; in half a century there could be 9 billion of us)?

Writing about ethics in an era of global consciousness, where we are daily made aware of the existence of innumerable others and of our own tiny singularity set amidst their surging millions, Fiona Robertson has suggested that "globalization means that we are increasingly confronted with moral dilemmas about our relationship with strangers". For me, Darlene has become the face of the most marginalised of strangers, a kind of totem representing in her isolated, unwanted, permanently injured state, the fact of other lives, replete with desperate needs, that are being lived concurrently with our own. And I wonder about the adequacy of my response during our brief and accidental acquaintance. It is a source of some unease that even when met with face to face, when want was seen up close, my response was well short of useful. Of course, in comparison to the situations of many whose lot can be calculated when we run the raw computation of suffering-by-numbers, Darlene was secure and comfortable. She had enough to eat, if she was ill a doctor would be summoned, she had somewhere to live. There are millions for whom such basics are unknown luxuries. Yet her situation still strikes me as totemically precarious, underlining the vulnerability that attends us all, however shielded we may appear. Do any of us have a place in the scheme of things, our swarming billions, that is really any more secure than that of this awkward, damaged, unloved child, or of an individual insect in a cloud of Lough Neagh flies massing for a while like smoke over a County Antrim tree line before crossing that inevitable threshold which separates the living from the dead? What are we all here for? What purpose can be read out of the human totality of which each of us is such a tiny part? Are we one of six billion variations on a theme? Can either theme or variations claim to partake in anything approaching sense? In what relationship do we stand to the crowds of strangers that stand beside us? And what of our relationship with the life-swarms of other species – apes, insects, birds, plants – whose existence (and our impact on it) is likewise something with which we are increasingly confronted?

Curiously, as well as sparking thoughts about how little we know of our purpose and end, as well as providing a perspective which may encourage us to take survey of the vertigo-inducing swarm of our fellows scurrying below in all their daunting millions, looking down also creates a sense of emptiness and absence. As well as sparking a glimpse of the dwarfing multitudes in the midst of whose enormity we are marooned, aerial views also show apparently unpeopled vistas from which it seems everyone has fled, giving the world a kind of deceptive toy-town simplicity. W.G. Sebald again:

> No matter whether one is flying over Newfoundland or the sea of lights that stretches from Boston to Philadelphia after nightfall ... it is as though there were no people, only the things they have made and in which they are hiding. One sees the places where they live and the roads that link them, one sees the smoke rising from their houses and factories, one sees the vehicles in which they sit, but one sees not the people themselves. And yet they are present everywhere upon the face of the earth, extending their dominion by the hour.

If you look at aerial photographs of Ireland, which allow you to examine such perspectives for longer than is possible when you're actually airborne, Sebald's point about the invisibility of people is powerfully driven home. Federica de Luca and Antonio Attini's *Ireland from the Air*, and Esler Crawford's *The North from the Air*, two beautiful books that provide new ways of seeing the landscapes and cityscapes with which we're so familiar at ground level, powerfully underline how hard it is to see people, even in the busiest urban settings. These seemingly unpeopled vistas press home the point of individual insignificance in another way, for it is simply the ant-like littleness of our physicality that is emphasised by looking down. Go further up, consider the earth from space, and even the things we have made, with only a very few exceptions, become invisible. It does not take much distance before we are blotted out. Years and miles soon swat our individual conceits. Faced with light-years and aeons, even the swarm evaporates, vanishing into the mystery of its ultimate beginnings.

Not long after I left Mullaghcartin Cottages, I happened to be flying into Aldergrove, Belfast's International Airport, on a clear December day. For a while, shortly before we came into land, you could see Lough Neagh spread out in its glittering brightness and get a proper sense of its real scale, which is nowhere easily apparent from the ground. I tried to pick out the row of cottages, glimpsed them for a few seconds before we banked and turned, and thought about what Darlene was doing at precisely that moment, at the self-same second as I was thinking about her, looking down from the plane, remembering how she had stood on my windowsill staring in, spying on another world. Perhaps she looked up as I went over, attracted by the noise of the plane and, each unknown to the other, our gazes collided somewhere in the icy winter sky. More likely she was going about her usual routines oblivious to much of what was going on around her. Grown a little older, but no wiser, still stuck in the same closed-orbit of her simple-minded outlook, where did she fit into the universe that dwarfs both of us with its dimensions, whose numbers seem to shatter any safety we might calculate from what is near at hand?

VI

There are other sources of terror-by-numbers beyond the enumeration of humanity, the dwarfing scale of the tribe we all belong to. Once admitted to our ordinary calculations of duration, for example, a geological sense of time soon ruptures the framings within which we normally enclose ourselves behind bulwarks scaled to the pace of our proximate purposes. Darlene is vulnerable enough even when time is measured by birthdays, Christmases, marriages and deaths. But when you see her held tight in the grip of aeons (a grip which has us all in its hold), her aloneness, her tiny isolation, her mysterious finitude becomes massively magnified.

Set beside the customary array of implements we use to butcher time, hacking its enormity into digestible portions, the vision offered by a geological purview introduces such gargantuan dimensions that all our careful cuts – hours, days, minutes, months, years – are rendered uniformly microscopic as the distinctions between them blur into a minuteness from which it is hard to salvage much sense of individual meaning. Our graspable currency of duration is suddenly and spectacularly bankrupted when the individual balance sheet is set not in history's context of mere centuries, but according to the co-ordinates suggested when we introduce the scales of Quaternary, Tertiary, Cretaceous, Jurassic, Triassic, Permian and so on, right back to the Pre-Cambrian Era. It is as if someone had thrown onto our temporal butcher's slab, used to slicing into weeks, seconds, centuries, a carcase as big as the planet itself. What does Darlene mean when viewed under the aspect of almost eternity that's nudged into view when we consider that the earth is some 4,600 million years old, that the first living cells appeared maybe 1,500 million years later? If you bring to mind the age of the rocks on which we have built our transient fictions of name and form, if you reflect on the fact that at least 400 million galaxies are detectable from earth, dotted through the immensities of space, if you remember the billions of other humans who have breathed the air of this planet and then vanished from it, if you recall the billions of cells of which we are constructed and the fact that we are creatures of a universe that came into being some 10 – 15 billion years ago, so much of what we cleave to seems laughably minuscule. Is there any story that could parse and divide these huge measures into sense? Is there any safety to be found in the numbers that hold us in the vice of their awesome quantity? Can we calculate from their enormities any sum of sense that might provide our passing moments with some carapace strong enough to withstand inundation by so great a mass that all the specifics of person, place, and psyche are instantly pulverised?

I wonder what happened to Darlene. And I wonder, sometimes, if she sometimes wonders, without words, what happened to me and to all the other people who have vanished from her life. Perhaps somewhere, now, as I type these reflections, she is bringing back to memory in whatever manner her mind performs such operations, traces of those vanished days at Mullaghcartin Cottages. *I wonder what happened to Darlene,* how she will meet life, how she will meet death, how she has made her way in the world. I wonder what will happen to any and all of us as we traverse our tiny journeys across gargantuan vistas of space-time, surrounded by multitudes that sometimes seem to defy even the basic computation of their number, let alone any triangulation into individually-scaled meaning.

Writing in *Numbers: Their Meaning and Magic*, Isidore Kozminsky, heavily influenced by Kabalistic mysticism, holds that the number one is "the mighty unknowable God of the Universe, it is the number of creation for out of One come all others." Though I would love to find some guiding symbol that might conjure the sum of things into the safety of clear purposes and values, that might secure a place for Darlene and all those others existing even more obviously on the edge than, in truth, we all do, I doubt the legitimacy of any of the equations offered by the great religious systems of the world. There seems little fit between the stories they would have us follow and the script that's offered in the daunting arithmetic of existence. Kozminsky's equation of singularity and divinity might seem to offer the promise of meaning, but in fact it only names a number; its unknowability, and the mystery of its multiplications, remain unchanged.

Assuming that neither the accident nor abduction I once feared cut short her life, Darlene would be almost forty now, her view of the world still filtered through the dense gauze of her disability, as masking of what's there all around her as a net curtain. (But I suppose every member of the human swarm sees things through their own particular array of obstructions; none of us enjoys a clear, unimpeded view). Wherever she is, I hope she has found some supportive niche in which to flourish, some safety in which to dwell amidst the kind of fractions we can handle, that the darker scenarios I often imagine for her have not come to pass, and that she will never be troubled by the terror of numbers swollen far beyond the finger-counting she could manage. I wish her safe and well. I know the littleness and futile impotence of such a wish, but I wish it, with all my heart, just the same, one vulnerable creature to another, two specks in an ocean of incomprehensible, incalculable ciphers into which we will vanish as surely as we came but where, for a moment, we enjoy the crazy buoyancy of consciousness.

Chris Arthur grew up in Bangor, Co Down. His second collection of essays, Irish Willow *(Davies Group), was published in 2002. He lectures in Religious Studies at the University of Wales, Lampeter.*

THE AMERICAN DARK
(excerpt from a novel)

Askold Melnyczuk

Rimbaud in the Second Empire.

Author's Note: What follows is an excerpt from a novel, The American Dark, *whose three narrative strands bob and wave in a violent dance choreographed to the music of George Bush's New Imperial Symphony. Ex-forger Peter Savitzky, newly released from a prison in El Paso, Texas, borrows money from a former fellow-inmate. He intends to use it to help him reconnect with the family he abandoned nearly two decades earlier. His thirty-three year old daughter Cassandra Friedlander nervously awaits the return of the father who abandoned her two decades earlier. A poet, she examines (in a novella-within-the-novel) her troubled feelings toward him through a series of unabashed meditations on the poet Arthur Rimbaud, who himself had been abandoned by* his *father.*

CHAPTER VI
A Bakery With Books

And I eat men like air.
Sylvia Plath

Several days later, before the third and final reading of her "book tour," over a hundred miles south of Clinton but still in the neighborhood by Texas standards, Cass sat on the bed of her motel room in bright mid-afternoon. It was hot. She hadn't turned on the air-conditioner or drawn the curtains on the windows. So her father was already in town. Now what? She watched a portly family of four, father and son with caps on backwards, load a bloated, lime-colored SUV while she smoked, bending a paperclip between the fingers of her right hand. *Daddy daddy, you bastard...*

The previous summer, as her mother lay dying, Cass began writing again, and she hadn't stopped since, the new material accumulating in pieces swept into a dozen blue folders. She'd intended to cancel the readings for her book, but then decided movement might be good for her. Sky, her problematic soon-to-be-ex, agreed.

She wrote a sentence, scratched it out, then rose to close the stiff green curtains.

A couple of days ago, in Archer City, she'd scoured the stores and even thought she'd spotted Larry McMurtry in the stacks.

That evening, she recognized a familiar figure in the back of the bookstore. The minute she saw Gus in the audience, Cass knew: given the chance, she'd humiliate him.

What was he doing there? They'd broken up almost a year ago.

She grabbed the water glass to show she wasn't nervous — it was only a poetry reading — and even though she was hung over, her hand didn't shake. Typical bookstore crowd — a dozen angular women of all ages, including one in her seventies seated up front staring at a café menu; a scattering of beards, and two unregistered voters fidgeting compulsively toward the back. Brisk intro by a man she'd never met who, thank god, made no cracks about the velvet skirt or cowboy boots. Sometimes they riffed on her hair — wise guys; the clever, roaring boys.

Cass knew her boho days were numbered. The Serious Years loomed ahead.

A blond in overalls yawned and scratched under her arm as though waking from a delicious nap.

In the beginning only friends came to her readings — had she really had so many once? Here strangers stared as though she were television: men horny, women analytical — each rehearsing a crack for their partner.

She couldn't wait to get home.

"Could we turn off that music?" she said to her host, who hurried toward some back room.

Sunlight streamed through plate glass behind her.

She smiled at the woman who'd looked up from her menu as though surprised to find someone there.

At least the men paid attention; she could still bank on that. She fingered a button on the snug blue cashmere sweater. Her thick-lashed green eyes and black hair (albeit shorter than before) had charge yet.

Her host returned. The music, softer though audible, was key to customer mood control.

Launching into a poem she glanced at Gus standing near the children's section. She met him in Marie's workshop when the idea of being a poet had begun seeming abstract, despite her training. The real thing was something else, something they couldn't teach in school. All she had to go by, beyond intuition, were the letters and poems of Keats and Rilke. Had either of them ever faced the gauntlet of po biz? Skeptical publishers, horny colleagues, tenure review committees, and empty chairs in bookstores with high ceilings which appeared to stock every book ever written except hers – until tonight, of course? Maybe. Maybe it was ever thus. Gus, she noticed, had shaved his head and pierced his fine straight nose.

While they were together Gus had kept threatening to escape to New York where she herself had gone to college until finally, with her encouragement and goading, he did, for several miserable months. He'd packed up his pick-up and driven by himself across the country, covering the distance in what must have been a near-record thirty-two hours. He stayed with a buddy of his who worked in the meatpacking industry. He'd gone to readings and performed at open-mike nights and met some of the Nyuorican crowd and, through one of Cass's old contacts, got invited to a few gatherings uptown at George Plimpton's house, where he attended his first catered affair. His letters from this period, which she still kept, had been erratic as the cardiograms of heart-attack victims. For one hundred days he was over-stimulated, underfed, and disoriented. One night he punched his hand through somebody's wall. There was a break in the torrent of mail; then a lone post card arrived; and then there was the man himself, looking remarkably unchanged, though she knew better. He'd returned full of bitterness about cliques, preppies in leather quoting Auden, and literary parties hellish as high school where everyone's eyes anxiously followed whatever published authors were cruising the room.

He'd loved threats, made a lot of them: against himself, the literary world, her.

Her bully-boy-poet, grilled in a culture of swap meets and swagger, gulping Borges with his Bud.

She responded to his paranoias firmly: "Of course it helps if you're rich. If you're good-looking. If you went to Andover, then Harvard, or Yale, or Brown, or Columbia, or Bennington. It helps if your grandfather owned a newspaper, if your mother's in publishing, if the family of your best friend from high school has ins at *Time*. Every damn thing helps.

"And another thing," he'd gotten her going, "Never be nice to preppies. Makes them suspicious. They start thinking you want something from them. Can't help it. It's what their parents taught them. Anyway, you probably do. Their money, their connections, their women. Confess, you scheming shit.

"But so what? You know, that's the bullshit. There's more to this than any of that."

On his return, Gus began getting into Waco, bringing it up at every turn: "You know they used CS, a kind of tear gas banned from warfare anywhere in the world after January 1994? Chemical weapons! *Achy-Breaky Heart* day and night, on the advice of trained psychologists!"

"What's your source?"

"*New Yorker,* babe."

"They were scared of another Jonestown."

"So they broke in and killed a hundred people to keep them from hurting themselves? You don't see them doing that to Rabbi Schneerson in Crown Heights, and he's been claiming to be the Messiah for years. People in Brooklyn believed him. You just don't get it. This is Nazi Germany squared."

"Oh come on. Nobody's going to send you to a concentration camp."

"Just wait."

She remembered how sad her father-in-law Jake had been, watching the standoff in Waco.

As her mother grew sicker, Cass's time was eaten up by homecare, leaving her no strength or appetite for suturing this wounded ego. When she finally told Gus to get out, it had been like turning off a dentist's drill that had been running nonstop for years. They hadn't spoken since. She began seeing Sky soon after. She was therefore surprised to notice that her reaction to Gus included not merely the wish to inflict one last retaliatory insult but also a dose of curiosity about what he'd been up to.

She read slowly, marking her place with her finger, finishing lines with a lilt while images from the night before flashed through her mind. She'd let herself be taken clubbing by a couple hosting the dinner "honoring" her. After advertising their tattoos and piercings, the pair, young academics from southern California, invited her to see the real Brillo, where women writhed in cages and buff boys groped each other. At the Fourth Alarm, she watched an orgy on stage; if she hadn't insisted she was tired, the evening would have ended in the master suite of the couple's split-level ranch. They offered Tequila and pot and said they had a hot tub open to the stars. Fortunately, they didn't press her. Alone in her room, she lay in bed thinking of her mother's thin drawn face against the hospital sheets, mouth puckered like an infant ready to suck.

Already at thirty-three she was finding a past she barely recognized nodding in her direction. Walking through the indoor mall in downtown Clinton a few days ago, hadn't she remembered when the building had housed her elementary school?

The next poems, she explained, were from a sequence, now spilling over into the second book, called *Bad Boys of the Nineteenth Century*. Rimbaud was part of that, though what she read revolved around Sir Richard Burton – not the actor but the traveler and orientalist. She'd gotten interested in him back in college after a friend, a graduate student in Arabic studies from Egypt, had told her about Burton's sexual adventures – which wasn't something she shared with the audience. Kamil even promised to take her to Africa with him. Then one night – it was her junior year – he never showed for dinner. Years passed before she heard from him: a few months ago a weathered postcard arrived with *please forgive me* in eight languages scribbled on the back. He must have gotten her address from Barnard with whose alumni group she stayed in touch, keeping a link to a life once almost hers.

She'd passed Kamil's postcard to her sister-in-law, Lana, who snickered "Fat chance." Though she was two years older than Cass, Lana reminded Cass of Tiffany, her friend from junior high who'd been killed by the tombstone. Cass felt protective of her. Lana seemed to have even worse luck with men than she did. Her marriage to Bela had been hellish and now she had some new dick creeping around.

Cass glanced at her watch – useless, since she'd forgotten when she began.

Toward the back, Gus smiled. When their eyes finally locked, she raised her chin in cool acknowledgment.

She feared boring the audience. The poems were difficult – fragmentary meditations on men and women, and even women and women.

In Sindh, Burton found a passion for Islam that eventually led him to Harar, capital of Somalia, where no whites had ever been. For four months he disappeared inside the heart of African light. When he surfaced, he reported his conversations with the king and rehearsed countless adventures. His second visit was aborted when a tribesman planted a javelin in Burton's jaw.

Should she mention that translating the Kama Sutra, Burton checked each position against his experience? She admired his study habits. Dreading boredom, he never focused on anything longer than fifteen minutes, laying his projects out across eleven desks.

She fumbled a line, apologized though she was sure nobody noticed, started over. Muzak audible. Was it corn muffins she smelled? A bakery with books, that's where she was. She imagined the authors on the shelves around her – Dickinson, Austen, James – huddled in a corner, sniffing the air, dismayed and amused by the ritual. She scratched her thigh as if trying to erase a spot in the velvet skirt.

At the last minute she decided to read a few poems about Rimbaud.

As she began, she wondered what she'd say if Gus asked her out for a drink – and what Sky would, if she agreed.

BLIND ANGEL

(from the novella-within-the-novel)

I drifted on a river I could not control.
Rimbaud

1 *The Blind Angel, Emanations from the Left,* or
Nobody's Serious When They're Seventeen

The young stowaway steps onto the platform at the Gare de Strasbourg in Paris in late February 1871, wearing short trousers and blue socks, hair punked with natural spikes. His lips and face are ripe, forehead a half-moon echoed in the brows. In photographs, the deadpan gaze speaks judgment. The eyes, so clear and cool, reflect a child's rage for justice and a touch of omnipotence.

God Jr.

I cannot be happy until all beings are happy, I cannot enter heaven until every last soul is ready to go, thinks the boy.

It's his third assault on the city. The first ended when he cursed a cop, earning himself several weeks in solitary, seasoned with buggery – all for riding a train without a ticket. Not bad for a sixteen-year-old from the sticks.

What lures him is the Paris Commune. The Emperor, a sometime opium addict, has surrendered to the Prussians, whom he attacked in the first place to shore up his own rule, and whose arrival the boy, a traitor by nature, kept hoping for. Then, as now, bullets spiced the longeurs of suburbia. Then, as now, young men had violence in their veins. Then, but not now, Hugo's *Les Miserables* was considered a subversive book.

He eats with the rats and sleeps among vagrants under bridges. When a summons is issued for God's arrest, he volunteers to deliver it. Drinking, he flirts with boys and girls both. A prototype.

Eventually he returns to the slap-happy palms of a single mother bewildered by the brilliant boy going bad before her eyes. What was all that Latin for?

2 *Merde a Dieu*

The word feminism was coined by Fourier in 1837 but while Dumas railed against French women for emasculating men, driving them to sport with whores, Arthur's mother raged and fumed. Many a morning she wished she could abandon her children and join a foreign legion herself.

Instead, she rose at dawn and slogged to the market where she bought leeks and lettuce and a little pork. She swept the kitchen and heated the milk and washed down the table and only then did she go and wake the boys, one of whom planned to sleepwalk his whole life. He'd run off to Paris twice already. Before going into the bedroom she always took a deep breath – she could never be sure she'd find Arthur there. He believed her the incarnation of evil masquerading as God and broke bread with the devil because of it.

It was the times in which they lived, *les temps moderns, les temps moderns.* Those sins of empire, racial mixing and intermarriage, had softened the iron of the Gallic soul, she knew it. Had not the Franks spawned Charlemagne, the Great King, whom she doubly revered for discovering brie? It had been after a campaign against the Lombards in 744, while pausing on the Plateau de Brie near the Abbey of Meaux, where the monks served him a platter. Enthusiasm became fiat. The cheese was made there until the 1790s, when revolutionary terrorists sacked the joint, murdering most of the monks. Should have been the lords of Europe, the French; they alone had poise of spirit, force of body, and wealth. But the Second Empire's decadence, the consumption of absinthe, endless sex – these weakened *les citoyens.* Catholics seized the day and bonded with the state, insisting on moral and religious education and Catholic universities; as a Jansenist herself, Mrs. R. supported it. Every mother needed help.

Vitalie Cuif suspected her husband the Captain had had African lovers.

He'd received medals for murdering Bedouin tribesmen in the conquest of North Africa, but no one as yet had given him any awards for fucking, so she couldn't be sure. All she knew was she had good reason to resent the senses, which had lured her into this: four children, an ancient family line in ruins, living above a bookstore. Naturally she hated the revolutionaries.

Oh the Commune, *mes Hercules, quelle disastre*: angry young people, lacking discipline, incapable of personal hygiene, never mind of running a government. Bohemianism, the romance of poverty, scorn for order and the needs of others: these appealed to the young, none of whom would be caught dead making a bed. They became expert destroyers with no idea how to replace the wares they swept from the shelves.

"I hate God," the boy had said to her the other day.

She slapped him.

"There is no god!" he shouted, and she slapped him again.

"You see, there's my proof," the child – and he was a child – spat.

She raised her hand again while he thrust forward his chin, strong and shapely as the spine of a book, his father's chin.

"Who are you? Who are you?" she hissed back, dropping her hand. Had she dragged him down into the world from the spirit realm so he could torment her further by repeating his father's rejection of all she loved?

"I am the mind of Europe," the boy replied blandly. He'd been studying mystical texts and reading Voltaire. The end had come for parent-gods and priests and kings, who served only themselves. *I cannot be happy until all are happy – doesn't she know that?*

"Then Europe is out of its mind," she replied, shaking her head and folding her hands before her submissively. There was no battling such madness.

When the boy farted, she burst into tears.

If he wanted everyone happy, why was he cruel to his mother, he wondered. A paradox.

Yes, there were reasons Louis Napoleon and the political classes mistrusted the intelligentsia, who depended on the labors of the citizens they damned. Surely the mandarins' contempt arose from guilt before their own rejection of manual labor. Too smart for the salt mines, or the office – how were they to earn their place in this imperfect world except by enumerating its imperfections?

Luckily, there he was, the clean white linen sheet over his head: her demon Arthur.

3 *The Secret Tradition*

Rimbaud never cared about sex as a discrete experience. Indiscretion was everything. He hated secrets – hadn't his mother concealed all from him? She even called herself a widow! Bouts of round-the-clock masturbation had been a way of hiding from the fear at his core, a fear of attachment to his mother, a frustration at not knowing what else to do, even an anger at being forced to figure so much about himself out for himself – why didn't school offer a class: How to Live? How to Live without a Parent … How to Live with Too Little Money …With Eternal Longings … How to Cheer Up a Depressed Mother … How to Murder Your Brother …Questions to the point, things he needed to know. Because his reality was so far from what he longed for, he nourished freakish fantasies about angels sporting in exotic climes. Dakas and dakinis. Consorts of Heruka Vajrasattva – he was reading everything he could about sex and the spirit. His desire drove the imperial and colonial forces outward

– because Europeans were desperate, sick of structures, institutions, fed up by all imagined pasts and heavens. They needed to see how others lived, seeking something better. In the heat of the colonies they found fresh miseries while learning new and often twisted ways of ministering to their senses, because the boundaries of moral law were drawn along the pouting lower lip of the Mediterranean. Below it stretched a formless realm where every violation was permitted – so they sucked up undervalued resources, from oil to diamonds to cooze.

His friend Auguste Bretagne brought him books and bought him beer at the café where they sat smoking pipes, talking kabala and other mystical texts popularized by Hugo and Baudelaire while Prussian soldiers stalked the dusty streets of Charleville. Bretagne was twenty years older, unemployed, with an uncombed beard and a passion for ideas. *Whatsover is found on earth,* Bretagne read aloud from the Zohar, *has its spiritual counterpart on high,* explaining to Arthur it meant that the Christian and the Jewish God were one; that God and Satan were one, to those who could see. And Arthur certainly did.

5   *The Manufacture of Orphans*

The French *chassepot* was far better than the Prussians' rifle, while the *mitrailleuse*, a prototype of the machine gun, with twenty-five rotating barrels, should have given them every advantage. But the discipline wasn't there, their goal was unclear, and they were outnumbered – so the Prussians hammered the French. Vicky, Crown Princess of Prussia, wrote her mother, Queen Victoria, that the French were getting what they deserved for their frivolity and depravity, which had set such a bad example for the rest of Europe. Nevertheless Victoria welcomed Empress Eugenie, Louis Napoleon's Spanish wife, and sheltered her when she fled, after the humiliating defeat, which ended with Bismarck of Prussia smoking a cigar under the Arche de Triomphe.

Empress Eugenie wasn't cowed. Born during an earthquake, she found the rest of life anticlimactic. After she and Louis Napoleon quit having sex, once the heir was born, she'd concentrated on throwing parties lasting months, crowded with elaborate games requiring three changes of clothes a day, which was when the English tailor Frederick Worth, who favored stiff clouds of crinoline and colors like pink or bottle green, with violet and jade for widows, rose in the world. In a way, giving all that up was a relief – and as to exile, her whole life had been lived in exile from her home, in the unofficial harem of a hapless man – for the moment she was minus the man, that's all.

The Comedie Francaise also fled to London, where its stupidest farces were its most popular hits.

Paris was now cut-off from the world. Mail service ran via hot-air balloons sewn from huge strips of calico, and freighted with equipment weighing several tons. They worked.

Food was a different matter: one menu offered minced saddle of cat, mayonnaise, and cutlets of dog *avec petit pois*. While the Jockey Club tempted Rothschild and the Vicomte de la Panouse and the British Consul with a *carte* proposing roast beef, chicken, duck, and crème brule, the denizens of the zoo were auctioned to vendors. A dwarf zebra fetched 350ff; two camels 5,000ff; and a pair of elephants named Castor and Pollux weighed in at 27,000ff. Several rounds from the chassepot were needed to subdue the screaming creatures, whose meat turned out to be tough, coarse, oily, utterly unsuitable for the discerning palate. The elephants' wailing so haunted the butcher that, days after sculpting them to bricks, his wife found him in the meat locker with both wrists filleted.

Pudding of horse marrow was popular, coupled with salami of rat. In front of the Hotel de Ville, a rat market sprang up.

Arthur licked his lips, walking by.

7   *A History of Western Thought*

Verlaine came in drunk, threw me aside, grabbed our child, his own son George, and swung the boy against the wall. My heart closed then, and while it would reopen many times again before it finally shut for good, because I was seventeen, and had faith, and a father sweetness itself (inside the limits of the day) and I was bored, because Paul had the spirit of poetry inside him whereas my own family were no more than consumers of culture, what did they know of what this took? Humanity and kindness had to go, if these men were to master life, though why their experiments habitually turned to violence against my kind I can't say – unless it is so obvious I'm missing it from fear. I see a man out of his senses, his cravat wrapped round his head in a bandana, his jacket pocket torn, his shoes covered in mud, beyond my orbit, spinning inside adolescence once more, that period when boys discover their own sexual organs. Many become organists for life and never grow up – because you need to be a true conductor, and not just of the last candle, to turn the scandal of your body into the symphony God meant it for.

He throws his own child at the wall, and what am I to do with that? Can genius really claim such privilege? And what's the value of the poems he brings to light through his debauches? They're pretty, certainly, but are they worth my pain? To which men answer, Yes. Yes, because what is my pain to anyone but me? Whereas a good poem pleases thousands, and for years to come, if he and you are lucky. So men say. To a man, a woman's pain's a figment, an unreal thing, crude hyperbole of the *what is*, which is determined by a man, cheri. Of course it is. A man decides – and men have trained to be berserkers for millennia or more, so it will be a while before they can adjust.

And yet his rage is not without a cause, although that cause has not a thing to do with me. He and Arthur yank each other. They're man and wife, who know neither the church nor I (nor any family) approve. He calls it all bourgeois, and maybe so. Maybe I want my husband mine, just like that chair, this mauve, flounced dress. And then I ask myself what right I have to temper his desire. He has free will, denying his desire's surely a mistake. That's what it is, his free will against ours. Because I too have it, and want him here, and mine, forever. He screams, insisting law's not God's but man's, imprisoning with guilt, demanding bodies fly their natures, natures' laws, and even gravity itself, which are what else but pure desire?

Perhaps.

11   *The Sorrows of the Courtesans*

The last century imagined itself sexually tolerant but Paris was precocious. The Second Empire found work for 30,000 prostitutes, able and obliging, eager to be ogled. The population was declining and the Emperor urged the cultivation of sexual vigor. Flaubert's friend, actress Suzanne Lagier, when asked why she preferred sex with women to men, said it was because among females she could fart so much more freely. La Pavia, the Polish-Jewish courtesan, who lived in a mansion on the Champ Elysses supported by a Prussian count minting his fortune in Silesian mines, and who had her ceilings painted with mythological scenes showing Zeus and Europa, Paris on his wedding night, Helen pursuing solitary pleasures while outside Troy's walls men murdered each other for her sake, claimed to have sequestered herself in her mother's home for three years, nearly starving to death, until the vision of how she might live came to her, and now she was merely playing out that dream, laughing away those stalkers, ageing and death, whispering: "Whores, honey, everyone's friends; cheap too – they work free."

It wasn't long, however, before free love priced itself out of the market. A revolution begged focus while hookers fucked anyone, even Prussians and Counts, and it became necessary to police them.

At the same time, the Communards abolished titles: no more Dukes or Lords; newspapers were closed; bastards were granted the same rights as legitimate children – and Arthur, reflecting on the madness around him, wept with joy. We would be equal, we might be one despite ourselves.

He loved especially *les petroleuses,* teenage girls, many of them orphans, who set fires with kerosene from milk cans, drove ambulances, and poured boiling water over the troops from Versailles. After the Commune was put down, they were raped, then shot along with the men.

Askold Melnyczuk is the Director of the Creative Writing Program at the University of Massachusetts, Boston. His second novel, Ambassador of the Dead *(Counterpoint), appeared in 2001.*

PORTFOLIO

———

Paul Seawright

Landscapes of absence.

Camels

These photographs are taken from a series entitled "Hidden: Photographs from Afghanistan," exhibited at the Irish Museum of Modern Art, Dublin, during the autumn of 2003. Commissioned by the Imperial War Museum in London after the fall of the Taliban regime in 2001, the exhibition consists of postwar landscapes littered with mines and ordnance evoking a malevolent aftermath.

Paul Seawright was born in 1965 and grew up in Belfast. Earlier series of photographs include "Sectarian Murder", "Cages, Walls and Fires" and "Police Force". He is the Director of the Centre for Photographic Research, University of Wales, Newport.

Column

Mounds

Passage

Sign

Valley

IN OTHER WORDS: FROM THE NEPALI

In the land of Buddha and Lenin.

I WOULD DONATE DROPS OF MY SEMEN...

Like the fusion
of sunlight and rainfall we came together,

became one
like entangled profusion of wild clouds

in which
later a rainbow flared.

And then
the sky shook in wrath

and storms roared in to uproot the trees of sunlight.

Again we grew silent,
vast blue of a mature sky.

In depths
of your moments of solitude, love,

I have lost
the tumultuous pinnacles of youthful heights.

Often we have broken together,
to laugh or to cry.

But today's waking seems
struggling to unravel the secret heart of our clogged skies.

In the excited tumult of our Waking
we have to listen to the clear calling voice of reason.

That's why from today onwards
instead of saying *I love you*, I would be saying:

I donate drops of my blood
To feed the hungers of your embryo.

Yes, love, it's made in the jungle too.

But here, in these
shacks of society, love itself doesn't seem sufficient.

Here we have to have
a pure donation of semen for healthy wombs.

Here you have to create a Buddha.
Here you have to give birth to a Lenin.

Is there a mirror better than
the eyes of our children to see truths of our lives?

Here we have
to have a self-revelation.

Yes, young girl, next time
on meeting you, I would openly say –

I donate drops
of blood for your embryo.

Or, on meeting someone else
just as glamorous as you,

the one who can
pull the reins of my heart's lusts

I would
boldly declare:

I donate drops of my semen
to feed the hungers of your savage womb.

THE STORY OF MY LOVE

I had a dark one then,
the one who couldn't dare to face

the magnificent
daggers of my gallant grace,

couldn't ejaculate
a gasp in my awesome presence.

I was her King
but she couldn't be my Queen.

Doorkeeper's daughter she was,
could speak only to doorkeepers.

To some cannibal world she belonged,
savagery being her religion.

Could she dare to face
the glowing pinpoints of my shimmering eyes?

But then I had others too,
like this dark one, the ones who plotted in their dreams

to possess me
since in reality it was no better than an obscene joke.

In dream thus they laboured to save me from myself,
like in dreams they had tried to tame me.

In dreams their vicious schemes flowered.
In dreams they conspired to kill me

to suck the blood
tingling in the veins of my rebellious heart.

Times of the dark ones
came and passed away.

Now the white ones are dancing in the castles of filth.
And with them I am dancing too.

But aren't such games
nothing but figments of fantasy?

Can such games choke the stars of my conscience?
Haven't I sought a divorce from harlots of illusion?

I am used to dancing with the dames of revolution.
That's why to me love and revolution seem equal.

That's why revolution has yet to accept my sacrifice.
That's why revolution has yet to become my bride.

I have already offered my salute to revolution.
I am thirsty of revolution. I am its ardent lover.

Revolution has yet to make love to me.
I am hungry.

It has yet
to serve the storms of my hunger

Gopal Prasad Rimal

A COLD SLEEP AND BROAD DAYLIGHT

In the *Wanted* columns
of daily newspapers am I waiting

to glimpse the face
of my days to come.

In each procession, rally and file of
each fresh plan am I hankering for

a platform
to step on to survive.

In the lips of each fresh budget
am I searching assurances

and from the promising declarations
of daily radio-broadcasts am I expecting a word or two of
consolation.

In each fresh pay scale
am I measuring the age of my family.

The opportunity of each fresh
vacancy invigorates me and makes me young,

and on hearing the result of each interview
life festers like some armpit reeking from sweat.

Even in my mother's tender kiss
someone has poured gloom.

In my father's speech of support
whistles a chilled exhaustion.

From the part of my young sister's hair
auspicious vermilion seems to have been frightened away.

My wife, it seems, serves
satire on my plate of daily rice.

An age has passed,
and I, carrying my application-like face,

am rambling in the gloom of each and every street
am reaching the frozen threshold of each and every house.

And a cold slumber seems
to be slowly coming over my limbs.

But I know if I sleep this time
it would be a long sleep.

That's why, O you lining up like caterpillars!
O you words of a slogan, cry aloud!

Shout my slogans!
O you words, rend open the sleep of this air!

Oh! I do not want to sleep now,
not in the glare of this broad daylight.

Wake me, O words, wake!

BAISAKH (NEW YEAR)

Like a postman just
transferred, carrying the parcel

of a bright sun
in his tarpaulin bag

Baisakh trudges
over the tin-roof of the shack.

Motioned by its heavy footfalls
the pendulum of time on the wall-clock swings

tuck, tuck, tuck, tuck, tuck.

Making a haggard, lightless face
the lonely sun lies crestfallen.

Untimely rain.
An unseasonal roaring in the clouds.

Drinking choleric waters of the Vishnumati
the sky is suffering from diarrhoea.

Out from the dismal notes of a clarinet
come innumerable, invisible germs of an impending plague.

Under the scorching sun of the mid-day,
the trees are feverishly scratching their limbs.

Once again
new year has come.

Once again have I
to hang up life's visa on the wall's new calendar.

Once again have I
to prepare a list of the companions of a lifetime.

Once again under
the lethal shadow of jets

carrying fatal bombs have I to write
in the name of the dear ones

the greetings
of success, peace and long, healthy life.

Bhupi Sherchan

AN ILLICIT AFFAIR

Sweet son,
you could be a Hamlet,

a dangling
diadem of dying and being,

of cause
and confusion,

could be
a sword of decision,

could sharpen your
new blade on the rocks of my body,

could dip its emblazoned point
in a bowl of potassium cyanide

to pierce my soft
throat with its poisoned end.

Squirming
in the point of poison

I would love to die

for secretly
I have been rearing

an illicit affair with my age,
an illicit affair with my age.

REALITY

Pregnant
with the wails of a hundred huts

the hillranges
beyond the brook are aflame.

Can't the smell
of a burnt human hair be a reality?

PROSPERITY

Drunken feet
dance to the rhythm of maize grains

bursting
in the seething cauldrons.

In the light
of the crackling hearth

grandma's tale
makes kids clutch

their fingers
between their jewel-teeth.

In the eye
of greenery the night consumes

pitchers of local wine,
softening fogged hilltops.

The singing virgins
accept the rhetoric of the sturdy youth.

Wouldn't you
call it bliss, prosperity?

Banira Giri

CONSTITUTION

Constitution isn't a book's name,
nor is it a fresh weapon from some nuclear arsenal,

a blue stretch of a sky,
a bird's exuberant attempt to fly,

a cry of a gurgling brook,
a prism of some jubilant vision.

Or is it some plastic plaything?

The questions like showers
of monsoons are battering plains of our mind.

Tell me which book of mantras,
which fragment of a blue sky

or which network
of some novel game you would distribute.

Do you know constitution isn't
the name of some new chocolate advertised by television?

Constitution is a country's youth.
It's a turbulent brook and its quaking banks.

It's an idea, an outlook and a vision;
a boat and its continuous journey.

Don't tell me it's just a book.

It's a sun.
It's a sky and its blue dream.

Shailendra Sakar

MUSEUMS OF TORTURE

Your face
stinging from the scratches of atrocity

is throbbing
to eke out droplets of blood.

Did some soft-nailed civilian do this?

A gleaming dagger
has been thrust deep into your ribs.

Is it a dagger of pure steel?

Your belly
is a bleeding sieve of bullet holes.

Did some imported rifle do this?

Your dusty body
lies splashed in gore and you cry aloud.

Is it a line from the national anthem?

The juice of your
lips has been squashed.

Your eye-sockets
are slimy ponds of dirt

Your rough-skin
is taut from tensions

The round moons
of your palms tremble weakly

Did your people
from the museums of torture return?

TEAR GAS

In our eyes tears haven't exhausted yet.
Our eyes haven't yet dried completely.

Even today there remains in our eyes
some grains of salt and tiny little drops of water.

Look, it's wet,
the soil of Narayanghat,

Pokhara, Janakpur, Katmandu,
Bhaktapur, Patan and Kirtipur.

It's wet
from the showers of our tears.

Tears turn into blood
and blood into tears.

Now there isn't any
difference between tears and blood anymore.

Blood and tears,
tears and blood,

out from thousands of eyes
are cascading brooks of blood.

Bloodied is this earth
and blood bathed Nepal.

O you traders of tears!
O you who make our eyes bleed!

This is tears' address to you,
this the resolution of blood.

This is the time,
this the time when blood would

clutch the winds
and demand accounts of tears from you.

Bimal Nibha

Translated, from the Nepali, by Yuyutsu R. D. Sharma.

TRANSLATOR'S NOTES

——

Gopal Prasad Rimal

Gopal Prasad Rimal was born in Katmandu in 1918. During his adolesecence he came under the influence of revolutionaries aspiring to overthrow the despotic Rana regime. Although Rimal had begun his career as a successful poet in 1930, and as playwright in 1940, it was in 1941 that Rimal emerged centre-stage in Nepal's literary and political life. In that year, the brutal execution of the patriot Dashrath Chand and his friends fired Rimal's imagination – and revolution became the bedrock of his creative ventures. Rimal founded a creative organization, *Praja Panchayat* (People's Democracy), to protest against the suppression of the Nepalese masses by the Rana rulers, and was imprisoned on several occasions. He played a pivotal role in the foundation of the successful Democratic Movement (1950-1951), but soon after grew disillusioned. His dreams of a democratic Nepal were shattered as the "harlots of anarchy" in the garb of democracy began occupying the "castles of filth". Rimal lost his mental balance and was sent to an asylum in Ranchi, India. Later he was returned to Nepal, where he spent the rest of his life, still insane, roaming the streets of Katmandu. He died in 1973.

Unlike his contemporaries who were influenced by the English Romantics and employed a Sanskrit metre, Rimal, even before the 1950 Revolution, shed Sanskrit usage and wrote fiery poems dealing with the struggle of the Nepalese people. He also introduced the prose poem to Nepali literature. "Rimal's contemporaries could hardly digest the English Romantics and Shakespeare," Nepali poet Krishna Bhakta Shrestha has written, "whereas Rimal succeeded in writing the first Nepali prose poems, using native symbols and folklore to capture the agony of Nepalese people." It was Rimal's literary boldness that encouraged Nepali writers like Laxmi Devkota and Baladrishna Sama to begin writing prose poems and social-realistic plays in the years immediately preceding the 1951 Revolution.

Bhupi Sherchan

Bhupi Sherchan, the true successor of Rimal and the most popular Nepali poet of modern times, was born to a well-off family in Tukuche, in the Mustang region of Nepal. He was educated in Benares, India, where, in 1956, inspired by communist ideology, he began writing poems under the *nom de plume*

Sarvahara (*Proletariat*). He subsequently published *Naya Jhyaure* (New Folksongs), a collection of songs in the popular *Jhyaure* metre. Around 1960 Sherchan moved to Katmandu, where he came in contact with the poets Krishna Bhakta Shrestha and Basu Shashi, and founded a literary organization, *Rodi* (Session). In the early sixties he participated in the protests of the Civil Resistance Movement (Bhadra Avagya Andolan) against the one-party Panchayat system and was jailed. During this period, he also published *Nirjhar*, a collection of poems aspiring to voice a revolutionary wrath, through the conventions of traditional metre.

But the real Shercan — a great satirist in the tradition of Rimal — was born when he shed his *nom de plume* and began publishing poems that ingeniously voiced Nepalese suffering under the autocratic yoke of the Panchayat regime. His later work explores the taboos of Nepalese consciousness; attacks the vainglorious traditions of Gurkha heroism; and evokes delicate questions of nationalism, sovereignty and geopolitical isolation. In 1969, he shot to nationwide fame with his collection, *Ghumne Mechmathi Andho Manche* (Blind Man on a Revolving Chair) which won the prestigious *Sajha Puruskar* prize.

Dissatisfied by city life, Sherchan subsequently left Katmandu and moved to Nepal Terai, where he worked as a building contractor until he was awarded membership of Royal Nepal Academy in 1979. He died in 1989.

Banira Giri

Banira Giri was born in 1946 at Kurseong, Darjeeling, India, but moved to Nepal when she was a student and has associated herself with the country in her writing. She attended Tribhuvan University and was the first woman to receive a PhD in Nepali Literature. Her work consists of three collections of poems and two novels. She became widely known in Nepali literary circles with her first novel, *Karagar* (The Prisonhouse) which explores exploitation of women in a patriarchal society. Widely travelled, she works as Associate Professor of Nepali at the Padmakanya campus of Tribhuvan University.

Shailendra Sakar

Shailendra Sakar was born in Bhojpur Bazar, Eastern Nepal, in 1947. While at school, he came in contact with a group of political activists who had sought refuge in his remote village. He moved to Katmandu in search of a job and later studied at Tribhuvan University, where he received a Masters in Nepali Literature in 1972.

In 1979, Sakar founded a movement for communities impoverished by the Panchayat system. In the 1980s, he was influenced by the Beat Poets and joined the Boot Polish Movement that campaigned for freedom of press and championed non-elite writers. He also edited *Mantra*, a literary magazine.

In 1979, Sakar published *Collage*, a collection of short stories where he experimented with traditional narrative and created an anti-heroic persona depicting the cruelties of Nepalese social life. In the same year, he also published *Shailendra Sakar Ka Kavita* (Poems of Shailendra Sakar), a collection of poems establishing him as a major voice for the dispossessed, and altering the élite definition of poetry. In 1991, his second collection of poems, *Sarpaharu Geet Sundainan* (Many Unheard Songs) returned to the cruelties of Nepal's one-party regime. Currently, he works as an official with Nepal's Agricultural Development Bank and lives in Katmandu.

Bimal Nibha

Born in 1953, Bimal Nibha was raised and educated in Birgunj, a small town on the Nepalese-Indian border. At university, he became involved with leftist politics. In the 1980s, he published his first collection, *Aagonira Ubhiyeko Manis* (A Man by the Hearth, 1984) and wrote a popular column, *Debre Kuna* (Left Corner) for Nepal's national weekly, *Dristi* (Seeing). In 1989, he published *Chautho Column* (Fourth Column), a collection of satirical essays. He has also edited several literary magazines. In 1990, he was active in the democratic movement, and was arrested for his involvement. Seeking the restoration of a multi-party democracy, Nibha founded a political weekly, *Pratipakh* (Review). He was for many years the Director of Nepal's leading semi-government publishing house, Sajha Prakashan. His most recent collection of poems is *Euta Bahula Nabhayeko Bushirt* (A Shirt Without Sleeves).

Yuyutsu R. D. Sharma

Yuyutsu R. D. Sharma has published three collections of poems, including *A Prayer in Daylight* (1984) and *Hunger of Our Huddled Huts and Other Poems* (1988). Sharma was educated at Baring Union Christian College, Batala, Punjab and later at Rajasthan University, Jaipur. He taught English Literature at Tribhuwan University for more than a decade, but in 1995 retired in order to pursue his writing. He has translated extensively from Nepali, and now edits *Pratik*, a magazine of contemporary writing. He currently divides his time between Katmandu and New Delhi.

THE REMNANT

(short story)

—

Robin Glendinning

Why the Remnant never learns.

It is said that even the crow thinks its offspring the most beautiful chick in the wood but as she fought to attach the new collar round her son's thick neck Sammy's mother despaired of his shape.

"You're hurting me, Ma," he protested.

"Well stop your wriggling then," she said, trying to prise the stud through an opening so small and tight that it seemed to have been deliberately designed to frustrate her.

"You're throttling me," he squeaked.

"Well the morrow you'll hae to throttle yourself," she said working away vigorously at the second eye-hole. "You can't come charging down to me in a fank every morning. I've enough to do as it is." He gulped at the tightness of the thing. She rammed a forefinger in next his neck and gave the offending collar and the shirt to which it was now attached a good strong pull.

"Aw!" he yelled as his head jerked forward.

"Ach, you'll get worse afore you're better," she said employing an expression he often heard from her when hurt or when mishap must be shrugged off without ceremony. She knotted the new tie at his throat with the determination of a hangman.

He twisted his head about inside the restricting halter and gingerly inserted his own finger where the stud pressed uncomfortably against his throat. "You bought them too small," he said.

"Didn't I have you measured?" she said and stood back to examine her handiwork.

"But I've grown since," he said plaintively.

"Well ye'll hae to thole," she said. "Money doesn't grow on trees you know. Where's your cap?"

"I don't know," he said and looked about him in surprise. How could he have lost the brand new cap with its peak and button and its red and black quarters to match the broad stripes of the same colour on his tie?

"Well I do," she said. It was another of her little habits to be smug with him and he waited patiently for her to tell him what she hadn't needed to ask. "It's in your room. You were wearing it in bed last night."

He blushed and his mouth opened to make a denial. She stopped him with a warning finger on her lips, "Now, Samuel," she said sternly, "don't be hurting Jesus with a lie."

He didn't.

"It's no shame to be excited," she said with a smile. "I looked in on you last night and there you were, fast asleep with your new cap perched on top of your head. It must have fallen off you before morning and you missed it in your rush."

He stood before her in silence. He was stocky, stout, round-shouldered and long-armed. But what is said about the crow is true. This was her only child and he had passed the new exam that would let him and others like him who were not from the families of the better-off, into the grammar school and this was the morning of his first day. Naturally she was proud. However, there was an angry red mark on his bull neck and she spent her precious moment wondering if she could persuade Small's in Market Street to take back the other collars in the box for some of a larger size. "Way up and get your cap," she said.

In the front row of the scrum that bull neck which had been too big for a collar was now a wonderfully effective offensive weapon. Sammy's rounded shoulders so unprepossessing on that morning over a week ago now fitted perfectly. His arms, which had then hung simian-like at his side, now stretched, bound and grappled him to his task. For once his short thick legs were no disadvantage and his girth suddenly ceased to be a subject of mockery.

Sammy McConkey planted his feet in the mud and braced his back. The taller, heavier, more conventionally athletic boy opposed to him heaved and grunted and shoved to no avail. Sammy's unique shape made it easy to be lower and straighter in the push than the larger boy. He felt a sudden thrill in the mechanical power of being able to hold that struggling, puffing, ill-designed engine with ease. He waited while frustration and discomfort took their toll and then with a snap drove forward. His unlucky opponent buckled and slipped and the whole scrum of which he was a part slid backwards and crumpled in an ignominious heap. Sammy trampled gleefully through the twisted mayhem of eight bodies, sixteen arms and sixteen legs.

"Well done there, McConkey," shouted Mr Clarke and Sammy grinned as he ran to the next scrum eager for his next triumph.

That first afternoon on the rugby pitch Samuel McConkey found his second home. Outside his first he had never felt at ease anywhere else, had never suited anywhere else, had never fitted anywhere else. He was the only child of a late marriage and his upbringing had been even lonelier than might have been expected under such circumstances. His father belonged to a particular sect of evangelical Protestantism whose pessimism about the fate of all but a very few on the Day of Judgement led to exclusive religious and social practices. The family did not worship in any of the churches or tabernacles of the small town but each Sunday went by train to Belfast where the sect held its meetings. Thus Sammy had never been a member of the local Cub pack nor of the Scouts, nor the Life Boys, nor the Boys Brigade, nor of the Young Covenanters and neither had he attended any of the town's many bible classes nor Sunday schools.

Neither did Sammy make friends with the other children he met in the big gloomy hall in the city centre. He only saw them once a week and they all seemed to know one another, indeed many of them were related. Their fathers were solicitors or linen merchants or doctors and though Sammy's father placed great reliance on the sect's egalitarian belief in the priesthood of all believers he was clearly not of the same as them. No matter how often his good suit was cleaned and pressed it was never as smart as those worn by the professional Christians. He spoke to the other men with great care, choosing words that often had a biblical ring to them for he had acquired most of the language he now used by dint of study.

Sammy's mother changed the ribbon on her one hat and wore it bravely each Sunday and smiled and nodded to the other women. She barely spoke a word, even to Sammy; except when she secretly dug him in the back with the knuckles of her clenched fist and hissed at him, to "sit up straight" in his chair.

As the sect did not have the numbers to run its own schools Sammy had had to attend the primary school with local children. However, his father followed the precepts of the sect to the letter and insisted that his son be withdrawn from Miss Cathers' Scripture class so that even there he had been a boy set apart.

The idea of being "set apart" was central to Mr McConkey's religious beliefs. He read to Sammy from Judges the story of Gideon who had, on the instructions of the Lord, reduced a force of many thousands to a mere three hundred and still put the Midianites to flight. To Sammy's surprise the three hundred were chosen because they had cupped water in their hands and lapped it with their tongues "as a dog lappeth," unlike the majority who had stuck their heads in the river. "Sammy, don't bend over your soup like a cat lapping milk," his mother would say at mealtimes. "Samuel, raise your spoon on a level to your lips and tip it so," his father would pronounce and demonstrate.

"You see, Samuel," his father often used his full name when he had serious information to impart, "You see, Samuel, we are like a remnant."

Sammy thought of the cheap pieces of cloth that his mother sometimes bought in Small's to economise but before he could develop this into a satisfactory exegesis his father quoted from Isaiah: "Except the Lord of hosts had left us a very small *remnant,* we should have been as Sodom and we should have been like unto Gomorrah."

The little town with its small shops, its many churches and its square and flagpole from which the Union flag flew every July seemed very dull in comparison to the infamous cities of the plain, and although the many gloomy public houses were undoubtedly places which might well be destroyed in the last days, Sammy found it difficult to imagine how Miss Cathers with her kind, soft voice, her mousy hair, her twin set, old tweed skirt, thick stockings and brogues could threaten anyone with eternal destruction, but that it was so he did not question.

Mr McConkey talked often of the *remnant* and how, though apparently small and feeble, the *remnant* might redeem the rest of the people, including Miss Cathers. After all only the *remnant* had been capable of re-founding the Temple in Jerusalem. He quoted further, from Jeremiah and from Ezekiel and from Joel and from Micah and from Hagai and from the Revelations of St John the Divine. This last reference told how a terrible earthquake had killed thousands of people and how "the *remnant* were affrighted and gave glory to the God of heaven." Sammy read a book in which there was a picture of an earthquake with buildings toppling and screaming people tumbling willy-nilly into a vast fissure that had suddenly appeared in the ground. One of them might have been Miss Cathers clutching vainly at her handbag. It was easy to be "affrighted" at such a prospect and he remained an unquestioning member of the *remnant* and did his best to give "glory to the God of Heaven."

Mr Clarke, or Clarky to the boys, was a chain-smoking Scotsman with a passion for rugby football. He was a purist in a world dominated by pragmatists. In Clarky's rugby world you ran with the ball, you passed the ball and you only kicked the ball as a last desperate defensive resort. The school did well for its numbers but the game in Ulster was very competitive and although Clarky had been capped three times by his native land he had never been allowed to coach the firsts. It was felt that Clarky's team would be more concerned with the way the game was played than the result and his colleagues and the headmaster and the school governors and the old boys, especially the old boys, were all agreed that the only thing that really mattered was the result. The story was often told, with good humour certainly but with a serious point to it also, of how a precocious fly-half of Clarky's had once dropped a goal. The cheering from the touch-line had been stilled by the sight of Clarky striding purposefully onto the pitch and the simpering smile had been wiped from the face of the fly-half when Clarky had roared at him in his broadest Scots, "The guid Lord gave ye hauns tay pass wi' an feet tay run wi' so cut out the music-hall stuff, Boy!"

Clarky's talents and enthusiasms seemed best-suited to the first year team where the basics had to be instilled, but over the years his contempt for the way the game was being played elsewhere had made his mission a lonely one that he felt only he could do. As he ran about on cold wet winter afternoons the solitariness of his purpose and the asceticism of his spare frame would have done justice to one of the Minor Prophets that Mr McConkey was so fond of quoting. Perhaps he was the ultimate *remnant* and on that first afternoon in early September he saw the potential of Sammy McConkey with a visionary's eye.

"I tell ye, Vera," he said to his wife at dinner, "there's a wee laddie in the first year that's going to go far."

"Yes, dear." Vera heard this or something like it every September.

"He's the perfect shape for a prop forward and he can run and he can tackle and he can pass and what's best of all, Vera," here Clarky paused for emphasis, "what's best of all the wee bugger's fearless!"

"Alasdair, please don't be coarse."

Clarky did not apologise but leaned back in his chair and took a cigarette from the packet at his elbow, shook his head and said, "Do you know, Vera, he didn'ae have a pair of boots."

"Alasdair, I do wish you wouldn't smoke between courses."

"I don't mean he'd forgotten them, you understand. He just didnae have any."

"I don't know how you can taste anything you eat."

"I had tae get him a pair outa the lost property."

"I sometimes wonder why I bother," she said.

Clarky was looking up into the smoke that he had blown in great clouds through mouth and nostrils. "Think of it, Vera: all that potential and no bloody boots."

"Alasdair, really!"

"Clarky says I have to have my own boots."

"It's Mr Clarke to you, Sammy," said his mother.

"Mr Clarke says I have to have my own boots."

"What for?"

"Rugby."

"Rugby? You're no playing rugby."

This was both a statement and a question. "I am," said Sammy.

"But your father spoke to the headmaster about it afore you went. You were withdrew from scripture and games."

"I don't want to be withdrew... withdrawn."

"But Sammy, what would your father say?"

"I don't know."

"Sammy, ye know fine well."

"Ma, I might be picked for the team."

"The team?" He heard the panic in her voice. "Sammy, ye canna be on a team."

"Och Ma!" She saw the tears in his eyes but though her heart went out to him her duty was painfully clear. "Son dear, ye know what it says in the scriptures."

"Yes," he said miserably.

"There is a remnant," she began and knew for his sake and her own that she must prove the point as her husband would have proved it with the apposite quotation. "There is a remnant," she struggled, "a remnant ..."

"According to the election of grace," he said.

"Well, if ye know it so well why don't ye act on it?" It was annoying not to have got it right herself.

"But why can't the remnant play rugby?"

"Because ... because it's chosen."

"So is a team."

She was sure there was an answer to his glibness but couldn't think what it was.

"There were three hundred in Gideon's host and fifteen on a team," he said.

"You must ask your Da," she said and immediately remembered that the table still had to be laid for supper.

He watched her for a moment dashing hither and thither with plates and cups and saucers and rattling vigorously in a drawer for cutlery. "Have ye no hands on ye?" she said. "Or do I have to do everything in this house myself?"

He went to the dresser where three linen napkins lay in three prized silver plate napkin rings and said as casually as he could, "But if *you* bought the boots there'd be no need for him to ..."

"Sammy!" She dropped the knives and forks onto the table with an impressive clatter. "Sammy, I am surprised at you."

He was surprised at himself.

"If I told your Da what ye've just axed me to do you know well what would be the upshot." He knew well. He hung his head. "Ye'd get lilty my lad. And don't think I'd raise a hand or say a word to stop it."

He shuffled his feet and felt shame and fear but placed his hope in that first *if*. "I'm sorry, Ma," he said.

"Well," she said and was grumpy to show that she was making a big concession, "I suppose I could forget ye said it."

"Thanks, Ma."

"But either ye ask your Da to buy ye those boots or ye tell Mr Clarke that ye're not playing any rugby nor getting on no team. Do ye hear me?"

"Yes, Ma."

"Hello, McConkey." Clarky was surprised to see the boy waiting on his own outside the classroom. "Did you get your boots yet?"

"No, sir."

"And why not, McConkey?"

"I'm not allowed to play, sir."

Clarky spoke very slowly. "Not allowed to play? Why so?"

"It's my religion, sir."

Clarky said nothing.

"My father spoke to the headmaster about it, sir. Before the term begun, sir."

"Began, McConkey, began."

"Began, sir."

Clarky lit a cigarette and considered the matter. He was of Calvinist stock himself, brought up in a land long riven by strict sabbatarianism and exclusivism of the narrowest sort and knew well where to tread carefully.

"It's the remnant, sir," said Sammy, by way of explanation.

"Ah, the remnant, McConkey," said Clarky as if a light had dawned. "The remnant," he said again rolling the *r* with particular relish.

"Yes, sir."

"'The r-r-remnant shall return, even the r-r-remnant of Jacob, unto the mighty God.' Isn't that so, McConkey?"

"Yes, sir."

Clarky hunkered down so that his head was level with Sammy's. "Did ye ever consider, McConkey," he said, and the acrid stink of the tobacco puckered up the boy's nose so that he wanted to sneeze, "Did ye ever consider why the Mighty God gave ye wee stumpy legs wi' strapping thighs and a backside like a carthorse? Did ye ever consider why your back is so strong and your neck is so short and your arms have the reach of a daddy orang-utan? In short, McConkey, did ye ever consider why the Mighty God made ye so ugly and blessed ye wi' the heart of a lion? Did ye, McConkey?"

"No, sir."

"Do ye no think that he might hae wanted ye tae prop for Ireland?"

"I was surprised at work today, Samuel," said Mr McConkey and went to hang his coat on the peg near the door. "What do you suppose surprised me?"

"I don't know, Da."

"Don't say Da. It is common."

"I don't know, father."

"Mr Dodds, my superior, asked me if I was going to the match," said Mr McConkey and sat down beside his son and lifted a Latin book in apparent interest. "Naturally I said that it was not my habit to go to matches." Sammy's mother, who had just risen from a chair to prepare the supper, stopped in her tracks, a half-darned sock still in her hand. "I did not add that I thought matches mere foolishness and vanity and that I was surprised at a man in his position repairing unto them." Mr McConkey closed the Latin grammar that lay on the table under Sammy's nose. The clock chimed. He took his watch from his waistcoat pocket, checked the time and then wound it slowly and methodically. "Mr Dodds said that his son and mine had both been picked on a team and were playing in a rugby match this Saturday. I was so sure of myself and my son that I told him that this could not be so, and Mr Dodds demurred. Tell me Samuel that he was indeed mistaken."

Some moments later, the red-and-black jersey, the matching socks, the black shorts and the new boots laced and dubbined were set out on the table like exhibits in a trial. Sammy and his mother dared not look at them. They must have both been mad to think that they could get away with it for long. Perhaps they had preferred not to think and had just hoped. But even the old piece of blackout material in which the forbidden boots had been wrapped when they were hidden in the chimney of the front room where a fire was never set was laid before them as evidence of their dishonesty and stupidity. Mr McConkey spoke slowly, reflecting on each word as he did at Sunday meeting in Belfast. "I have been made a fool before my superior. That hurts me but it is of little consequence. I do not mind being thought a fool for the sake of The Lord. What I do mind is that my son has been deliberately and systematically deceiving me. What have you to say about this, Elizabeth? What have you to say about a boy who will go to such lengths to deceive his father?" At that he picked up the string that had bound the cache together. It was a long twisty piece of string and it dangled from his finger and thumb. "Well, Elizabeth?"

Sammy looked at his mother and saw her red face and bowed head and was suddenly sorrier for her than he was for himself. He was just about to make a heroic gesture to take all the blame when she spoke. "Ye know well I bought him the boots."

"I simply wished to hear you say it, my dear," he said.

"Well shame on you for that," she said with an unexpected show of belligerence.

"Shame? Me? Why should I be ashamed?"

She said nothing.

"Unless of course you speak of the shame I undoubtedly feel in my betrayal. There is shame a-plenty, is there not, in being betrayed by one's wife and son? Is that the shame of which you spoke, Elizabeth?"

Sammy watched his mother's face contort in a manner that he had never seen before. She bit her lip, quite cruelly.

"Well, Elizabeth, why should I be ashamed?"

"Because you're a bully."

Her husband could not have been more shocked if she had suddenly slapped him hard across the nose and eyes. Indeed he gasped, and took a half-step backwards as if she had. Although her face was glowing hotter and redder by the minute her head had come up and her shoulders had squared and her jaw had tightened. "I don't mane you're rough," she said. "You've never raised your hand to the child except it were needed, but there are other ways of bullying."

"What ways?" Extraordinarily, this was a genuine inquiry.

"You say what's to think. You say what's to do. You lay down the law and no-one else is axed."

"Asked," he corrected.

"Axed!" she said defiantly.

"Elizabeth, I hardly think this is…"

"I'm usually Beth in the house."

He looked at her in utter astonishment. A second blow had staggered him. He took a breath and tried to summon his intellectual resources. "Beth dear, I…"

But she was at him like a terrier with her words; "Mr Clarke says Sammy's good at the rugby. Says he's got a talent for it. Says God gave him the talent so why shouldn't he use it. Well, why shouldn't he? It says in the Good Book that if ye're given a talent ye're to use it and not hide it in the ground, doesn't it? It says it's a sin to hide the talent in the ground, doesn't it?"

"But Beth, a talent is a coin, an ancient Greek or Roman coin." He had recovered his poise. "The parable of which you speak, Beth, is about faith, not a mere human faculty or attribute. Why did you not speak to me about this? I could have elucidated."

"Because I was afeared!"

"Afea ...afraid?"

"Do ye not understand?" He clearly didn't. " I was afeared ye wouldn't listen. That ye'd argue me out of it. I was afeared ye'd thwart the boy. Afeared ye'd spoil his chances. He's no brothers nor sisters and no friends. Do ye want him to grow up lonely? Always special? Always withdrawn? Always this ... this ... this remnant?"

"Be..."

"And anyway, why can't the remnant play rugby?"

The terrier-like shaking had been so thorough that he struggled to recover his sense of wounded dignity and lost the calmness that had made his righteous indignation so terrible to them. His voice was shrill and lacked authority and he sounded merely piqued and querulous. "You went behind my back, you bought boots and ... and ... and a shirt and ... and socks and you ... you hid them in the chimney!"

"Yes." She said neutrally, without guilt, without truculence.

"But where did you get the money?"

"My Post Office savings book."

"Your saving's book?" he squeaked.

"I supposed it were mine. It has my name on it anyhow."

He knew she was careful with the housekeeping and had commended her for it and had encouraged her to save but he had never anticipated her spending without his approval. "How much is left?"

"One shilling and eleven pence halfpenny."

"One shilling and ... ," he began, but the odd pennies were such a paltry sum he couldn't bring himself to repeat them and stared stupidly at her with his mouth open.

The silence extended. They both knew that the situation was unprecedented and they were both afraid. Each thought of words to say and then decided better of saying them. Sammy wanted to flee, but dared not move a muscle. He counted the flags on the floor all the way to the window and back. He heard his father's feet and raised his eyes to see him walk slowly to the special shelf where the big family Bible sat. He watched him take it reverently in his hands. Its black bulk restored authority to where it rightfully lay and as an earnest of that authority his father recovered his composure and spoke in measured tones. "I shall seek guidance," he said. The front room door closed.

"Come on, Sammy," hissed his mother, as she did at the Sunday meeting when he slouched in his chair. "Come on quick."

"Where?" he said.

"Onto the floor," she said.

"Why?"

"To pray, ye eejit!" and she fell directly onto her knees. "Why should himself be the only one giving Jesus an earful?" she said, and pulled him down beside her.

It was not the practice of the sect to kneel. They preferred to remain seated as if they were having a conversation with God and merely inclined the head a little in deference but in the crisis she had reverted to an old habit of her Church of Ireland upbringing. "Oh Jesus," she began. "Jesus help us this day. Forgive my lie, Jesus. The child had no part in it , Jesus, not really, for he's too young yet, and Jesus, forgive my pride but forgive his too, I mane my man's, not the child's, he's too young yet." Sammy felt the familiar dunt in his ribs. "Say after me, Our Father which art in heaven…"

They repeated the Lord's Prayer together, their fervour doubling then trebling as they reached the end … "For thine is the greatness, the power and the glory, for ever and ever, Amen."

"What about the rugby?" whispered Sammy.

"I think we've said enough," she said.

They got to their feet.

"Ye never told me a talent was a coin," she said.

"I didn't know either," he said.

"Ye live and learn," she said.

He helped her get the supper. The cloth was flipped out over the deal table and smoothed onto it without a word. Without a word each knife, fork and spoon was carefully and silently placed. He carried cups and saucers as if they were not chipped and homely delft but were of the rarest china. All the time he kept listening for any tell tale sound from the front room. Whoever was communicating with whom behind the door he was taking his time about it. Eventually there were no more cups to carry or red or brown sauce bottles to find so he sat down to wait. It grew darker outside and the shadows stretched into each corner of the kitchen but neither he nor his mother thought to turn on the single bulb hanging below its cheap plastic shade. He watched her lift the lid of the saucepan and slowly stir the soup for far longer than was necessary. Her lips made a tight line and her eyebrows were raised as if this might help her ears. He had been shocked when she had called his father a bully. That had never, would never, have occurred to him. Her impromptu prayer had also amazed him. She looked rock-like in the gathering gloom. He remembered the words:

"There is a remnant according to the election of grace." Suddenly he felt like running to her and throwing his arms round her. And he would have done so if the front room door had not opened and light flooded into the kitchen.

For a moment his father was silhouetted against the new brightness. He carried the open Bible in his hands. "Why are we in the dark?" he said, and switched on the light. "I struggled long with the Lord," he said, "and sought his guidance and he has spoken to me through some words of his apostle Paul." He raised the Bible slightly and read. "When I was a child, I spake as a child, I understood as a child, I thought as a child: but when I became a man I put away childish things." He paused and smiled at Sammy. "You, Samuel, are a child; you speak as a child and you understand as a child and you must be a child. Children play games, so you must play games, until you become a man, that is. And Samuel when you do become a man you will, like the apostle Paul, put away childish things." He closed the Bible and held it to his chest and beamed upon his little family.

Sammy glanced quickly at his mother. Her prayer, and his, had been answered. Surely God had designed him for the front row of the scrum as Clarky had said. He would be able to play in the match. A grin began to spread across his face but suddenly vanished. His father was preparing to speak again.

"I was told a lie," he said his tone changing from beneficent righteousness to stern solemnity. "And it was not a simple lie, it was a complicated lie, a lie that demanded continuous and sustained subterfuge. I confess that I was hot with anger but I read in Jeremiah, 'O Lord correct me, but with judgement; not in thine anger, lest thou bring me to nothing.' I have prayed to the Lord to take away my anger and he has answered my prayer. I have prayed also that he forgive you, if you ask his forgiveness. Do you Samuel ask the Lord for forgiveness?"

"Yes," said Sammy with enthusiasm. Tomorrow he would be wearing the red-and-black jersey and the new boots.

"And you El … Beth?"

Sammy's mother raised her head and looked his father straight in his face and said, "Yes."

"Very well then," he said, the warm mood of beneficence again suffusing his face. "If the meal is ready I shall see to my ablutions."

When his father had stepped out into the tiny scullery and the single tap could be heard spurting into the jaw-box sink, Sammy noticed that his mother had doubled up as if a pain had suddenly gripped her stomach. "What's wrong, Ma?" She was clutching the head of a chair and was shaking all over her body. "Ma, what is it?" Her cheeks puffed out and her eyes went round as if the inside of her head would explode. "Ma?"

His mother tried to open her mouth to answer, but thought better of it and shook her head vigorously instead. Suddenly she clapped a hand over her mouth and uttering a strangled little scream ran from the kitchen. Sammy heard her feet clattering up the stairs and creaking on the floorboards above his head.

"Where's your mother?" said his father, coming in and folding down his shirt-sleeves and refastening his cuffs.

"She went upstairs."

"Ah," he said as if he knew what exactly what this meant. "No doubt she will be down presently." They listened for a moment. There was no sound from above. Mr McConkey placed a hand on his son's shoulder. "Do you remember the parable of the shepherd who had lost one of his hundred sheep and left the ninety and nine and went in search of it?"

"Yes, father."

"How does the story end, Samuel?"

"The shepherd finds the sheep."

"And?"

"He carries it home." Sammy paused; not because he didn't know what happened next but because of the sound from above. It was a rippling, bubbling sound, the sound of uncontrollable human laughter. His father showed no sign of having heard it, however. His eyebrows were raised as he waited for his son to recite the remainder of the parable and he was on the point of summoning a regretful tone with which to finish the story himself, when Sammy rattled out: "He carries it home and calls in his friends and neighbours to rejoice with him for he has found the sheep which was lost."

The laughter was getting louder and less inhibited. Sammy had never heard his mother laugh like this.

"'Likewise, there shall be joy in heaven over one sinner that repenteth,'" summed up his father, "'more than the ninety and nine just persons which need no repentance.' Isn't that so Samuel?"

"Yes, father," said Sammy; and as the laughter above heaved and rollicked, he thought he heard the bed squeak.

Robin Glendinning, a playwright (for stage and radio) and short-story writer, was born in 1938 and attended Trinity College, Dublin. In the early 1970s, he worked for the Alliance Party of Northern Ireland, which he helped to found. His stage plays include Jennifer's Vacation *(1982),* Mumbo Jumbo *(1986),* Culture Vultures *(1988), and* Donny Boy *(1990). He lives near Comber, Co Down.*

THE WAR NEXT DOOR

Gerald Dawe

Remembering the variable figure.

My talk ends where it began, literally next door, in the house I moved to as a young boy in the Belfast of the 1950s. The terraced row was fairly typical pre-First World War not particularly graceful houses. What made the row important, looking back over forty years, were the people who lived there. Next door was an Austrian woman who had fallen in love with a dashing Northern Irish soldier who had been stationed in liberated Vienna at the end of the Second World War. She was an incredibly tall woman who always seemed to be dressed "up"; she bred pedigree poodles and spoke with a pronounced accent. Next door to this lady and her exceedingly quiet civil servant husband was a large family with whom I became very friendly; indeed, at one stage of my boyhood, I was almost a foster son of this family. They were a Catholic family, unlike my own, and I loved being with them. My mother did not "mind", nor my grandmother with whom we lived, and during the 1950s and 1960s this little patch of Belfast – that terrace, the encircling avenues, main roads, that district – was my home. I knew it like the back of my hand.

I count myself lucky to have been brought up in that particular place and time because from my boyhood I was experiencing difference; cultural diversity, as we would say now, but without the heavy shades of contemporary self-consciousness. The Catholic family became very much a part of our life. So too with the Austrian lady, who fascinated me with her domestic rituals of thick rich coffee in little small cups and her strange mix of formality and vulnerability. By the mid-sixties I also became very friendly with several Jewish families who lived in our immediate district; there was a synagogue, delicatessen, hair stylist – all part of the local fabric. The cultural mix was a good thing; it freed up the mind, maybe not back then, but later on.

It is important to state this as bluntly as possible, given what we now know was to happen in Belfast by the late sixties and early seventies as the city turned into a bloody site of sectarian warfare and a struggle for political and cultural supremacy (and retribution). Indeed, the particular area of North Belfast I am describing became one of the most bitter interface areas of sectarian conflict, with Protestant families accusing Catholic families of seeking to "ethnically cleanse" them from the area. Catholic families, on the other hand, counter such accusations with their experience of constant sectarian attacks from Loyalist gangs. This tragic outreach of the peace process, rather then being at the top, seems to have slipped off the agenda of the professional reconciliation lobby.

It is also important to recall that the history of the city since its emergence as an industrial hub in the mid-nineteenth century was very much wrapped up with the economic destiny of Britain. The city drew into its constricted low-lying basin hundreds of thousands of unskilled and skilled workers from the rural Irish hinterlands, from Scotland and England. Unplanned, unhappy often, communities had to learn how to get on with one another. It should not be forgotten that for long tranches of the people's history they did precisely that – get on – without any enlightened leadership from their respective power-brokers.

With the foundation of the Irish State in 1922 and the partition of Ireland into two separate if related states, the substantial Catholic minority remaining inside the new Northern Irish "Protestant" state felt isolated and marooned within a hostile political culture. The abject failure of the Northern state to seriously address and integrate the Catholic minority was to ultimately lead to the eruption of The Troubles. A thirty-year conflict left over 3000 dead and countless thousands maimed both physically and psychically, primarily in Northern Ireland, but also further afield, in the Republic, Britain and Europe.

Against this bloody backdrop, the cultural mix I mentioned as being part of my own upbringing in Belfast, has been largely destroyed. In its place has emerged a patchwork landscape of exclusionist districts, Protestant or Catholic, loyalist or nationalist, literally ring-fenced against each other, with the grotesquely named Peace Lines demarcating a divided city which in turn reflects the realities of a divided Province. Northern Ireland lives in a kind of cultural flux of emblems, mutually excluding one another, either physically or symbolically. It is a war of nerves now as much as anything else. The net result of past political antagonism and the resultant paramilitary violence is a city of internal walls.

So one can see the Belfast situation (or the Northern Irish situation) as a scaled-down political analogue to what was to happen throughout Eastern Europe by the time the Communist states crumbled and the refrigerated ethnic tensions resurfaced without any sufficiently powerful civic intervention and mediation. As parts of Belfast were parceled up by paramilitary or para-political forces on the ground (with fall-out in terms of law and order, drug problems, localized power struggles, political exploitation and patronage), the overarching political system stalled. What we are currently seeing in Northern Ireland is the latest protracted attempt to restore some form of accountable democracy to a people who do not know how to imagine what other communities have been living through during the past thirty years. Behind the parliamentary language of compromise and mutual understanding, of medial interviews and sound bites, there is still a huge gulf of mistrust and ignorance upon which the bigots and violence-junkies prey.

Like hundreds and thousands before and after me, I was schooled in British history; to most of my generation the Second World War was still part of our psychic and social landscape. The public figures of that time, the names of battles, the sense of war and destruction in countries and cities across Europe, filled my mind and imagination at a very early age. Yet it was a "Europe" in fundamental ways distant. It only started to take on a much more personal meaning when I saw in the mid-sixties a photograph in *The Observer* newspaper commemorating the beginning of the Second World War. It was of a young Jewish boy being rounded up by Gestapo, his arms raised, his large cap seeming too big for his frightened face.

Somewhat later I followed with fascination developments in Czechoslovakia and wrote a poem in homage to Jan Palach, the young student who set himself on fire in St Wenceslas Square in Prague in protest at the Russian invasion and the ensuing closure of the borders between Czechoslovakia and the outside. Much later on holiday in Santorini with my wife and family I met a Czech *émigré*. His sense of where he came from and what he belonged to, exposed my own frail knowledge of what this place "Europe" actually was. I was also probing my own family background and discovered that on my mother's side we had arrived in Ireland as part of the exodus of French Huguenots, while my maternal great grandmother's people had also arrived in Belfast from we know not where, bearing the surname *Quartz*. Alongside this mixture, there were on my maternal grandfather's side well established roots in Fermanagh. My own father's people, whom I had never met, had roots in the borders of England and Wales.

There was, if you like, an inherited cultural dispensation (or coding) which I now take to be a valid part of where I come from; but such diversity has been sidelined as irrelevant to the big historical picture. Little enough of this consciousness would have come through formal schooling. Random and unstructured, it is related more to chance – the Austrian neighbour, the Czech holidaymaker – as much as to genealogy. But probe ever so lightly into most families and one finds the variable figure, the different strain, influence or background. The problem comes when this difference is locked away, either literally or metaphorically, in the interests of one exclusive political or cultural identity. What then happens can become shocking beyond belief, as the Second World War demonstrated, and as the end of the twentieth century showed in abundant measure, in Bosnia, Kosovo and elsewhere.

This is an extract from an address given at The Conference on Identities and European Unity, Nicosia, Cyprus, organized by the British Council.

Gerald Dawe's sixth collection of poems is Lake Geneva *(The Gallery Press, 2003). He is the Director of the Oscar Wilde Centre for Irish Writing, Trinity College, Dublin.*

COMPLICITIES IN TOW

—

Fred Marchant

Okinawa and now.

"And when it was claimed / the war had ended, it had not ended."
Denise Levertov, "In California, During the Gulf War."

I

Ignominious Icon: The helicopter-borne evacuation of the US Ambassador's residence during the fall of Saigon in 1975. The Vietnamese who were literally dying to get out of the country and become refugees, but who were locked out at gunpoint by the last Marines in-country. The helicopters lifting off from the tiny rooftop platform, and heading out to an offshore carrier. Some of the evacuation helicopters rolled overboard, dumped at sea because there was no more room on the flight deck, and there were no landing zones for them in Vietnam anymore. The long war was finally over.

The War Continues: Bruce Willis, and the newly released *Tears of the Sun*. This film is set in the present tense, in Nigeria during a civil war. A sketchily defined (but definitely Muslim) "rebel army" has assassinated the President and nearly all his family. A European doctor, a woman who was an American via marriage, directs a jungle hospital and must be rescued by a team of U.S. Navy commandos. They are led by a taciturn, lantern-jawed, and above all honorable character played by Willis. Not only does he complete the mission in rescuing the doctor, but he also disobeys his orders and turns back to rescue also scores of "natives" who had been at the hospital. Willis orders the feeblest patients to be flown out on his own unit's rescue helicopters. Then the commandos begin a long trek over the mountains to the border of a neighboring country. Along with them come the others from the hospital, in whose group is hiding – with the knowledge of the doctor – the remaining son of the assassinated president. The murderous rebels, trailing this group, are out to capture and kill the heir-apparent. Half the commandos and half the refugees die in firefights during this march, but Willis and the others restore everyone's faith in American honor by their humane intervention and noble self-sacrifice. There is no craven rooftop escape for the Americans in this film.

Limited as it may be, such a movie allows us to peer awhile into the contemporary, mainstream American mindset. There we glimpse with startling clarity one of its most dangerous elements: the propensity to think of ourselves as permanently innocent and fundamentally good. This film is a paean to American exceptionalism, offering a consoling, post-September 11 image of ourselves as the good guys on the world's stage. We may not know much about Third World politics or history or why anyone might hate us, but we are always and only on the side of righteousness. If there must be an imperial presence in this chaotic world, so says this film, thank God it is us.

II

I probably should have gone to jail. It would have meant more. I think sometimes I should have just disobeyed orders and refused duty. I would have been court-martialed, reduced in rank, given a few months in a federal penitentiary, slapped with a dishonorable discharge, and booted out. That would have made my conscientious objection into a larger and louder anti-war statement. As it happened, I slipped quietly out of military service, the first Marine officer in history (so I heard later) ever to be *honorably* discharged as a conscientious objector. It was September 1970, and the American war in Vietnam was in full fury, even if the American troop levels were beginning to recede. I had been an infantry lieutenant, stationed on Okinawa for a year. I was getting on a plane to fly back home to be discharged. I was free, elated, and relieved.

I had enlisted in the Marine Corps in the spring of 1968 just as I was about to graduate from Brown University. I had signed up for a three-year stint, gone to officers' candidate school, become a lieutenant, and opted for the infantry as my military occupational specialty. I had wanted to be a "grunt," and I had wanted to go to Vietnam. At Brown I was a scholarship boy, and a "Townie," the name we had for anyone who had grown up in Providence, Rhode Island, where Brown is located. I was from a thoroughly working-class family and joining the Marines was returning to my origins. There was where I came from a tacit norm that a young man shouldn't miss out on the action. My father had been in World War II, for instance, and a grandfather and an uncle were in World War I. Going to a war, even a bad one, was the male rite of passage par excellence.

I was not alone in these root attitudes. In the year I graduated, there were half a million American soldiers in Vietnam, each on a year-long tour of duty. During my two years of service, I don't recall meeting anyone under the rank of Major who was motivated by a desire to kill Communist insurgents and win the Cold War against the Soviets. The people who carried rifles and knapsacks were either reluctant draftees or youngsters who thought of going to Vietnam as the next step in the adventure of their lives. As historians have noted, poor people and working-class people were overwhelmingly the Americans who fought in this war. People who could afford to stay in school did so, and were thereby exempted. In the language of those days, they had a "deferment." Those who didn't have a deferment were drafted. Or else they enlisted. I remember thinking that being drafted was too passive, and that by signing up I had made an existential choice about my fate.

But what about the war itself and the massive, student-led opposition to it? Where was I in all of that? I think now I was at least half out of my mind. I had only a vague sense how wrong the war was. But I also had an acutely negative reaction to mass demonstrations, student organizations, and political rhetoric. I thought of myself as someone above all that. I spent my undergraduate years discovering and falling in love with literature. When I first arrived at Brown, I had just begun to conceive of myself as a poet. Later I became the class poet of 1968, and wrote the graduation poem. It was addressed to all the "dark fathers" who had sent us marching down the hill toward death. I meant the image to be sufficiently ambiguous to include war-resisters as well as enlisters such as me. The fact that there were so few enlisting was to me a sign that it was my unique calling to go to this war and write about it. If it was a morally bankrupt enterprise, then – so I reasoned – I would bear witness to the bankruptcy. I would walk the ground and carry a weapon. There would be no buffer, nothing to protect me from the reality, and I would learn what it had to teach. It never occurred to me I was lining myself up to kill another human being. Instead, I thought I was more or less like Ishmael, signing up for a long, dangerous voyage around the world, under a madman captain.

III

A year and a half later I was stationed at the Headquarters Battalion of Camp Smedley T. Butler on Okinawa, in the Ryukyu Islands, south of mainland Japan, and off the coast of China. There had been so many injuries and deaths among junior officers in Vietnam that when I arrived on the island, in transit to the war-zone, I was arbitrarily shunted aside and appointed Deputy Provost Marshal for the Marine Corps on Okinawa, a billet normally reserved for a Captain or above. I became operations officer for a platoon of Marines and a battalion of hired Okinawan security guards. We guarded six major garrisons, and patrolled the roads between them. We also had a Criminal Investigation Division with a half-dozen detectives. The crimes we worried most about ranged from the specifically military – AWOL, Desertion – to brawls, petty larcenies, and drug busts. Occasionally there would be a violent crime to be investigated. Or there might be an escape from the Brig. We would hop into our vans, shotguns loaded, and hunt the prisoners down in the island's vast fields of sugar cane. Considering the alternatives, it was superb duty. All my troops had recently been in combat in Vietnam, so for them this job was a heaven of regular working hours, hot meals every day, bars and bar-girls on any given night, and nobody shooting at them, at least not very often. For me, though, the Provost Marshal's job was at first tremendously frustrating. I was "stuck" on the island and would have to wait four or five months before I could put in a request for a transfer "down south" to Vietnam.

One of my very first clear moments of opposition to the war in Vietnam came while I was sitting at my office desk in early December 1969. I was leafing through *Life* or *Time*, and came upon the terrible photographs of the My Lai Massacre. I had done marksmanship training. I had studied my small-unit tactics. But I was unprepared for those bodies strewn along the lane, the women and children, that bare-bottomed dead toddler. As I recollect the moment, I felt a moral vertigo precisely because of my proximity to the scene. I knew who the killers were, if not by name, then by training, by military culture, by every time my instructors had spoken of "wasting some gooks." The ambiguity as to who was civilian and who was not, along with a too-typically American obliviousness to the Vietnamese history of anti-colonial struggle, had produced a climate ripe for atrocity. I could all too easily picture the junior officer "supervising," and those young soldiers who did what they were told. I wasn't off the hook just by saying "there but for the grace of God." I knew that by virtue of being in uniform I had indirectly contributed to the deaths before me. That was what the military meant by a war-effort. For every foot soldier in combat, we all knew, there were nine other soldiers whose support jobs kept him there.

Things seemed, however, to have been shifting deep within me in the weeks before my encounter with My Lai. For instance, one weekend I devoured Saul Bellow's *Herzog*. I remember being particularly taken by the scene in which Moses Herzog decides not to kill Valentine Gersbach, his former best friend. Gersbach has "stolen" Herzog's wife, and has moved into what used to be Herzog's own apartment. Herzog meanwhile has climbed up the back stairs of the apartment and is peering in through the bathroom window. Though he has a pistol, he is stopped in his tracks by seeing how tenderly Valentine bathes Herzog's infant daughter. He decides not to kill Gersbach. Bellow's novel predates the war, and it is not a pacifist tract. But in that scene Herzog's flawed but passionate intellect spoke to me about war and peace, specifically in Herzog's affirmation of the value of any human life. It showed a man pulling back from the precipice. The novel worked subliminally on me. I didn't really want to kill anybody either, but, unfortunately, I had put myself in a position where I would most likely have to, unless I too pulled back.

One Sunday morning not too long after I had encountered the My Lai story, I lay in bed staring at the cinder-block ceiling. I was doing a strange sort of mulling. I asked myself exactly what non-fatal wounds would I find tolerable. Could I lose a toe and not miss it? What about an eye? What if a good piece of writing emerged from such losses? How much of my life was I willing to sacrifice for that writing? The next thought surprised me by the ease with which it appeared. What about the arm or leg or life of another person? Would the piece of writing be worth *that?* Here too was moral vertigo, like the moment when the priest slides back the screen-window in the confessional, and you know you have mortal sins to report. Something was stirring down deep, as Emily Dickinson might have said, where the meanings are. The answer I said out loud was "No."

IV

During the ten years of the American war in Vietnam, upwards of three million Vietnamese people lost their lives. That morning all I could imagine was someone nameless and almost faceless, but definitely Vietnamese. Realizing I had been not only reckless but wrong, I rose and went to Sunday Mass for the first time in a long time. Afterwards I waited to speak with the chaplain, Jim Harris, a Catholic priest who had served in Vietnam for two tours of combat duty, earning a Bronze Star medal, with a V for valor. I told him that I thought I was going to have to quit the Marine Corps. I can still see him wink and say, "Me too." I could not have been more lucky. Given his sense of the Church and its responsibilities in matters of war and peace, he was the best pastoral counselor I could have met. He had, for example, a substantial library of contemporary anti-war writing. In the months that followed I read Thomas Merton, Daniel Berrigan, and Martin Luther King, Jr. It was also through him that I learned about some very practical aspects of the anti-war movement. Because of Jim, the Chaplain's office had a subscription to the radically anti-war *National Catholic Reporter*, wherein I read about the Central Committee for Conscientious Objectors, a Quaker organization in Philadelphia. I wrote to them, and quickly developed a correspondence with a stateside adviser who monitored cases of active-duty personnel applying for CO status. I had never even thought there was a creature such as a conscientious objector within the military, though in fact that was what I was becoming.

The path was arduous but mapped. The various service branches each had policies and regulations governing situations such as mine. The military's greatest concern was to make certain the person requesting CO status was not faking it. The process initially required me to be interviewed by each superior officer in my local chain of command. They were required to write a report evaluating my sincerity. I also had to be interviewed by a psychiatrist to make sure I was not insane. I had a military lawyer assigned to me to verify that the right procedural steps were followed on both sides. The most important part of my application for discharge was, however, an autobiographical statement in which I had to account for my change of heart. By April 1970 I finished a ninety-page essay that sketched out my life and my beliefs, paying particular attention to my religious background. Though I had lapsed during my college years, I had sixteen years of Catholic education preceding. I drew upon the Catholic traditions of pacifism, claiming them as one might a recently discovered member of a family tree. I had to address whether I was against all wars or just this one. The Pentagon policy made no provision for a "selective" conscientious objection. Although at times I felt tentative about it, I claimed unequivocal conscientious objection to war in general. I didn't quibble over questions of personal self-defense or the need for a civilian police force. Instead I argued that I was opposed to the actuality of organized, state-sponsored violence. I presented my sense of the Vietnam War as the prime and pressing example of why war itself was the problem.

In addition, I had to gather letters of support from teachers and friends back in the States. These would be added to my file, as would the reports from my superiors. The person whose word would carry the most weight was the base commander, General Robert Barrow, the last of my interviewers. For our conversation he put aside three hours. He was a tall, languid Southerner. Highly decorated, and apparently well respected: a few years later he would himself become the Commandant of the Marine Corps. He had read my biographical statement, but he wanted to know more about my background. He also seemed eager to talk about his own combat experience, to assure me that he too was troubled by the taking of life. At times there were tensions in the air. He felt, for example, that My Lai was more anomalous than typical. He believed in the "domino theory." If not in Vietnam, he argued, then someday we would be fighting Communists in Australia or closer.

He expressed no contempt for the position I was taking. He seemed to enjoy the philosophical aspects of our discussion. The climactic moment came when he wanted to know if I would oppose a war in direct defense of my nation, my town, or my family. I said in those cases I would still oppose war itself, and resist in non-violent ways. The General said he was confident that in such a situation there would come a moment when even my principles would have to give way. "Every man," he said, "has a tipping point." I replied that I had already reached a different sort of tipping point about the war we had on our hands right now.

"Son," he said, "you owe something back to this nation that has given you so much."

"I don't belong to any nation on earth," I replied, my emphasis on the word *belong*.

VI

Site of one of the most bloody battles in World War II, Okinawa is a beautiful sub-tropical island, some ninety miles long. Today it is the southernmost prefecture of Japan. In addition to several American military bases, there are spas and resorts for wealthy tourists. On the eastern coast is one of the world's great coral reefs. In the early evenings, especially during the weeks in which I was waiting for a response from Washington, I would go snorkeling.

A few days after my conversation with the general, I was floating out on the reef, pondering our exchange. Around five in the afternoon, several squadrons of B-52 bombers appeared on the horizon, lumbering home after the all-day bombing run to Vietnam. As I treaded water and looked up at these airplanes just a few hundred feet above the water, I was more than a little haunted by my assertion about not belonging to any nation on earth. Perhaps too grand and sweeping a verbal gesture, the statement wasn't totally false. But it wasn't totally true either. The fact was that I was irrevocably connected to these airplanes and the republic for which they stood. The shock of appalled recognition that had begun with those photos of My Lai was now being writ large with these returning airplanes. As I say in "Tipping Point," my poem that recounts this moment, I recognized that I would have a long swim back to shore, with "my complicity in tow."

It has been that way in my life ever since. I am glad I never fired a weapon at another person, and I was happy to get out. But my single conscientious objection, however consoling or valuable, could never in itself be enough. I would have to make conscientious objector-like decisions over and over again throughout my life, even now, thirty years later. The gradual right-wing takeover that began with the election of Ronald Reagan has heralded a resurgent militarism. The xenophobic and nearly fascist impulses that bubble under the surface of our response to the Sept. 11th attacks seem related to what feels like the breakdown of democratic principles in the United States. There was a stolen election. Then there were lies about the threat Iraq posed to us, and now there is our invasion and occupation. A candid general concluded we have a guerrilla war beginning there. We might well think someday that the war in Vietnam was just a precursor of our empire.

This all means that the B-52's are still coming in low overhead. Most Americans feel the terrorist attacks on us justify anything we want to do on the world's stage, even pre-emptive acts of war. We are aggrieved, and a set of pre-emptive strikes is how many Americans think we can make the world safe for our democracy. As the cover stories about weapons of mass destruction start to unravel, we seem to have become a deeply frightened people, and our fears are what make this nation so dangerous to itself and others. Let us imagine the United States even more thoroughly militarized. Let us also imagine a worldwide American imperial presence, buttressed at home by the ideology of exceptionalism. In such a grim future, what is to be done?

Some remarks Susan Sontag made recently might point the way. She was speaking at the Vassar College commencement and advised those young people to despise both violence and national vanity. She urged them instead to "protect the territory of conscience" and "try to imagine at least once a day you are not an American." This utterly practical advice about the nature of the moral imagination reminded me of *The Adventures of Huckleberry Finn*. The most important element in that boy's adventure was his moral awakening to the reality of slavery. His floating down the Mississippi with the runaway slave Jim taught him daily what it was like not to be white. By the end of the novel, Huck declares, "I'll go to hell" rather than return Jim into slavery. One cannot help but think of Thoreau, another conscientious objector in American literature, who said that in an unjust society, a jail cell was the right place for an honest man. Sontag's idea about protecting the territory of conscience reminds me also of the real "lesson" of the Vietnam War. It is a lesson about hubris. In the world of tragedy, hubris is an unyielding certitude, a willful failure to remember that everything human has limits and every mind is prone to error. This is as true of nations as much as individuals. For those who live in the United States, we need to remember that no nation's destiny has ever been truly manifest.

TIPPING POINT

Late blue light, the East
    China Sea, a half-mile out …
        masked, snorkelled, finned,

rising for air, longing for it,
    and in love with the green
        knife-edged hillside, the thick

aromatic forest, and not ready
    for the line of B-52's coming in
        low on the horizon, three airplanes

at a time, bomb-empty after
    the all-day run to Vietnam.
        Long, shuddering wings, and predatory,

dorsal tail-fins, underbelly
    in white camouflage, the rest
        jungle-green, saural, as if a gecko had

grown wings, a tail-fin, and
    nightmare proportions. Chest deep
        on the reef-edge, I think of the war smell

which makes it back here:
    damp red clay, cordite, and fear-salts
        woven into the fabric of everything not

metal: tarps, webbed belts,
    and especially jungle "utes,"
        the utilities, the fatigue blouses

and trousers which were not
    supposed to rip, but breathe,
        and breathe they do – not so much

of death – but rather the long
living with it, sleeping it,
not ever washing your body free of it.

A corporal asked me if he still stank,
I told him no, and he said,
"With all due respect, Lieutenant,

I don't believe you." A sea snake,
habu, slips among the corals,
and I hover while it slowly passes.

My blue surf map wraps its rope
around me, tugs inland
at my hips while I drift over ranges

of thick, branching elkhorn
over lilac-pale anemones,
over the crown-of-thorns starfish,

and urchins spinier than naval
mines, over mottled slugs,
half-buried clams, iridescent angelfish.

The commanding general said,
"Every man has a tipping point,
a place where his principles give way."

I told him I did not *belong*
to any nation on earth, but
a chill shift of wind, its hint of squall

beyond the mountain tells me
no matter what I said or how,
it will be a long swim back,
complicities in tow.

1994

THE SECRETARY OF

I love his creases, and the angle the carriage
Of his body projects, the fine dolmenesque
Of his shoulders, tilting into the future,
Side vents on his jacket flaring in dispute.

I love the wide English collar of his dignity,
His cravat a blue rose blooming under the chin.
As they cross the boundary-lines of his body,
The pin stripes of his suit read like fine print

In a punitive treaty. His shoe-leather gleams
So brightly the laces seem to be smiling.
He labors on the brink without thanks or dreams.
I know there is more to the actual man than this,

For in this dank world, he is the designated realist.
He is free of shit. He is full of shit.

February 2003

In 1970, Fred Marchant became the first officer to be discharged honourably as a conscientious objector to the Vietnam War. His second volume of poems is Full Moon Boat *(Graywolf Press, 2000). He is the Chairman of the PEN New England Freedom-to-Write Committee and lives in Arlington, Massachusetts.*

PROSE POEMS

Bruce Weigl

An incinerated empire.

EDDY

My friend Eddy had a younger brother who definitely had something fucked up in his brain. Eddy's mother prayed out loud all day in her bedroom, lit with candles. I never heard his solemn, steel-mill father utter one single syllable. Not ever, though he'd smile sometimes, and shake his head, and that meant something.

Because no one else would, I loved Eddy. I went to his house where the other children feared to go. I listened to his mother pray and weep so loudly, I almost had to run away until Eddy held me by my wrist and said to take it slow. I didn't know then what immaculate beauty I was among. We tried to teach his brother how to use a fork and spoon; how to zip his own fly and pee like a man; how to swing the bat, but he only never learned. He stayed who he was and he never changed, which I came to envy, though I didn't know then that love could be about two boys like that. What Eddy held fast before the waves of prayer, and the stony father's silence, and the world's small indignities, is called brother. What he gave up is called everything.

IRAQ DRIFTING *July 2003*

I have to bother you with a story about how it feels when the dead speak to me. I have to annoy you with the facts. They press their greasy faces against the inside of a glass bubble. They press their faces against some kind of net, or web of dim light, and ask of me favors, and call me friend. This feels like the loneliness of fireflies which rise and rise for love but then surrender to the last darkness. This feels like the urn emptied of its oil for the last time. No mercy. No tongues cut out. No wivery or wine. No dumb fucks. No democracies. No dead bodies any more.

SAY GOOD-BYE
for Nguyen Phuong

Say river. Say bloody current. Say not enough rice. Say mother and father. Say village bell, calling. Say music through the trees from someone's lonely radio. Say mango sliced into the woman's open hand. Say rice, steaming just in time. Say paths worn by the naked feet of lovers. Say lovers who must hide in the mango groves, even to say good-bye.

ANNA, IN MOURNING

We die and we die so many times and still we want to live. I looked at the face of death more than once from the corner of my eye, and his countenance was always calm and reassuring, like the old woman who smells of lavender in her sleep, and who dragged the boy I was to the funeral home to pay our respects to dead strangers from her old country. She made me walk to the casket and its perfumed, powdered body. I had to open my eyes. I had to pray for the souls I imagined even then must be lost. Mr Death has a face like an angel because he believes in his work.

When we came home from viewing the bodies – I must have been four or five – I lay myself out in the tub of hot water my grandmother had drawn, closed my eyes, and pretended that I was dead, floating there like the boy I'd seen, killed in a car wreck with his family.

My grandmother had found their pictures in the newspaper. Their name sounded vaguely European. She cut their faces from the paper, and waited for me to come.

THE HEAD OF THE COMPANY

The Head of the Company wanted me out. An almost tiny man, he had come to hate excellence and accomplishment, and he had made a cult of the same, who gathered around him like fearful baitfish around shadow. He wore a grand and flamboyant hat to cover his baldness, which he suffered badly on other men, especially tall men, like me, with hair.

This little man had contrived for himself some little power, which he used badly, because he was small, and because he hated his smallness. I still had faith that the truth mattered in those days, like breathing matters. Some lies of his I hope I've lost forever.

The teacher on the mountain outside of Hue told me to water my garden every day and to imagine I was watering goodness and compassion inside of me when I asked him about forgiveness. I don't forgive the small man his many small indignities. When he was fired for refusing to step down after his corruption had become intolerable, even among his acolytes, he disappeared into his regret, and into the unimaginable loss he must have felt when his power was gone

He was left with only his smallness, and with his theories that had grown tired and out of fashion, and with his great hat, and with the map of his self-hatred, woven into his skull, and with the wreckage, in his wake, of some good lives. Woe is the traveler, lost after dark. Woe are the spirits who long to come home. That was then. Even the waves of evil flatten out over time until they almost disappear.

WHAT YOU WOULD DO

Think about what you would do when you are handcuffed out of nowhere in the middle of the bloody foreign airport, what it feels like to sit back on your handcuffed wrists in the back of a black and white, no siren or lights, no talk from the officer who may or may not love the law blindly.

Think about being in the cage one morning and all of one long day, caught in the splendid optics of the modern police, measuring, before you know it, how many steps back and forth and across, as if on a rope bridge over nothing.

They will let down the veil between you and them so that nothing means what it is, and nothing is what it means. They will do themselves in many different voices.

I CONFESS TO ENJOYING THE FLESH OF OUR COUSIN, MR PIG

I once watched some pigs eat another pig who had died. They just ate him. I was twelve and I rode on the back of a big boy's bicycle straight into a funnel cloud that picked us up and threw us clean into the ditch. I could hear the pigs squeal behind us. The wind was shipping shingles from the barn, and still they fought each other for the flesh.

My young father saved us. He found us in the blitz of rain and wind, and he carried us to the house. Roughly he dried my hair with a towel, and shook me as if he were still not certain I was alive. I could not stop thinking about the pigs, eating the other pig. My father told me and the big boy, who should have known better than to ride us into a yellow sky like that, that we could have died in the storm, but it didn't sink in. Not for a long time. Not until now.

I don't know what happened to those pigs, caught in the storm. Afterwards, I saw some sticks of straw driven through a phone pole by the wind. They probably kept on eating because they were pigs, until there was nothing left.

SELF-PORTRAIT AT FIFTY-THREE

There's a fire in the vestry beyond hope.

Don't leave the boat, the sergeant said.

When she tangos I'm insane on the floor.

Into the sanctuary of trees we marched, canopy over our heads, oh la, canopy over our heads.

(Do not call. Do not write. Do not wire. Do not e-mail. Do not send an emissary. Do not even think of me.)

You live and you live. Spirit of the broken banister, spirit of the dark cellar, spirit of the lies, spirit of the mad woman, beating her door with her bloody fists after everything had come to loss. Spirit of the man who hanged himself, do-da, do-da.

You live and you live and you know so many things. In the end I want opera played in the trees, and in the thick underbrush that you may reach where the river is deep, where the blossoms follow the moving water.

HOW I LIKE IT

I like it awake and I like it asleep. I like it long and I like it short. I like it fresh and I like it old. I like it wet and I like it dry. I like it weak and I like it strong. I like it black and I like it white. I like it dressed and I like it undressed. I like it hot and I like it cold. I like it far and I like it near. I like it gay and I like it straight. I like it hidden and I like it open. I like it green and I like it burned brown by sun. I like it open and I like it closed. I like it in and I like it out. I like it up and I like it down. I like it under and I like it above. I like it to hurt and I like it when it stops. I like it quiet and I like it loud. I like it hungry and I like it fed. I like it hungry, and I like it fed.

WHATEVER

You could be at the airstrip on Pongo Pongo, like me, sitting in the fallen terminal's café, across from a woman whose ass, like a sweet plum, every man and many of the women sitting nearby would want to hold in the full of their own hands. That's the way it is in the fast lane. That's the way it is on the road.

Under some heavy stars, bright as my showcase, I think about how to behave among the ruthless, and among the betrayers of our faith, yet nothing redemptive unfolds.

You could be in my shoes, though I would not put on you my fleshy baggage, or the bullet-torn time, like a scene, now, from a movie. But you may have the rivers, alive at night with dark shapes and mirage. Something splendid might happen. Whatever.

MY AWARD

I thought if I ever won one of those big awards they give to writers, which include not only a large sum of money, but a fancy dinner, and a ceremony where you're presented with your award, and where you're encouraged to say a few words (just keep it brief) to the many truly swell people gathered there.

I thought that if I ever won, I'd wear a classy outfit, like the one the monopoly guy wears. I'd have a monocle too, and an accent. I'd have things in my pocket, connections in high places. I would seem to float above the stage when I walked.

IN LOVE WITH EASEFUL DEATH

That was surely a spirit just now, a flicker and then gone into the dusk of trees at the edge of the party I can no longer bear witness to. In the small pond with its faux waterfall and lights at night, I feed the imported fish into boredom.

That was surely a hummingbird, flit of color and then vanished into the trees. I don't ask any more what's real, and I told no one about the absolutely white rabbit I watched hop through my vision at the Shawmut T-stop in Dorchester one midnight. I told no one, but I caught myself wondering, and then I stopped.

NOTHING MORE

The porcelain attitude of the women was merciless that Saturday. We were in a cottage by the ocean; the cars were nineteen and fifty-seven. Oh the prices of things. Oh the ease with which we lived with our spirits and with our selves. The mist around the moon was only that. The wolf was just a wolf, however at our door. All things were what they were, and nothing more.

CON GAI BO (DAUGHTER)

Amazing to me that you're not afraid, even when the night holds such touching shadows as these, in the way we make them, in our minds. That you would interrupt my short time alone, my hour of recovery before spiritual death, is funny to me, but here you are, in your bright pajamas we bought in Hanoi, the words misspelled in English across the front, and in your black eyes, the rivers of Binh Luc still churn and swell and twist to the great sea of your coming.

I wanted to say that you were my river there, or that you were my flower, or that you were my yellow bird, but I didn't want the words to hold you down the way words do. I didn't want the words to bend you, so I kept quiet. I watched you – do you remember – for a long time as you squatted by the fishpond and dragged a stick across your reflection. Way, way back in another time I watched you, and way back to the memory of a green place I don't know why we may not name.

PORTAL

In our hallucination, the children are instructed in the ways of finding shelter when the rain of our bombs comes down on their small villages and schools. The children can identify our planes, and what our planes can do to them. They sleep the sleep of weary warriors beaten down and left for nothing in their lonely deaths that come so slowly you would wish your own heart was drained of blood.

I watched the people gather in the street to stop the war that is the war against ourselves, and against the children who practice finding our planes before they're touched up into dust that nobody sees, but that makes a sound like the vanquished.

OH NATURE

Today some things worked as they were meant to. A big spring wind came up this Mother's Day and blew down from the verdant neighborhood trees, billions of those little spinning things with seeds inside of them. And my heart woke up alive again too, as if things could be unprinted from your brain. Fat chance of that, yet things work sometimes as they were meant to work, like the torturer who finally can't sleep, or the god damn moon who sees everything we do and who still comes up behind clouds spread out like hands to keep the light away.

HOME OF THE BRAVE

First many people died, and then many other brave people went to save them and they died too. There was a short but stunning moment. The smoke blacked out the sun. The people's noses, mouths and eyes were filled with the dust of an incinerated empire. Some faces were streaked with blood, but the people picked themselves up and began to walk in a great migration like a battalion down the highways empty of traffic, towards their homes and their televisions.

So much was taken from them, and a hole had been torn into their world. One man hung a thousand flags from his house. You could not see the windows, or the doors. So many flags, you would think we were American.

Bruce Weigl served in Vietnam for two years in the Third Air Calvary. He is the author of a memoir, The Circle of Hanh *(Grove Press, 2000) and ten collections of poems, most recently* The Unraveling Strangeness *(Grove Press, 2002)*

ZEN WISDOM POEMS

—

Nguyen Chung & Kevin Bowen

Older than Chaucer.

Much of Vietnam's ancient literary heritage in Classical Chinese is preserved in Zen texts associated with temples throughout the country. This selection of twelve poems and accompanying photographs was assembled by the poet and photographer Nguyen Duy. A similar selection will appear in Vietnam in the format of a calendar in the near future. All twelve poets were either Zen masters, or Buddhist rulers. The following poems are published here in English translation for the first time.

The Editor

Phap Thuan (915 — 990)

THE NATION'S DESTINY

The Nation's destiny — intricate as a thicket of cane.
The Southern Land opens a new era to Peace.
If the spirit of the Way guides the Royal path,
All bloodletting stops, all strife withers.

A structure within the Temple of Literature (Van Mieu) in Hanoi, built in 1070 in honour of
Confucius and his more famous disciples

The Zen Master Phap Thuan was born in 915. His native village and given name remain
unknown. He belonged to the tenth generation of the Vinitaruci School of Vietnamese Zen
Buddhism, which was founded in 580 in the Red River Delta by the Indian monk Vinitaruci.
Recognized for his deep knowledge and understanding of the world, Phap Thuan served as advisor
to King Le Dai Hanh (980-1005). This poem is the only poem of the author to survive.

Dieu Nhan (1041 – 1113)

FAREWELL ADVICE TO DISCIPLES

Birth, old age, sickness and death.
The cycle has always ruled us.
The more we fight to escape,
The tighter the net tangles.
In confusion we chase after Buddha.
In error we seek the Way.
Seek neither the Buddha nor the Way.
Lips pursed, say nothing.

The Constellation of Literature Pavilion (Khue Van Cac),
in the Temple of Literature, Hanoi

The Zen Master Dieu Nhan was born in 1041 in Phu Dong village, Tien Du district. The daughter of Phung Can Vuong, King Ly Thanh Tong's brother, she was raised by the King in the royal palace. When she came of age the King gave her in marriage to a highland tribal chief in Chau Dang (now Hung Hoa Province). After her husband passed away, Dieu Nhan joined a Buddhist order and later became Head of the 17th generation of the Vinitaruci School. She was also recognized as one of the two most distinguished woman poets of the time. The above poem is the only one extant today.

Man Giac (1052 – 1096)

CONFESSING TO FALLING ILL

Spring passes, a hundred flowers fall.
Spring arrives, a hundred flowers shine.
Worldly events fly past our eyes.
Old age scatters dust on our heads.
Don't say when spring departs all flowers fade.
Only last night, in the courtyard, an apricot bloomed.

*Return-the-Sword Lake (Ho Hoan Kiem), in the center of Hanoi,
commemorating the legend of the turtle who took King Le Thai To's sword
after his victory over the Ming troops in 1428*

Zen Master Man Giac's given name was Ly Truong. He was born in 1052 at Lung Trieu village, An Cach. Widely known as a great scholar while still young, he was quickly inducted into the royal household by King Ly Nhan Tong. He soon decided, however, to become a monk, and left the Court to travel up and down the country, seeking out friends of similar bent. He gathered about him a great number of disciples, and became one of the most prominent monks of the 8th generation of the Vo Ngon Thong School. This is the second school of Vietnamese Zen Buddhism, which was founded by the Chinese monk Vo Ngon Thong (Wo Yen Tong). This poem is the only one by the author that remains extant.

Cuu Chi (born circa 1065)

A FAREWELL POEM

Please remember: deep inside mind and body are one.
From their stillness comes the wonder of all things.
From their stillness, Yes and No are born.
From their stillness the innumerable universes grow.
The emptiness of space brims over with their presence.
Yet, nowhere do they stop to take shape or form.
Countless lifetimes cannot compare,
Here and there, to their luminous calm.

Miniature bronze pagodas on top of Yen Tu Mountain, Quang Ninh Province,
marking where King Tran Nhan Tong, founder of the Bamboo Grove School of
Zen Buddhism, reputedly sat and meditated

Zen Master Cuu Chi, or Dam Cuu Chi, was born in Phu Dam village, Chu Minh district, Bac Ninh Province. His family name and exact date of birth remain unknown. As a young student, he is said to have complained that "Confucius, Mo Tsu are biased on Yes; Lao Tsu, Chuang Tzu are biased on No. The world's small schemes cannot bring about freedom. Only Buddhism, biased neither on Yes nor on No, can end the cycle of birth and death, but it will require utmost self-discipline and efforts." Cuu Chi studied with the great Zen master Dinh Huong at Cam Ung Pagoda and belongs to the seventh generation of the Vo Ngon Thong school. King Ly Thai Tong three times asked him to make a visit to the capital, and three times he declined. To meet him, the King made several trips to his temple. This is his only poem to survive.

Tu Lu (born circa 1100)

—

YES AND NO

If we answer yes, even a speck of dust has existence.
If we answer no, then the entire universe is void.
Yes and No. Like the moon's face in the river,
We cannot say it's there, we cannot say it isn't.

Main bronze pagoda, Yen Tu Mountain, Quang Ninh Province,
enclosing statues of the three Bamboo Grove Patriarchs:
King Tran Nhan Tong, Phap Loa and Huyen Quang (13-14th centuries).
Inside the miniature pagoda is a statue of Huyen Quang (see p. 154).

—

The Zen master Tu Lo, or Tu Dao Hanh, belongs to the 12th generation of the Vinitaruci School.
There is no record of his native village or his given name. He resided in Thien Phuc Pagoda
(popularly called Chua Thay) on Phat Tich Mountain, Quoc Oai Province. He was known to
practice Tantrism and became an almost legendary figure in the national folklore. Only four of
his poems are still in existence. The above is one of the most popular and quoted.

Khong Lo (born circa 1100)

THE FISHERMAN'S IDLENESS

A hundred miles of blue river. A hundred miles of blue sky.
A hamlet of mulberry. A hamlet of mist.
An old fisherman deep in sleep. No one to stir him.
He awakens past noon, his boat brimming with snow.

A stupa on Yen Tu Mountain, Quang Ninh Province

The Zen Master Khong Lo, or Duong Khong Lo, was born in Hai Thanh Village, Nam Ha Province. Born to a family that had been fishermen for many generations, he joined a Buddhist order and become part of the 9th generation of the Vo Ngon Thong School. He devoted his time to the practice of both Zen and Tantrism. Known for his preference for a simple and unattached life, he took to the road, often visiting the most remote temples and landscapes in the company of another famous poet, Zen Master Giac Hai. Only two of his poems are still extant.

Khanh Hy (1067 – 1142)

RESPONSE TO PHAP DUNG ON THE QUESTION OF MATTER AND NON-MATTER, THE WISE AND THE WORLDLING

Don't waste your breath asking of Matter and Non-Matter
If you follow the Path just study the ancients.
Look in the sky: you'll never see the Mind's face.
Cinnamon trees planted in fields never become cinnamon forests.
The entire universe stands on the tip of a feather.
Sun and moon revolve inside the tiny mustard seed.
All that can be manifest rests in the play of these powers.
Who can tell the West from the East, the Wise from Unwise?

A Buddhist statue, most likely the female Quan Yin Buddha,
Yen Tu Mountain, Quang Ninh Province

The Zen master Khanh Hy's given name was Nguyen Khanh. Born in 1067 at Co Giao village,
Long Bien district, he was known to chant the Buddha's name as a child and have a preference
already for vegetarian food. He joined a Buddhist order and became head of the 14th generation
of the Vinitaruci School. Well-known for his straightforwardness and integrity, King Ly Than Tong
(1128-1137) often asked for his advice. He was appointed the National Bonze. This is the only
poem of his to survive.

Tinh Gioi (born circa 1200)

A FAREWELL POEM

The autumn light cool and spacious.
Great poets gaze on the moon and write.
Laughable dupes drunk in the Zen land:
What's sealed in Mind to stamp in words.

One of a row of 700-year old pine-trees,
Yen Tu Mountain, Quang Ninh Province

The Zen Master Tinh Gioi's given name was Chu Hai Ngung. He was reportedly born in Giang Mao, but exactly where and when is unknown. From a poor peasant family, he initially pursued the study of Confucianism. At the age of 26, he became a novice at Quoc Thanh Pagoda where he was famous for his talent of praying and divining the weather. He was often asked by kings of the Ly Dynasty to perform the rituals. Only two of his poems have come down to us.

Tran Thai Tong (1218 – 1277)

TO THE MONK DUC SON AT THANH PHONG SHRINE

The wind beats at the pine door, the moon shines on the yard.
Heart and landscape one: clear, calm, and bright.
What great joy and no one knows.
Alone on the peak the monk sits in bliss till dawn.

Scene of a typical ancient pagoda, North Vietnam

Tran Thai Tong was born in 1218 at the end of the Ly Dynasty. His uncle Tran Thu Do prepared the ground for his marriage to Queen Ly Chieu Hoang, who abdicated to make him the founder of the Tran Dynasty in 1226. He commanded the armies that defeated the first Mongolian invasion of Vietnam in 1257. He was the grandfather of King Tran Nhan Tong, the founding Patriarch of the Bamboo Grove School (see p. 153), who in turn was the dharma student of Tue Trung Thuong Sy (see p. 153) and the teacher of Huyen Qunag (see p. 154). Learned in both Confucianism and Buddhism, Tran Thai Tong ruled the country wisely and authored several profound works on Buddhism, the most famous of which is Khoa Hu Luc *(Instructions on Emptiness), a Zen manual. A prodigious writer, he left behind a substantial number of works. However, only a small part of these remain today.*

Tue Trung Thuong Sy (1230 – 1291)

SUDDENLY INSPIRED TO WRITE A POEM

Suddenly inspired to write a poem
I sit up straight in the room in silence.
A coil of smoke rises from Con Luan Mountain.
When we're tired, the mind comes to a stop.
No need to sit or chant the Buddha's name.

The Lom Son stele, honouring the founder of the Le Dynasty,
King Le Thai To (1385-1433)

Tue Trung Thuong Sy's given name was Tran Tung. He was born in 1230, the elder brother of the Great Marshal, Tran Hung Dao. He led the resistance against two Mongolian invasions, in 1257-58 and 1287-88. At the end of the latter war, he served for a short time as a provincial governor, but then retired to his beloved Duong Chan Trang (Nurture Truth Farmstead) and devoted himself to the practice of Buddhism. He became the teacher of King Tran Nhan Tong, who later founded the Bamboo Grove School of Zen, the first genuinely Vietnamese-inspired branch of Buddhism. A lay practitioner, Tue Trung Thuong Sy was widely acknowledged as an enlightened spirit, free from tradition-bound rituals and dogmas. His writings were collected by his senior students into the collection Thuong Sy Ngu Luc *(Recorded Sayings of The Eminent Tue Trung).*

Huyen Quang (1254 – 1334)

DIEN HUU PAGODA

The temple-bell's call fades into the autumn night.
Moonlight falls in waves over the red maples.
A dragon's feet reflect upside down in the pond
as if sleeping quietly on a chill mirror.
The pagoda's two towers loom like icy jewel-crusted fingers.
A life freed of snares escapes worldly desires.
Eyes without cares see wider.
Good and evil know the same hearth.
The Devil's Home and the Buddha's Land are one.

My Son, the principal religious centre of the Champa Civilization,
4th to 13th Centuries, Central Vietnam

Huyen Quang's given name was Ly Dao Tai. He was born in 1254 at Van Tai village, Nam Sach district, Lang Giang Province. Recognized in childhood as a great literary talent, he easily passed the regional examination in 1274, and a year later was the first laureate of the third examination (the ancient equivalent to a doctoral degree). He was appointed to serve in the Court, but after a short time decided to leave to become a monk. King Tran Nhan Tong, founder of the Bamboo Grove School, took him under his wing. He later became the Third Patriarch of the School. He is considered one of the greatest poets of the era. Twenty-four of his poems have been found.

Tran Quang Trieu (1286 – 1325)

—

THE DESERTED PAGODA AT MAI HAMLET

The pagodas of past dynasties sleep covered in wild grasses.
Old battlefields lie exposed to cold autumn winds.
Stelae dissolve in evening rain.
Ancient statues grow mute in fading light.
In the stone hall, the Buddha's clothes are stored.
As the field adds its fragrance to the flowers,
The Nirmanakaya has no fixed home,
But rises and falls one with the world.

A headless statue in the religious centre of My Son, Central Vietnam

—

Tran Quang Trieu was born in 1286 at Tuc Mac village, Thien Truong district, now in Ha Nam Ninh Province. A nephew of the great Marshal, Tran Hung Dao, and brother-in-law of King Tran Anh Tong, he was well-positioned in the Court. He excelled in both literary and military fields, leading troops to pacify the border area. After the death of his wife, he asked to be allowed to retire to his retreat of Bich Dong near Quynh Lam Pagoda, in Quang Ninh Province. There, with his colleagues, he founded the Bich Dong Poetry Club. In 1324 King Tran Minh Tong asked him to return to the Court. Unfortunately, he died shortly thereafter. His sudden departure stunned his friends, who edited his poems posthumously into the Cuc Duong Collection. *Of that collection, only 11 poems remain in existence.*

TRANSLATORS' NOTE

Buddhism established roots in Vietnam, or *Giao Chau* (Jiaozhou) as it was known in those days, about the second century C.E. As early as the rule of Si Nhiep (Shi Xie), Governor of Giao Chau from 187 to 226, a part of the official court entourage was a retinue of Indian or Central Asian monks. When Ly Nam De (Ly the Southern Emperor) wrested independence from China between 544 and 602, one of his first acts as King was to build Khai Quoc Pagoda (Founding the Nation Pagoda). Despite this brief period of sovereignty, Vietnam remained a part of the Chinese Empire until 939 C.E., when Ngo Quyen, at the naval battle of Bach Dang River, established Vietnam as a permanently independent nation.

Eleven centuries of occupation and rule by China brought a profoundly Confucian orientation to the forms of administration, education and classical literature practised by the Vietnamese élite. Still, it was the homegrown adaptation of Buddhism, initially brought to the country directly from India, that molded Vietnam's cultural core, its unique and synthetic blending of Confucianism, Taoism, and Buddhism. The fusion of these systems of thought with local and native beliefs provided Vietnamese culture with its deep roots, and set the stage for the golden age of the Ly and Tran Dynasties that stretched from the 10th to 15th centuries.

The twelve poems translated here have been chosen from the first and second volumes of the massive three-volume *Tho Van Ly Tran* (Poetry and Prose of the Ly-Tran Dynasties), an historic compilation that took 17 years (1960-1977) to complete. The poems capture both the joyous sense of self-discovery of the Ly-Tran period and the sorrows of witnessing the fall of these dynasties. Above all, they raise, in a poetical and sometimes almost playful mode, issues as to the meaning of human life – issues as relevant today as when they were first written.

The poems reveal an outlook that might now be called "engaged": in the world and with the world, though not necessarily of it – although this very distinction may not make sense in Buddhist discourse (*Good and evil know the same hearth / The Devil's Home and Buddha's Land are one*). Four are farewell poems, a kind of poetic testament from a Zen Master to his or her disciples.

These translations aim to follow closely the originals – written in Classical Chinese – but not always literally, where possible attempting to convey the native vigor, significance and playfulness without relying on a special Buddhist terminology.

A Zen poem, to borrow an oft-quoted phrase, does not *say* but just *is*. It captures the reflected ray of a moment when the I and the world cease to exist as contradictions – the ray streaming back to us, locked in our world of differentiation, in order to remind us – through its energy – of a possibility always open, like Man Giac's flower blooming when its season had long passed.

A distinguished poet and translator, Nguyen Chung left Vietnam for the United States in 1971. His most recent books are a work of translation, Distant Road: Selected Poems of Nguyen Duy *(Curbstone Press, 1999) and* A Thousand Years Old at Birth *(1998), a collection of poems in Vietnamese. Kevin Bowen was drafted and served in Vietnam for two years. His selected poems,* Eight True Maps of the West *(The Dedalus Press), appeared in 2003. He divides his time between Massachusetts and Achill Island, Co Mayo.*

BUSON

(from the Irish)

—

Gabriel Rosenstock

Yosa Buson (1716-83), Haiku Master.

There is probably no Haiku master, except Basho of course, whom the Japanese regard more highly than Buson. His reputation is easily defended. He was a great painter – Basho's pilgrimages were often among his themes – and an excellent poet, and the painter's eye was obvious in his beautiful creations. Before we focus on his haiku – which weren't haiku at the time but *hokku*, the first verse of a connected component poem called *renku* – let us look at a fine poem of his unknown to many westerners. He met a girl – a servant girl – returning to her family home and this is how the poet pictures the young woman's perceptions.

BY THE BANKS OF THE KEMA, A SPRING ZEPHYR IN THE AIR

Returning home this day –
Leaving Osaka behind, here I am
By the Nagara River

A spring breeze blows
The bank of the river stretches far, further still
Is my native village

I walk the banks, gathering herbs,
And the path is bristly on the way.
Are the briars so jealous
They would tatter my clothes and scratch my thighs?

The river is speckled with rocks –
I venture out and pick a fistful of parsley.
Thanks to those jutting rocks
The hems of my kimono remain dry

The willow tree
Beside the lonesome teahouse
How old it's got

The old woman of the teahouse, when she sees me
Good luck to you, says she, and praises my appearance

She has two customers who are on the point of leaving,
They rattle on in the southern dialect,
Throw three coins on the table as payment
And leave a space for me on the bench.

This boundary village has no more than two or three houses –
A cat howls for its mate
That does not appear

Outside the fence a hen calls to her chicks.
The whole world is grass.
Little chickens trying to get over the fence,
A few of them fail – it is too high

Three paths lie ahead
And through the spring grass
I see a shortcut that will do me fine

Dandelions bloom, groups of three and five,
Here are five that are yellow, three that are white,
                              I remember this path well

I pick one of the dandelions
Fondly and milky juice
Ejaculates from the thin stalk

I remember far-off days, the love our mother had for us,
The sweet smell of spring in her bosom

My springtime is over and I live in Osaka now
In Whiteflower Manor by Naniwa Bridge,
As a young woman I picked up city ways

It was three years ago that I left my home and my little brother.
A grafted plum tree, its branches blooming, the roots forgotten

My home village besieged by spring, I walk ahead.
Adorned with cherry trees, the path sweeps down along the bank

Twilight, craning my neck, I catch a glimpse of the old abode.
With her back to the door stands an old woman, my brother in her arms,
Waiting for me the whole long days of spring

Remember what Old Tigo said?

> Returning home –
> She is asleep, and beside her
> The lone parent still alive

(In the Irish, Rosenstock gaelicizes *Tigo* to *Tadhg*, the personal name that also means "a poet", anglicised by Ulster Protestants as *Tague*, meaning a Catholic. Such is the catholicity of translation and back-translation. – *Managing Editor*)

There's a certain atmospheric sorrow there and a facility to tell a story that would remind you of the Riora T'ang poets of China and, of course, Yuso Bosun was greatly influenced by the best of Chinese culture. To the marrow. There is much that could be said about that poem. The little chickens, for example. This is an example of what is called *hogan biiki*, empathy with small unimportant things. It is a characteristic excellently developed by the master Issa (examples of whose work may be read in *Eachtraí Krishnamurphy*, 2003). I notice also that there is *hon'i* here, a poetic description of a particular place.

It's a masterly poem in many ways and I thought of our own spailpíns and servant girls that were of other days, and all the changes they noticed on returning home. It's a universal theme that reminds me of another poem, the title poem in Peter Huchel's book, *An Spealadóir Spáinneach* (The Spanish Reaper) published some years ago by Comhar. There is, of course, a touch of eroticism in Buson's poem and you would expect that from this painter-poet who celebrates all the senses.

It's surprising how often wandering is mentioned in classical Japanese haiku; Zen monks practised it often and Buson himself did his share of it as well:

The gate behind me
    I, too, am a wanderer again
        Autumn dusk

A word that tells you which season the haiku involves is called *kigo*. The season itself can be mentioned, of course, and it is often mentioned or a clue is given. If you mentioned, for example, snow drops, the reader would know that it isn't midsummer. Specialist dictionaries were published where all the signs connected with each particular season were mentioned. The four seasons, therefore, are very important as we read old haiku. I'm not sure the ancestral religion of Japan isn't involved in the matter: Shinto, where there is a close connection between supernaturalism and nature. And if the crow, say, is somewhat cheerless to look at, he often appears accordingly in autumn poems:

One by one
    they disappear from view, crows,
        Autumn gloaming

Everything is connected. The day is going from light and the crows are going from view. There is a poetic connection between the two things, a connection that a poet especially will recognise:

Lightning flash —
    the sound of dew
        dripping from bamboo

There is a mysterious sensitivity in the haiku above. The quality that brings things together that have no obvious connection is called *toriawase*. There is a particular texture about that example, and note that there is more than one sense operating there, both seeing and listening.

Autumn wind goes by
    the scarecrow
        bending with it

Certain images are commoner than others in classical haiku. The scarecrow is one of them. At times it arouses amusement, at other times loneliness. I know of two books of haiku from Eastern Europe which have the scarecrow in their title. Issa was a countryman who loved fine honest people. But, as for town and suburban people:

Don't speak to me of people –
even the scarecrows
all of them bent!

Buson must have been in good humour when he jotted down this haiku:

Sedge warbler
his song
has an extra syllable

No doubt the poet's friends and disciples enjoyed that one. Buson had noticed that the bird added a syllable to his song. Of course, haiku makers count syllables – to their dying day. These death poems are called *jisei*. Often a *haijin* (a haiku master) was found on his deathbed and it was clear from the shape of his hand that counting syllables was his last act in this world.

Syllables in European languages are not like the Japanese *onji;* that's why free haiku is practised in the West. Often about a dozen syllables will do in our haiku rather than the 7-5-7 we get in classical haiku. There are fifteen in the English version above, 16 in the one before it and the same in the one before that, but note that there are only 13 in the lightning haiku.

Autumn evening
a woman shines a mirror
with her sleeve

We know that Buson was fond of women. There is a graciousness or femininity in the above haiku. She's not a servant girl as in the long poem above. I'd say she's a noble woman, and she's cleaning the mirror to get a look at herself. Note it's an autumn evening. Leaves are withering. Is the woman trying to assure herself that she's as resplendent as she always was? That's certainly what I take from it. Haiku doesn't tell everything. It leaves us room to complete the picture.

Two plum trees –
wonderful their blossoming
one early, the other late

The painter's eye again, indeed. The haiku master opens the landscape for us, he opens our eyes for us.

Sedge warbler
     what's all that rustling?
        frosty bush

And he opens our ears as well. He can't see the bird but he recognises its voice and because of the frost, there's more than the usual rustling coming from the bush. Haiku poets often speak directly to animals, to birds, to insects. In the last haiku in Issa's haiku collection (in *Eachtraí Krishnamurphy*) the poet is leaving and it is a good example of the *hogan biiki*:

I'm off
     start your love-making now
        my flies

There's probably a trace of Shinto in the two haiku above — esteem for nature — and Buddhism teaches us to show sympathy for every perceptive thing. In the western world, you are either one thing or another, Catholic or Protestant for example. Often the people of the East have more than one belief, one person wearing the hat of Kung Fu (Confucius), the Dao's robe and Buddha's sandals. It is so with me: one system isn't enough for me. Interestingly enough, comparative study has been done recently on Animism in Japan and in Ireland. I go from A to Z — from Animism to Zen — and I see nothing odd about that.

Waterfowl
     changing its sleeping place-
        a croosting* of stones

*(This was the word used in Rosenstock's native Kilfinane when boys pelted stones: from the Irish, *crústaigh*. — *Managing Editor*)

Boys out and about, probably in high spirits. If Zen-haiku were taught in Ireland's schools there'd be a big decrease in all kinds of bullying.

A young trout
     in the valley stream
        there goes a bamboo leaf too

A sharp glance. It's not a trout, but a young trout. I notice that this makes a difference — even if it's a subtle difference. Its being small adds to the atmosphere. Any of us would notice a fish, or the shape of a fish. The haiku poet names it. And you could certainly say that there is no such thing as triviality in the mind of the haiku poet. Every thing has its own quality, its own beauty, its own dignity, its own life – a bamboo leaf in this case. The bamboo is mentioned often in the poetry of Japan and China – in the great poetry of Riora T'ang, say, in which Basho and Buson were highly skilled. Did you ever listen to the bambu flute, the *shakuhachi*? Little else would bring you closer to the spirit of Japan. The Indian flute, by the way, is called *bansuri*.

> "You'll find my house
>   where that kite is flyin"
>   she tells him

A prostitute definitely. (She's not necessarily speaking to Buson himself.) Prostitutes are found in profusion in Japanese and Chinese haiku. There's something airy, playful about that image of the kite.

> The year's close, almost,
>   filth and rubbish
>   in Sakura River

The problem of waste is not a modern day one. You'd have to understand the word Sakura, perhaps, to realise the poet's amazement. It means "cherry flowers". I stayed in a hotel called that in Tokyo, the cheapest hotel in the city.

> The lotus are all dead –
>   how miserable the pool –
>   winter shower

He's not often as bleak as that in his haiku. Basho was really the master of bleakness. Perhaps the above piece is in homage to Basho or to Basho's spirit. Basho (a pen-name) means "banana tree" or "plantain tree". The plantain is a rough banana. The tree bears no fruit in Japan and it has a wretched look in bad weather. His disciples had a hut of plantain leaves built for Basho – the *Basho-an* it was called. And what did Buson do but have a hut built long after Basho's death and he called it *Basho-an*. Poets used to gather there for renku sessions.

> First frost of winter –
>   an injured white crane
>   somewhere in the distance

Again, you'd probably have to know how beautiful a bird the white crane is, as it dances with its other half in the mating season, to grasp the pathos of this haiku. One of the most delightful pieces of music played on the *shakuhachi* is *The Dance of the White Cranes*.

> The willow is bare,
>> the bright stream dried up
>>> stones in scattered confusion

That is also quite bleak. However, it is a beautiful picture.

> How white the lotus –
>> to pick or not to pick –
>>> the monk's dilemma

Well, there you have seventeen syllables, if that's what you want – 5/7/5. There's great delicacy behind this haiku. We are forever interfering with nature. This is a picture of a Zen monk about to pick a beautiful flower. But wouldn't it be better to leave it as it is and not disturb its perfection?

> Ambush site –
>> a butterfly alights
>>> on neck armour

If flowers and women, refinement and delicacy pleased Buson, he was obviously attracted to heroism as well. The hero is probably dead in this haiku. A clawed crow or a black raven would descend on a Gaelic hero; here we have a butterfly. There's a fine contrast there.

According to the modern master Shiki, Basho's haiku characteristics are manliness (*yukon*), strength (*keiken*), beguilement or delight (*enrei*) and liveliness (*kappatsusa*).

> The wheat *meitheal* –
>> sadness in the eyes
>>> of the mad woman

(*Meitheal* is still widely used in Ireland to convey a party of reapers. Curious, is it not, that an Irish word not contained in the Irish versions should find its way into an English back-translation. – *Managing Editor*)

Because poets are not like other people, they have a fellow-feeling for those on the edge of society. And because poets are forever trying to take some meaning from life, they're particularly attracted to the lunatic. What does the lunatic think? What does the lunatic see? What does the lunatic hear? What does the lunatic feel?

> Ancient well
>> catching mosquitoes
>>> dark fishy sound

There is much happening in that haiku but there is also the unsaid thing there. A fishy sound? A poet would hear such – or a lunatic. However sharp the haiku masters are, everything in this world isn't black and white, or recognisable:

> Air shimmer …
>> the bright flight
>>> of an unknown insect

> White plum blossoms
>> absorbing the colour
>>> of morning

We often find in the haiku things painting each other, colouring each other, influencing each other, from season to season, from morning to night. Life and death:

> Flying squirrel
>> crunching a bird's bones
>>> bare cold field

Fragility and transience everywhere:

> Short summer night—
>> a drop of dew
>>> on the hairy moll

(*Moll*: one of many anthropomorphic names, in Irish and in the English of Ireland, for the caterpillar. – *Managing Editor*)

Views and sounds that excite, or astonish, us:

    Walking over the dishes –
        such cold rattling music
            made by the rat's feet

Things inside, things outside, and the long white roads calling him again:

    Farewell! I take to Kiso Road
        all on my own
            older than autumn

    Southern roads,
        on the thatched cottage, on the shrine,
            everywhere, swallows

A couple of views, a couple of adventures along the way that would make you laugh or reflect:

    No underpants,
        suddenly arse to the wind –
            spring gusts

    Bamboo hat, straw coat,
        Basho come alive –
            freezing rain

    The boat has gone off –
        Johnny come lately
            under winter's first shower

    Four or five dancers
        in a circle: the moon above
            about to fall

Like many other masters, Buson succeeds in generating echoes from unusual things. For example:

    Young bamboo trees –
        the courtesan in Hashimoto
            is she still there?

The graciousness of the bamboos reminds him of a prostitute. Or, perhaps she has grown old? A beautiful yearning haiku. His master, Basho, couldn't write the like. Basho mentions prostitutes sure enough, but with no liking for them.

It happens often in the poetry of the west that something unusual must happen before we mention it. In haiku, however, maybe there's not much at all happening, or the occasion involved so insignificant that no one but a haiku poet would consider saying anything about it:

> The snail has vanished –
> where, I wonder?
> not a sinner knows

And here comes another snail and the discernment that we see always in the good haiku which is more than just acuteness of sight:

> Hit squarely
> by a drop of rain –
> the snail closes up

It was only a split second, but a split second that will last as long as haiku is read. That keenness of sight strengthens the unsaid thing, the full picture that we must fill:

> Tethered horse –
> snow in both
> stirrups

Translated, from the Irish, by the Managing Editor.

One of the generation of "Innti Poets" that transformed Irish language poetry in the early 1970s, Gabriel Rosenstock was born in 1949 in Kilfinane, Co Limerick. His most recent book is a travelogue, Ólann mo Mhiúil as an nGainséis *(My Mule Drinks from the Ganges). His 12th collection of poems in Irish,* Krishnamurphy, Ambaist! *is forthcoming.*

TWO POEMS

Sarah Maguire

A BOWL OF TRANSVAAL DAISES
for Seitlhamo Motsapi

Time darkens the petals
from scarlet to madder,

the plush fringe of lashes
curling backwards,

brittle rims
latching onto air

onto oxygen,
tenderly fingering the white china bowl –

a last,
vagrant gesture.

When you entered my bedroom
they were erect,

tall
in the tall cool vase,

their long, slender stems
drinking, drinking –

pliant necks spilling up
into the shocked high rush

of red mouths wide open
in joy, in astonishment.

Ten flat wheels of redness,
hot feathers

spooling
from the spun hub of gold.

Small planets fallen to earth,
they shoulder

the grass
and fire into light,

fat pollen shaking
its thick yellow blessings on the wind.

I came back
to a cold place,

crockery stacked in the sink,
chairs pushed back from the table,

your book propped open.
The gerberas were falling —

heavy heads keeling downwards,
kissing the china,

their soft useless necks
gone, all over.

I slit their throats —
ten of them,

right through the core.
Fed them to a flat china bowl

as they jostled the whiteness
and gazed aloft.

A forest of soft eyes open below me,
memory pulsing the fading red veins,

the curved fabric hardening
into a map.

A bowl of Transvaal daisies
waning at dusk,

releasing the tincture
of over, a slight fug staining the air.

I am exhausted by relics,
by this beautiful display

of loss and dust.
Please come here and tell me

their ten red names —
moarubetso, beloved

Sarah Maguire was born in 1957 in West London, where she has lived all her life. Her third book of poems is The Florist's at Midnight *(Cape, 2001). Her translations from the Arabic of Zakaria Mohammed appear in the Inaugural Issue of* IRISH PAGES.

THREE POEMS

Charles Wright

AGAINST THE AMERICAN GRAIN

Stronger and stronger, the sunlight glues
The afternoon to its objects,
                    the baby pine tree,
The scapular shadow thrown over the pond and meadow grass,
The absence the two
                 horses have left on the bare slope,
The silence that grazes like two shapes where they have been.

The slow vocabulary of sleep
                   spits out its consonants
And drifts in its vowely weather,
Sun-pocked, the afternoon dying among its odors,
The cocaine smell of the wind,
The too-sweet and soft-armed
                 fragrance around the reluctant lilac bush.

Flecked in the underlap, however,
                 half-glimpsed, half-recognized,
Something unordinary persists,
Something unstill, never-sleeping, just possible past reason.
Then unflecked by evening's overflow
                 and its counter current.
What mystery can match its maliciousness, what moan?

THE SILENT GENERATION II

We've told our story. We told it twice and took our lumps.
You'll find us here, of course, at the end of the last page,
Our signatures scratched in smoke.

Thunderstorms light us and roll on by.
Branches bend in the May wind,
But don't snap, the flowers bend and do snap, the grass gorps.

And then the unaltered grey,
Uncymbaled, undrumrolled, no notes to set the feet to music.
Still, we pull it up to our chins; it becomes our lives.

Garrulous, word-haunted, senescent,
Who knew we had so much to say, or tongue to say it?
The wind, I guess, who's heard it before, and crumples our pages.

And so we keep on, stiff lip, slack lip,
Hoping for words that are not impermanent – small words,
Out of the wind and the weather – that will not belie our names.

THE SILENT GENERATION III

These are our voices, active, passive and suppressed,
                                    and these are our syllables.
We used them to love your daughters, we used them to love your sons.
We travelled, we stayed home, we counted our days out
                                    like prescription pills.
In the end, like everyone, we had too much to say.

We lived by the seat of our pants, we bet on the come
Only to come up short,
                    and see, as the smoke began to clear,
The life we once thought that boundless canopy of sky,
Was just the sound of an axe, echoing in the woods.

We hadn't the heart for heartlessness,
                                    we hadn't the salt or the wound.
The words welled,
                    but goodness and mercy declined to follow us.
We carried our wings on our own backs, we ate our dead.
Like loose lightbulbs, we kept our radiance to ourselves.

Not heavy enough to be the hangman's burden,
                                        our noosed names
Are scrawled in the dust discursively, line after line.
Too strange for our contemporaries,
                        we'll prove to be
Not strange enough for posterity.

            O you who come after us,
Read our remains,
                study the soundless bones and do otherwise.

Spring and Summer, 2003

Charles Wright was born in Pickwick Dam, Tennessee in 1935 and now lives in Charlottesville, Virginia. He is one of America's foremost poets. His fifteenth volume of poems is A Short History of the Shadow *(Farrar, Straus & Giroux, 2002).*

TWO ADDRESSES

Susan Sontag

Is Sontag the American Sakharov?

LITERATURE AS FREEDOM

*An acceptance speech upon receiving the Friedenspreis Peace Prize
at the Frankfurt Book Fair, Germany.*

President Johannes Rau, Minister of the Interior Otto Schily, State Minister of Culture Christina Weiss, the Lord Mayor of Frankfurt Petra Roth, Vice-President of the Bundestag Antje Vollmer, your excellencies, other distinguished guests, honored colleagues, friends … among them, dear Ivan Nagel:

To speak in the Paulskirche, before this audience, to receive the prize awarded in the last fifty-three years by the German Book Trade to so many writers, thinkers, and exemplary public figures whom I admire – to speak in this history-charged place and on this occasion, is a humbling and inspiring experience. I can only the more regret the deliberate absence of the American ambassador, Mr. Daniel Coats, whose immediate refusal, in June, of the invitation from the Booksellers Association, when this year's Friedenspreis was announced, to attend our gathering here today, shows he is more interested in affirming the ideological stance and the rancorous reactiveness of the Bush administration than he is, by fulfilling a normal diplomatic duty, in representing the interests and reputation of his – and my – country.

Ambassador Coats has chosen not to be here, I assume, because of criticisms I have voiced, in newspaper and television interviews and in brief magazine articles, of the new radical bent of American foreign policy, as exemplified by the invasion and occupation of Iraq. He should be here, I think, because a citizen of the country he represents in Germany has been honored with an important German prize.

An American ambassador has the duty to represent his country, all of it. I, of course, do not represent America, not even that substantial minority that does not support the imperial program of Mr. Bush and his advisors. I like to think I do not represent anything but literature, a certain idea of literature, and conscience, a certain idea of conscience or duty. But, mindful of the citation for this prize from a major European country, which mentions my role as an "intellectual ambassador" between the two continents (*ambassador,* needless to say, in the weakest, merely metaphorical sense), I cannot resist offering a few thoughts about the renowned gap between Europe and the United States, which my interests and enthusiasms purportedly bridge.

First, is it a gap – which continues to be bridged? Or is it not also a conflict? Irate, dismissive statements about Europe, certain European countries, are now the common coin of American political rhetoric; and here, at least in the rich countries on the western side of the continent, anti-American sentiments are more common, more audible, more intemperate than ever. What is this conflict? Does it have deep roots? I think it does.

There has always been a latent antagonism between Europe and America, one at least as complex and ambivalent as that between parent and child. America is a neo-European country and, until the last few decades, was largely populated by European peoples. And yet it is always the differences between Europe and America that have struck the most perceptive European observers: Alexis de Tocqueville, who visited the young nation in 1831 and returned to France to write *Democracy in America*, still, some hundred and seventy years later, the best book about my country, and D.H. Lawrence, who, eighty years ago, published the most interesting book ever written about American culture, his influential, exasperating *Studies in Classic American Literature*, both understood that America, the child of Europe, was becoming, or had become, the antithesis of Europe.

Rome and Athens. Mars and Venus. The authors of recent popular tracts promoting the idea of an inevitable clash of interests and values between Europe and America did not invent these antitheses. Foreigners brooded over them – and they provide the palette, the recurrent melody, in much of American literature throughout the 19th century, from James Fenimore Cooper and Ralph Waldo Emerson to Walt Whitman, Henry James, William Dean Howells, and Mark Twain. American innocence and European sophistication; American pragmatism and European intellectualizing; American energy and European world-weariness; American naiveté and European cynicism; American goodheartedness and European malice; American moralism and the European arts of compromise – you know the tunes.

You can choreograph them differently; indeed, they have been danced with every kind of evaluation or tilt for two tumultuous centuries. Europhiles can use the venerable antitheses to identify America with commerce-driven barbarism and Europe with high culture, while the Europhobes draw on a readymade view in which America stands for idealism and openness and democracy and Europe a debilitating, snobbish refinement. Tocqueville and Lawrence observed something fiercer: not just a declaration of independence from Europe, and European values, but a steady undermining, an assassination of European values and European power. "You can never have a new thing without breaking an old," Lawrence wrote. "Europe happened to be the old thing. America should be the new thing. The new thing is the death of the old." America, Lawrence divined, was on a Europe-destroying mission, using democracy – particularly cultural democracy, democracy of manners – as an instrument. And when that task is accomplished, he went on, America might well turn from democracy to something else. (What that might be is, perhaps, emerging now.)

Bear with me if my references have been exclusively literary. After all, one function of literature – of important literature, of necessary literature – is to be prophetic. What we have here, writ large, is the perennial literary – or cultural – quarrel: between the ancients and the moderns.

The past is (or was) Europe, and America was founded on the idea of breaking with the past, which is viewed as encumbering, stultifying, and – in its forms of deference and precedence, its standards of what is superior and what is best – fundamentally undemocratic; or "elitist," the reigning current synonym. Those who speak for a triumphal America continue to intimate that American democracy implies repudiating Europe, and, yes, embracing a certain liberating, salutary barbarism. If, today, Europe is regarded by most Americans as more socialist than elitist, that still makes Europe, by American standards, a retrograde continent, obstinately attached to old standards: the welfare state. "Make it new" is not only a slogan for culture; it describes an ever-advancing, world-encompassing economic machine.

However, if necessary, even the "old" can be rebaptized as the "new."

It is not a coincidence that the strong-minded American Secretary of Defense tried to drive a wedge within Europe – distinguishing unforgettably between an "old" Europe (bad) and a "new" Europe (good). How did Germany, France, and Belgium come to be consigned to "old" Europe, while Spain, Italy, Poland, Ukraine, The Netherlands, Hungary, the Czech Republic, and Bulgaria find themselves part of "new" Europe? Answer: to support the United States in its present extensions of political and military power is, by definition, to pass into the more desirable category of the "new." Whoever is with us is "new."

All modern wars, even when their aims are the traditional ones, such as territorial aggrandizement or the acquisition of scarce resources, are cast as clashes of civilizations – culture wars – with each side claiming the high ground, and characterizing the other as barbaric. The enemy is invariably a threat to "our way of life," an infidel, a desecrator, a polluter, a defiler of higher or better values. The current war against the very real threat posed by militant Islamic fundamentalism is a particularly clear example. What is worth remarking is that a milder version of the same terms of disparagement underlie the antagonism between Europe and America. It should also be remembered that, historically, the most virulent anti-American rhetoric ever heard in Europe – consisting essentially in the charge that Americans are barbarians – came not from the so-called left but from the extreme right. Both Hitler and Franco repeatedly inveighed against an America (and a world Jewry) engaged in polluting European civilization with its base, business values.

Of course, much of European public opinion continues to admire American energy, the American version of "the modern." And, to be sure, there have always been American fellow-travelers of the European cultural ideals (one stands here before you), who find in the old arts of Europe correction and a liberation from the strenuous mercantilist biases of American culture. And there have always been the counterparts of such Americans on the European side: Europeans who are fascinated, enthralled, profoundly attracted to the United States, precisely because of its difference from Europe.

What the Americans see is almost the reverse of the Europhile clichè: they see themselves defending civilization. The barbarian hordes are no longer outside the gates. They are within, in every prosperous city, plotting havoc. The "chocolate-producing" countries (France, Germany, Belgium) will have to stand aside, while a country with "will" – and God on its side – pursues the battle against terrorism (now conflated with barbarism). According to Secretary of State Powell, it is ridiculous for old Europe (sometimes it seems only France is meant) to aspire to play a role in governing or administering the territories won by the coalition of the conqueror. It has neither the military resources nor the taste for violence nor the support of its cosseted, all-too-pacific populations. And the Americans have it right. Europeans are not in an evangelical – or a bellicose – mood.

Indeed, sometimes I have to pinch myself to be sure I am not dreaming: that what many people in my own country now hold against Germany, which wreaked such horrors on the world for nearly a century – the new "German problem," as it were – is that Germans are repelled by war; that much of German public opinion is now virtually pacifist!

Were America and Europe never partners, never friends? Of course. But perhaps it is true that the periods of unity – of common feeling – have been exceptions, rather than the rule. One such time was from the Second World War through the early Cold War, when Europeans were profoundly grateful for

America's intervention, succor, and support. Americans are comfortable seeing themselves in the role of Europe's savior. But then, America will expect the Europeans to be forever grateful, which is not what Europeans are feeling right now.

From "old" Europe's point of view, America seems bent on squandering the admiration – and gratitude – felt by most Europeans. The immense sympathy for the United States in the aftermath of the attack on September 11, 2001 was genuine. (I can testify to its resounding ardor and sincerity in Germany; I was in Berlin at the time.) But what has followed is an increasing estrangement on both sides.

The citizens of the richest and most powerful nation in history have to know that America is loved, and envied ... and resented. More than a few who travel abroad know that Americans are regarded as crude, boorish, uncultivated by many Europeans, and don't hesitate to match these expectations with behavior that suggests the ressentiment of ex-colonials. And some of the cultivated Europeans who seem most to enjoy visiting or living in the United States attribute to it, condescendingly, the liberating ambiance of a colony where one can throw off the restrictions and high-culture burdens of "back home." I recall being told by a German film-maker, living at the time in San Francisco, that he loved being in the States "because you don't have any culture here." For more than a few Europeans, including, it should be mentioned, D.H. Lawrence ("there the life comes up from the roots, crude but vital," he wrote to a friend in 1915, when he was making plans to live in America), America was the great escape. And vice versa: Europe was the great escape for generations of Americans seeking "culture." Of course, I am speaking only of minorities here, minorities of the privileged.

So America now sees itself as the defender of civilization and Europe's savior, and wonders why Europeans don't get the point; and Europeans see America as a reckless warrior state – a description that the Americans return by seeing Europe as the enemy of America: only pretending, so runs rhetoric heard increasingly in the United States, to be pacifist, in order to contribute to the weakening of American power. France in particular is thought to be scheming to become America's equal, even its superior, in shaping world affairs – "Operation America Must Fail" is the name invented by a columnist in the New York Times to describe the French drive toward dominance – instead of realizing that an American defeat in Iraq will (in the words of the same columnist) encourage "radical Muslim groups – from Baghdad to the Muslim slums of Paris" to pursue their jihad against tolerance and democracy.

It is hard for people not to see the world in polarizing terms ("them" and "us") and these terms have in the past strengthened the isolationist theme in American foreign policy as much as they now strengthen the imperialist theme. Americans have got used to thinking of the world in terms of enemies. Enemies are somewhere else, as the fighting is almost always "over there," with Islamic fundamentalism having replaced Russian and Chinese communism as the implacable, furtive menace. And terrorist is a more flexible word than communist. It can unify a larger number of quite different struggles and interests. What this may mean is that the war will be endless – since there will always be some terrorism (as there will always be poverty and cancer); that is, there will always be asymmetrical conflicts in which the weaker side uses that form of violence, which usually targets civilians. American rhetoric, which doesn't necessarily coincide with public opinion, would support this unhappy prospect, for the struggle for righteousness never ends.

It is the genius of the United States, a profoundly conservative country in ways that Europeans find difficult to fathom, to have devised a form of conservative thinking that celebrates the new rather than the old. But this is also to say, that in the very ways in which the United States seems extremely conservative – for example, the extraordinary power of the consensus and the passivity and conformism of public opinion (as Tocqueville remarked in 1831) and the media – it is also radical, even revolutionary, in ways that Europeans find equally difficult to fathom.

Part of the puzzle, surely, lies in the disconnect between official rhetoric and lived realities. Americans are constantly extolling "traditions"; litanies to family values are at the center of every politician's discourse. And yet the culture of America is extremely corrosive of family life, indeed of all traditions except those redefined as "identities" that can be accepted as part of larger patterns of distinctiveness, cooperation, and openness to innovation.

Perhaps the most important source of the new (and not so new) American radicalism is what used to be viewed as a source of conservative values: namely, religion. Many commentators have noted that perhaps the biggest difference between the United States and most European countries (old as well as new according to current American distinction) is that in the United States religion still plays a central role in society and public language. But this is religion American style: more the idea of religion than religion itself.

True, when, during George Bush's run for president in 2000, a journalist was inspired to ask the candidate to name his "favorite philosopher," the well-received answer – one that would make a candidate for high office from any centrist party here in any European country a laughing stock – was "Jesus Christ." But, of course, Bush didn't mean, and was not understood to mean, that, if elected, his administration would actually feel bound by any of the precepts or social programs expounded by Jesus.

The United States is a generically religious society. That is, in the United States it's not important which religion you adhere to, as long as you have one. To have a ruling religion, even a theocracy, that would be just Christian (or a particular Christian denomination) would be impossible. Religion in America must be a matter of choice. This modern, relatively contentless idea of religion, constructed along the lines of consumerist choice, is the basis of American conformism, self-righteousness, and moralism (which Europeans often mistake, condescendingly, for Puritanism). Whatever historic faiths the different American religious entities purport to represent, they all preach something similar: reform of personal behavior, the value of success, community cooperativeness, tolerance of other's choices. (All virtues that further and smooth functioning of consumer capitalism.) The very fact of being religious ensures respectability, promotes order, and gives the guarantee of virtuous intentions to the mission of the United States to lead the world.

What is being spread — whether it is called democracy, or freedom, or civilization — is part of a work in progress, as well as the essence of progress itself. Nowhere in the world does the Enlightenment dream of progress have such a fertile setting as it does in America.

—

Are we then really so separate? How odd that, at a moment when Europe and America have never been so similar culturally, there has never been such a great divide.

Still, for all the similarities in the daily lives of citizens in rich European countries and the daily lives of Americans, the gap between the European and the American experience is a genuine one, founded on important differences of history, of notions of the role of culture, of real and imagined memories. The antagonism — for there is antagonism — is not to be resolved in the immediate future, for all the good will of many people on both sides of the Atlantic. And yet one can only deplore those who want to maximize those differences, when we do have so much in common.

The dominance of America is a fact. But America, as the present administration is starting to see, cannot do everything alone. The future of our world – the world we share – is syncretistic, impure. We are not shut off from each other. More and more, we leak into each other.

In the end, the model for whatever understanding – conciliation – we might reach lies in thinking more about that venerable opposition, "old" and "new." The opposition between "civilization" and "barbarism" is essentially stipulatory; it is corrupting to think about and pontificate about – however much it may reflect certain undeniable realities. But the opposition of "old" and "new" is genuine, ineradicable, at the center of what we understand to be experience itself.

"Old" and "new" are the perennial poles of all feeling and sense of orientation in the world. We cannot do without the old, because in what is old is invested all our past, our wisdom, our memories, our sadness, our sense of realism. We cannot do without faith in the new, because in what is new is invested all our energy, our capacity for optimism, our blind biological yearning, our ability to forget – the healing ability that makes reconciliation possible.

The inner life tends to mistrust the new. A strongly developed inner life will be particularly resistant to the new. We are told we must choose – the old or the new. In fact, we must choose both. What is a life if not a series of negotiations between the old and the new? It seems to me that one should always be seeking to talk oneself out of these stark oppositions.

Old versus new, nature versus culture – perhaps it is inevitable that the great myths of our cultural life be played out as geography, not only as history. Still, they are myths, clichés, stereotypes, no more; the realities are much more complex.

A good deal of my life has been devoted to trying to demystify ways of thinking that polarize and oppose. Translated into politics, this means favoring what is pluralistic and secular. Like some Americans and many Europeans, I would far prefer to live in a multilateral world – a world not dominated by any one country (including my own). I could express my support, in a century that already promises to be another century of extremes, of horrors, for a whole panoply of meliorist principles – in particular, for what Virginia Woolf calls "the melancholy virtue of tolerance."

Let me rather speak first of all as a writer, as a champion of the enterprise of literature, for therein lies the only authority I have.

The writer in me distrusts the good citizen, the "intellectual ambassador," the human rights activist – those roles which are mentioned in the citation for this prize, much as I am committed to them. The writer is more skeptical, more self-doubting, than the person who tries to do (and to support) the right thing.

One task of literature is to formulate questions and construct counter-statements to the reigning pieties. And even when art is not oppositional, the arts gravitate toward contrariness. Literature is dialogue; responsiveness. Literature might be described as the history of human responsiveness to what is alive and what is moribund as cultures evolve and interact with one another.

Writers can do something to combat these clichés of our separateness, our difference – for writers are makers, not just transmitters, of myths. Literature offers not only myths but counter-myths, just as life offers counter-experiences – experiences that confound what you thought you thought, or felt, or believed.

A writer, I think, is someone who pays attention to the world. That means trying to understand, take in, connect with, what wickedness human beings are capable of; and not be corrupted – made cynical, superficial – by this understanding.

Literature can tell us what the world is like.

Literature can give standards and pass on deep knowledge, incarnated in language, in narrative.

Literature can train, and exercise, our ability to weep for those who are not us or ours.

Who would we be if we could not sympathize with those who are not us or ours? Who would we be if we could not forget ourselves, at least some of the time? Who would we be if we could not learn? Forgive? Become something other than we are?

———

On the occasion of receiving this glorious prize, this glorious German prize, let me tell you something of my own trajectory.

I was born, a third-generation American of Polish and Lithuanian Jewish descent, two weeks before Hitler came to power. I grew up in the American provinces (Arizona and California), far from Germany, and yet my entire childhood was haunted by Germany, by the monstrousness of Germany, and by the German books and the German music I loved, which set my standard for what is exalted and intense.

Even before Bach and Mozart and Beethoven and Schubert and Brahms, there were a few German books. I am thinking of a teacher in an elementary school in a small town in southern Arizona, Mr. Starkie, who had awed his pupils by telling us that he had fought with Pershing's army in Mexico against Pancho Villa: this grizzled veteran of an earlier American imperialist venture had, it seems, been touched – in translation – by the idealism of German literature, and, having taken in my particular hunger for books, loaned me his own copies of *The Sorrows of Young Werther* and *Immensee*.

Soon after, in my childhood orgy of reading, chance led me to other German books, including Kafka's "In the Penal Colony," where I discovered dread and injustice. And a few years later, when I was a high school student in Los Angeles, I found all of Europe in a German novel. No book has been more important in my life than *The Magic Mountain* – whose subject is, precisely, the clash of ideals at the heart of European civilization. And so on, through a long life that has been steeped in German high culture. Indeed, after the books and the music, which were, given the cultural desert in which I lived, virtually clandestine experiences, came real experiences. For I am also a late beneficiary of the German cultural diaspora, having had the great good fortune of knowing well some of the incomparably brilliant Hitler refugees, those writers and artists and musicians and scholars that America received in the 1930s and who so enriched the country, particularly its universities. Let me name two I was privileged to count as friends when I was in my late teens and early twenties, Hans Gerth and Herbert Marcuse; those with whom I studied at the University of Chicago and at Harvard, Christian Mackauer and Leo Strauss and Paul Tillich and Peter Heinrich von Blanckenhagen, and in private seminars, Aron Gurwitsch and Nahum Glatzer; and Hannah Arendt, whom I knew after I moved to New York in my mid-twenties – so many models of the serious, whose memory I would like to evoke here.

But I shall never forget that my engagement with German culture, with German seriousness, all started with obscure, eccentric Mr. Starkie (I don't think I ever knew his first name), who was my teacher when I was ten, and whom I never saw afterward.

And that brings me to a story, with which I will conclude – as seems fitting, since I am neither primarily a cultural ambassador nor a fervent critic of my own government (a task I perform as a good American citizen). I am a story-teller.

So, back to ten-year-old me, who found some relief from the tiresome duties of being a child by poring over Mr. Starkie's tattered volumes of Goethe and Storm. At the time I am speaking of, 1943, I was aware that there was a prison camp with thousands of German soldiers, Nazi soldiers as of course I thought of them, in the northern part of the state, and, knowing I was Jewish (if only nominally, my family having been completely secular and assimilated for two generations, nominally, I knew, was enough for Nazis), I was beset by a recurrent nightmare in which Nazi soldiers had escaped from the prison and had made their way downstate to the bungalow on the outskirts of the town where I lived with my mother and sister, and were about to kill me.

Flash forward to many years later, the 1970s, when my books started to be published by Hanser Verlag, and I came to know the distinguished Fritz Arnold (he had joined the firm in 1965), who was my editor at Hanser until his death in February 1999.

One of the first times we were together, Fritz said he wanted to tell me – presuming, I suppose, that this was a prerequisite to any friendship that might arise between us – what he had done during the war. I assured him that he did not owe me any such explanation; but, of course, I was touched by his bringing up the subject. I should add that Fritz Arnold was not the only German of his generation (he was born in 1916) who, soon after we met, insisted on telling me what he or she had done in Nazi times. And not all of the stories were as innocent as what I was to hear from Fritz.

Anyway, what Fritz told me was that he had been a university student of literature and art history, first in Munich, then in Cologne, when, at the start of the war, he was drafted into the Wehrmacht with the rank of corporal. His family was, of course, anything but pro-Nazi – his father was Karl Arnold, the legendary political cartoonist of Simplicissimus – but emigration seemed out of the question, and he accepted, with dread, the call to military service, hoping neither to kill anyone nor to be killed.

Fritz was one of the lucky ones. Lucky, to have been stationed first in Rome (where he refused his superior officer's invitation to be commissioned a lieutenant), then in Tunis; lucky enough to have remained behind the lines and never once to have fired a weapon; and finally, lucky, if that is the right word, to have been taken prisoner by the Americans in 1943, to have been transported by ship across the Atlantic with other captured German soldiers to Norfolk, Virginia, and then taken by train across the continent to spend the rest of the war in a prison camp in northern Arizona.

Then I had the pleasure of telling him, sighing with wonder, for I had already started to be very fond of this man – this was the beginning of a great friendship as well as an intense professional relationship – that while he was a prisoner of war in northern Arizona, I was in the southern part of the state, terrified of the Nazi soldiers who were there, here, and from whom there would be no escape.

And then Fritz told me that what got him through his nearly three years in the prison camp in Arizona was that he was allowed access to books: he had spent those years reading and rereading the English and American classics. And I told him that what saved me as a schoolchild in Arizona, waiting to grow up, waiting to escape into a larger reality, was reading books, books in translation as well as those written in English.

To have access to literature, world literature, was to escape the prison of national vanity, of philistinism, of compulsory provincialism, of inane schooling, of imperfect destinies and bad luck. Literature was the passport to enter a larger life; that is, the zone of freedom.

Literature was freedom. Especially in a time in which the values of reading and inwardness are so strenuously challenged, literature is freedom.

TURNING POINTS

Hic clavis, alias porta.
(The key is here, the gate elsewhere.)

*A speech given at the Commencement Exercises
at Vassar College, 25 May 2003*

President Fergusson, faculty, trustees, students, parents and other family members, friends of Vassar, and, above all, members of the Class of 2003.

This is a wonderful occasion, an occasion of joy. Graduation from college is one of life's major turning points. There will be other turning points, but this one has to feel awesome. Something large and complicated has been at last accomplished. Something even larger and more complicated awaits – on the other side of a great door that officially opens today.

On these occasions, it is the privilege of a few designated elders to bore you, or amuse you, or provoke you, with admonitions and words of encouragement. But before I set out on my homiletic task, let me invoke the joy. Again.

You have been receiving something called an education – a very loose concept indeed. It includes matters as varied as information, ways of thinking, cultural references, skills of different kinds, pre-professional preparation. There is an idea of knowing. There is an idea of growing – aka growing up. (But let me tell you a secret. Growing up is something you'll be doing, or trying to do, all your life.) There is an idea of getting stronger, more independent, clearer. There is an idea of being safe, protected, cosseted … encouraged.

You will have learned something about the power of words, the power of thinking. Your teachers, the best of them, will have been trying – through the medium of various "subjects" – to form your attention. The formation of attention is the true definition of education – and, as Hannah Arendt once observed – of culture itself.

Part of the formation of attention is the courtesy you extend to what is different. The eagerness you have to receive new stimuli, and to be challenged. That, too, is part of an education.

Of course, to be educated, specifically to go to a liberal arts culture college, does not mean that one is automatically committed to the values of respect and dignity, and a civilized approach to discourse and debate. A college is anything but an ivory tower, as I'm sure you know, and what goes on inside has to reflect what is going on throughout the society. Nobody is "in" college without also being "in" the society at large, as well as "in" our circles of family and friends.

Nevertheless, some colleges try to offer a counterforce to some of the bigotry and narrow-mindedness and bellicosity of the society at large – and Vassar, with its long traditions of intellectual distinction, and its commitment to tolerance and intellectual openness, is surely one of the places where a certain "resistance" to conventional opinions is honored, if not actively promulgated.

It is not always so in American campuses. Just last week, on May 20th, at a small liberal arts college eighty miles north of Chicago, Rockford College, a commencement speaker was booed by a pack of students as he began his speech, who then cut the electricity that powered the podium's microphone and, ignoring the pleas of the college president to let the speaker continue, stormed the stage and forced the speaker off. Chris Hedges is the name of the commencement speaker who was not allowed to make his speech. He is a former foreign correspondent at *The New York Times*, and I spent time with him in Sarajevo, where Chris was stationed for about a year and where I lived for a good part of the three years of the siege. We both know, at first hand, what war is really like.

What did Chris Hedges say that turned a large number of college students into a potential lynch mob? He said, for one thing, that war is an addiction. He probably said, or was going to say, that the American invasion and conquest of Iraq – for that is how it should correctly be called (not: "the liberation of Iraq" or "Operation Iraqi Freedom" or "the campaign of the coalition of the willing to disarm Iraq") – was illegitimate, and unwise. He probably said, or was about to say, that the administration did not provide any credible evidence of an imminent threat from Iraq to the United States before the invasion – which may be explained, in the weeks since the conquest of this pitifully weak, nearly destitute, fiendishly ruled country of 24 million people, by the subsequent failure to find the fabled "weapons of mass destruction" that were, if one was to believe the administration, poised with the nuclear tips or chemical payload to strike at the American heartland.

He may have said these things. I don't know. It seems he did not get very far, before the students started booing, and shouting "USA Number One" and someone, a woman, according to the news report, began singing "God Bless America!" as Chris tried, in vain, to go on speaking.

As I say, I don't know how far he got. I haven't been in touch with him. I haven't read the speech he was prepared, but unable, to give. But you will have gathered, from my rhetorical elaboration of what I take to be his position, that I am actually describing my own position. And you will assume, as I do, that such behavior is inconceivable at Vassar, and that had I chosen to use my allotted time for a commencement homily to denounce the Bush-Cheney-Rumsfeld administration and to express my conviction that the United States is at a radical, a very radical, turning point – possibly the moment when the Republic may have ended, and the Empire begun – you would hear me out, all of you, including those who do not think as I do.

As I've said, I haven't read Chris Hedges' speech, but I would wager that I wouldn't find anything objectionable in it. So it's easy, maybe too easy, to condemn the behavior of the students at Rockford. But let's make it a little harder for ourselves. Would there never be an occasion when we might want to register our disapproval of a speaker? No one, I would wager, is likely to be driven off the stage at Vassar for opposing American bellicosity. But suppose someone took this platform and uttered stridently racist remarks or gleefully recounted misogynistic anecdotes. What would we – you, I – do then?

Should you not have opinions? Should you not care? Sure. But how would you act on them. Boo? Sing? Stamp your feet? Turn your back? Walk out? Cut the power and storm the stage?

Think about it. Do we care? Do we care? And what do we do when we care? These are the old questions, the questions central to 19th century Russian literature: *How do we live?* And: *what is to be done?*

—

One of the things you learn – you are supposed to learn – in college is the value of doing something for itself. That is the meaning of a liberal arts education. Yes, some of you were taking courses because you were preparing for a professional career, but there was always the idea that you might take a course just for the hell of it, because it was fun, or you were "interested" (a muddy word if ever there was one).

In college, you are encouraged to respond to the value of doing something for itself. And now you are going out into a world where this is not the case, where all action becomes more instrumental, more calculating, more practical. And mercenary.

If you continue to be a student, that is, go to a graduate or professional school, your education will become more focused; you will be studying and learning in order to prepare or qualify for a profession. If you leave here and go directly to a job, you are expected to set your sights on what is practical. What *works*.

Either way, you are not going to have the same incentive to just let your mind float, to follow your whim. Indeed, you will have powerful incentive to do just the opposite. The road to adult life and its responsibilities runs beneath a sign that says: "Abandon all dreams, ye who enter here."

At least, that's the myth. That's what you've been told. That's what you dread.

Ambition may flourish. But certain kinds of energy die.

Going out into the world means not having enough time to do what you "want to do" – "used to do" – that is, read, listen to music, have fun, hang out.

Is this true?

I'm here to say: not necessarily.

Don't buy into the myth of age. Maybe you're doing now what you think college students ought to do, have a license to do. The myth of the stages of life (reduced in our time to the notion of "decades" – hey, now you're beginning your twenties!) – may seem to be on your side now. But it will start turning against you, as you get older.

Oh, I can't do that, or, I don't do that, you'll say as you near your thirties. I wish I could. But I just don't have the time.

Don't believe it.

You can.

The most potent, the deepest form of censorship, in a society and in an individual life, is *self*-censorship.

—

Today is a great turning point for you. And the notion of turning points is a useful one. It can give permission for new energies to be mobilized. It can also mobilize the sense of loss ... a feeling of being thrust forward, of having to leave behind something you'll never be able to duplicate in its feelings of warmth and protected adventurousness.

You are going from a place – college, this college, Vassar, where the best is expected of you to a place – the world – where this is usually not the case. Here are some pieces of advice:

– Read a lot. Expect something big, something exalting or deepening from a book. No book is worth reading once that isn't worth re-reading. If you read right, you'll be doing a lot of re-reading all your life. (The same for movies, by the way.)

– Try not to live in a linguistic slum.

– Try to imagine the concrete, lived reality that words point to. Words like, for example, "war."

– Try not to think about yourself, or what you want, or need, or what disappoints you; try not to think of yourself at all – at least half of the time.

– Get about. I mean this, literally. Travel.

Live in another country for a while. But travel, never stop traveling. And if you can't get very far, then go deeper into places that take you out of yourself. As the critic Denis Donoghue wrote, "If time is the category of loss, there is always place. Places make up for times, as a garden, for instance, lets you feel that the past is no longer a burden."

– Commerce is the ruling activity and money-making the ruling standard in this society. Try keeping a place for ideas and practical actions that oppose or ignore commerce. Each of us, if we so desire, can be, in some small measure, a counterforce to what is shallow and heartless in the society that will welcome the attractive and the privileged which, as graduates of Vassar, you are.

– Despise violence. Despise national vanity and self-love.

– Protect the territory of conscience.

– Try to imagine at least once a day that you are not an American. Go even further: try to imagine at once a day that you belong to the vast, the overwhelming majority of people on this planet who don't have passports, don't live in dwellings equipped with both refrigerators and telephones, who have never even once flown in a plane.

– Be extremely skeptical of all claims made by your government. Remember, it may not be the best thing for America or for the world for the President of the United States to be the president of the planet. Be just as skeptical of other governments, too.

– It's hard not to be afraid. Be less afraid.

– It's good to laugh a lot, as long as it doesn't mean you're trying to kill your feelings.

– Don't allow yourself to be patronized, condescended to – which, if you are a woman, happens, and will continue to happen, all the time. Don't take shit. Tell the bastards off.

– Do stuff. Be clenched, curious. Not waiting for inspiration's shove or society's kiss on your forehead.

– Try not to become someone you now, the you that's here today, would be disappointed in. That's hard. Things aren't set up for you to do this without a lot of vigilance and obstinacy. Nothing is easier than giving up or settling for less, without meaning to give up or settle for less. Even the most beautifully launched life can founder.

– Pay attention. It's all about paying attention. It's all about taking in as much of what's out there as you can, and not letting the excuses and the dreariness of some of the obligations you'll soon be incurring narrow your lives.

– Attention is vitality. It connects you with others. It makes you eager. Stay eager.

You'll notice that I haven't talked about love. Or about happiness. I've talked about becoming – or remaining – the person who can be happy, a lot of the time, without thinking that being happy is what it's all about. It's not. It's about becoming the largest, most inclusive, most responsive person you can be.

⸻

From two poems by Wallace Stevens, two visions of life. First, from a late poem, "The Dwarf":

> Now it is September and the web is woven
> The web is woven and you have to wear it.
>
> It is all that you are, the final dwarf of you,
> That is woven and woven and waiting to be worn...

And this, from a late poem called "Architecture":

> What manner of building shall we build?
> In this house, what manner of utterance shall there be?

Remember: It's not September, it's May. Believe me, everything is possible. Don't let yourself down.

Congratulations on getting out of here. I wish you more than one life, and many passions, many turning points, in the years that lie before you.

Susan Sontag is an essayist, critic, scholar and novelist. An important voice in American letters since the 1960s, she is the author of 11 books, including such classics as Against Interpretation and Other Essays *(1968) and* On Photography *(1976). Her fourth novel,* In America *(Farrar, Straus & Giroux), was published in 1999. She lives in New York City.*

POEM

Michael Hamburger

POST-PASCHAL, 2003

1

After Good Friday this bitter wind,
Northeasterly, on to dead fibre warmed
Back into bud or leaf, blossom or nucleus.

After the last words, human,
Agony beyond words, too human now
That words are what they use,
Their counterfeit currency
Perverting all they price and sell to trash,
Even the outrage tainted.

To walk immune here in the rising light,
Our pathways quiet, skyline not blasted black
Was to be shamed by the sun's clear shining.

2

What sap stirs now, what moves?
Conquest projected from empty heads
Into long-distance missiles fuelled with money,
Their borrowed billions, unreal estate
That rules the residual real,
Electronically missed their would-be targets
And the limbs of a child exploded.
For bonus, the lying logo affixed
To the cluster-bombs of liberation
From home-grown tyranny to its imported replacement
When the ruins and relics, forgotten,
Can be buried in desert sand.

3

Pilate's power was more honest.
The pagan light, nature's,
Left him room for doubt.

Two millennia were needed for this:
Our new age crusaders
Too busy playing golf for their health
To prove what they profess,
Sent out their "boys" on the thuggish business,
"Girls," too, the new age demanded,
A mere handful of either to be killed or maimed,
Not counting the reporters, men and women,
Closer to true action in this pseudo-war.

4

For the next assault, here beginneth the lesson,
Where every beginning is almost the end:

Disarm the enemy who was your friend,
Starve the people, destroy the installations,
Blessed by a cowed, compliant United Nations
You can always bypass, should it grow brash.
Modernize, modernize! Pretend, pretend!
In that penumbra, Thatcherized New Labour,
Call him potential client, global neighbour
Whom out of deep affinity you bash
Into disorientated frenzy – first.
Then restore order, yours, and do your worst.

5

Ah, but it's words again, weary and wearisome.
The Kingdom has not come.
Satan, the salesman of dominion once,
Laughs at himself: that tempter was the dunce.
This world, distributed, incorporated,
Has been diminished, all the fuss inflated.
The very oil, they say, is running out.
So what was this expenditure about,

Whose mass destruction, whose individual pains,
Propaganda self-dissolving – while confusion reigns?

Silence that mocked could heal it,
Source of water stopped or polluted – drought could reveal it,
Lights that flickered, went out enhance the light that remains.

Michael Hamburger, a poet and translator, lives in East Anglia. His most recent collection is From a Diary of Non-Events *(Anvil, 2002).*

AMERICA AND THE WORLD

———

Michael Foley

From the American Archive, reflections on the global colossus.

THE DEMOCRACTIC IMPERATIVE
(1993)

An island race in a shrinking world.

I

Preamble

America's pronounced sense of national identity is derived from its geographical and cultural distance from the "old world" and from the country's allegiance to the idea that the peculiarities of its position and development gave rise to a model democracy. The belief in the exceptionalism of the United States and in the definitive nature of its democratic arrangements has led to two different, and often contradictory, conceptions of America's role in the world. First, that America is a unique entity which is not comparable to other nations and which must be protected from the corruptive forces of the outside world. Second, that America is a universal model whose social progress and political democracy can, and should, be applied to other countries and cultures.

This dual outlook has always generated tensions but, as the United States had advanced to the position of a global superpower, these strains have multiplied in scale and intensified in nature. Deep divisions exist between ideals and practice, principles and self-interest, obligations and expedience; between the rule of law and the law of competitive national advantage; between democratic choice and necessary response; between coercive American emancipation and national self-determination; between uniqueness preserved from without and universalism applied from within; and between American independence from the world and the dependency of America's identity upon that which is not American.

Such dichotomies afflict the United States' outlook on the world and disrupt the continuity of American foreign policy. In the same way that the world outside the United States can give credence to the American precept of democratic exceptionalism, so the pressures of international involvement can also serve to subvert the democratic order of the United States and, with it, the substance of America's example to the rest of the world. Opinions can swing markedly between, on the one hand, deferring to definitions of national security and strategic need for the sake of protecting American democracy; and, on the other hand, objecting firstly to the lack of democratic control and accountability in foreign policymaking, and secondly to the amoral and often illiberal nature of international power politics. As a consequence, the "solution" of American intervention can often coexist with the alternative "solution" of American retreat and retrenchment.

Even though the United States has now emerged triumphant as the dominant superpower, these types of tensions remain unresolved. In fact, with the end of the Cold War and the erosion of its related disciplines, American foreign policy promises to become more conspicuously subject to these contrary impulses and fluctuating postures, than ever before.

II

The United States and the External World

America's outlook upon the world has always been coloured by its conviction that whilst it is self-evidently in the world, it remains equally convinced that it is not of the world. Its identity remains strongly dependent upon the conception that America is separate from, and different to, everywhere else. Americans take pride in the fact that their society was formed and developed by multitudes of settlers who sought emancipation from previous conditions of European destitution and oppression through the simple recourse of physical flight to the protean expanse of America's "virgin lands". "New" rapidly became the leitmotif of everything American. In the eighteenth century, St John de Crevecoeur described the American as the "new man who acts on new principles". America itself was a new world of disaggregated peoples from other nations reconstituted into an alternative nation by nothing other than their collective experience of America. As a consequence, the United States could claim the title of the first new nation. It had been the first major colony successfully to break away from colonial rule by a process of revolution. This was more than a simple act of political independence. It provided public evidence that the peculiar dynamics of both America's social organization and its geographical isolation were sufficient to defeat the British army and, thereby, to defy the authority of a major power. America's successful declaration of independence not only seemed to substantiate a pre-existing separatism in outlook and conditions, but served to fuse American belief that in any contact between the United States and the "old world", it was assumed that the latter would in the end always have to come to terms with the providential and progressive nature of the former. A new world order to an American was a revised international order in the shape of the new world.

These inflated suppositions were not to become relevant in a global sense until the United States itself expanded to a point where its size could match its presumptions. During its first one hundred years, the American republic was almost wholly preoccupied with assimilating the vast landmass of the continent's interior. By purchase, treaty, war and annexation, the United States was rapidly enlarged in size, resources and population. The enormous acquisitions exacerbated pre-existing tensions to the point of a cathartic civil war between the North and the South. The union army's victory conclusively established the indissoluble nature of the American federation. It also ensured that the American republic would evolve as an integrated continental entity and, with it, generate the potential to be a world economic and military power.

That promise was largely fulfilled in the years of rapid industrialization and urbanization which followed the war. By the turn of the century, the number of businesses had grown to over 1,000,000 from under 250,000 in the 1850s and 1860s. Agricultural employment fell from two thirds of the labour force in mid century to just one-third by 1900. At the beginning of the twentieth century, the United States had become the world's leading producer of coal, iron ore, pig iron, steel and gold. The enormous potential of its natural resources and its massive internal market, allowed the US to become an economic giant within a generation. A laissez faire economy had produced an essentially laissez faire nation centred firmly on the spontaneity and dynamics of America's own purportedly inner-directed social experiment and organization. As unprecedented numbers of immigrants poured into the country, the American interior began to swell with towns and cities. At the beginning of the nineteenth century, Thomas Jefferson believed that there would be enough new land to satisfy a thousand generations of settlers. But by 1890, the frontier was officially closed. Within a hundred years, the United States had tripled its land possessions, its population had grown from 5.3 million to 75.9 million and the number of states had increased from 16 to 45.

The United States gave the impression of a nation so absorbed with itself and its own economic and social development that it inadvertently stumbled out into the world backwards. The outside world was always taken to be dangerous and corrupting, but it was also assumed to be distant and only accessible through choice. America had no consciousness of being a great nation in the sense of constituting one of the major powers. The nation had been formed *in vacuo*, as a nation apart from others. Its greatness, therefore, had come not from any aspirations to gain entry into Europe's power politics, but as a consequence of its internal consolidation and an abhorrence towards being entrapped in the responsibilities and restrictions of any international balances of power. The nation was vindicated by its own aggrandisement. It was conditioned to believe that America was so massive that it could always accommodate its own voracious economic developments without compromising its idiosyncratic status as not merely a new nation but a new kind of nation. In the twentieth century, however, America repeatedly had to come to terms with the ramifications of being an island race set on a subcontinent in a shrinking world.

America's ambivalence towards the Old World was compounded by an increasing ambivalence towards itself. America had always felt threatened by the world outside, but as a result of a number of paradoxical developments, the country was also threatened by its own size and composition. For example, the United States had become a nation by being apart from other nations; it had developed as a country by developing away from Europe both culturally and literally by westward expansion. And yet its success in this respect had increasingly brought it back into the orbit of international affairs and the European powers. By cutting itself off so effectively, it had succeeded in generating the growth that undermined its own isolation and brought it into closer contact with outside interests and obligations. Another example of this type of self-generated ambivalence towards the world was provided by the enormous influx of immigrants. For example, in the first twenty years of the twentieth century, 14.5 million people migrated to the United States. In 1920, over 15 percent of the American population was classified as foreign-born. This created anxieties over the extent to which such large numbers of newcomers could be assimilated within American culture. The fear was that the success in attracting large-scale immigration was also a sign of decay in that these new immigrants brought the old world to America, instead of leaving it behind. This suspicion led to spates of internal cultural conflict involving conspicuously homogenous American forces defending individual, liberty from the "Un-American activities" of those "subversive elements" who wished to challenge the orthodoxy of American society in the name of their constitutional rights to diversity.

Many other examples exist of the contradictory tendencies and interpretations generated by America's changing place in the world. For example, it can be argued that America's marked attachment to, and development of, science and technology not only served to integrate the nation and the economy, but neutralised the spatial boundaries of America's oceanic distance from other continents. It can also be claimed that America's very success in acquiring land in the nineteenth century gave the country a sense of being so open-ended in nature that it massively reduced the number of reference points in the new world demarcating which were areas of legitimate expansion and which were not. When its economic empire spilled out into the Pacific and Latin America during the late nineteenth century, it drew political interests and even military engagements in its wake. Later, American forces were sent to Europe, thereby, allowing the process of American expansion to transcend the society's original *raison d'etre* and to project the United States into the very centre of old world power. America's entry into World War I, to fight alongside the British Empire against German imperialism, marked the emergence of the United States as a world power. In doing so, it might be said to have signified that the United States had expanded into an ordinary nation as dedicated to imperial outreach as any great power. On the other hand, the American impulse to withdraw can be said to be even more consistent than its imperialist disposition to intervene. In spite of its considerable economic interests in Europe and the Far East, for example, the US nevertheless engaged in an emphatic, and quite unrealistic, isolationist stance in the 1930s. Stephen Ambrose could conclude that even as late as 1939 "the dominant political mood was isolationism. America's physical security, the *sine qua non* of foreign policy, seemed assured, not because of American alliances or military strength but because of the distance between America and any potential enemy".

These types of developments have generated a profusion of inconsistencies, and even contradictions, in the United States approach to the rest of the world. The unresolved nature of the strains entailed in these historical and cultural processes continue to cause marked fluctuations in America's approach to international affairs. But there is one element in America's composition that has had a particularly profound effect in this area. It could even be claimed to be the central feature in the United States' outlook upon the world and the medium through which most American anxieties and mixed reactions concerning its international position are expressed. The element in question is the United States relationship to its adopted values of liberty and democracy. These have the effect of couching the condition and behaviour of America in an indigenous moral framework, thereby, deepening even further America's ambivalence toward what lies outside itself; what is at risk with worldly contact; and what America's responsibilities are to itself and to the rest of the world.

III

The United States and its Internal Democracy

Central to America's self-image is the conviction that it is a wholly exceptional society not just because of its position in the new world, but because its unique social chemistry allowed it to become synonymous with the sort of advanced social principles which in most countries remain only aspirations. In the United States liberty, equality, and democracy are taken as merely traditional and self-evident features of America's indigenous experience. They are not regarded as a set of values to be striven for, so much as a set of pre-existing conditions to be protected and embellished. They are widely assumed to embody the essence of American — what makes America different, what makes it the new world.

These suppositions have a long and well-established pedigree. As early as the 1830s, Alexis de Tocqueville was pointing out that the United States had produced a democratic society that was extraordinary in scale and spontaneous in origin. "The great advantage of the Americans is that they have arrived at a state of democracy without having to endure a democratic revolution and that they are born equal, instead of becoming so." This theme of democracy as an expression of American existence became such a dominant feature in the identity of the United States that the main question raised by it has traditionally been that of causes rather than effects. For example, in his highly influential interpretation of American culture and ideas Louis Hartz asserts that the origins of America's overwhelming liberal tradition lay in the absence of a feudal past. Without an ancien regime, America "lacks a genuine revolutionary tradition ... and this being the case, it lacks also a tradition of reaction". As a consequence, America never developed the class divisions and political tensions that have traditionally afflicted European politics. Instead, it produced an intuitive social consensus centred upon liberal individualism, economic opportunity and widespread property acquisition – i.e., what Hartz terms "democratic capitalism":

> Amid the "free air" of American life something new appeared: men began to be held together not by the knowledge that they were different parts of a corporate whole, but by the knowledge that they were similar participants in a uniform way of life.

This view of American life arising spontaneously from the very nature of American conditions – arguably from a state of nature – is a common theme underlying the conception of society in the United States. In Daniel Boorstin's opinion, for example,

> The United States is the *land* of the free ... No nation has been readier to identify its values with the peculiar conditions of its landscape: we believe in *American* equality, *American* liberty, *American* democracy ... American ideals are not in books or in the blood but in the air, (where) they are readily acquired; actually, it is almost impossible for an immigrant to avoid acquiring them. He is not required to learn a philosophy so much as to rid his lungs of the air of Europe.

American democracy in this respect is not just a condition of democracy existing in the United States. It is a qualitatively exceptional form of democracy whose idiosyncratic nature is derived from the peculiarities of America itself. According to this perspective, American democracy is not comparable to other democracies. More precisely, America is not comparable to other countries because it is a democracy – the definitive democracy which other countries may seek to emulate but which never succeed in doing so because they lack the social chemistry of the new world. Democracy in this guise is the climactic end product of America's naturalistic experience and, therefore, the supreme expression of America's inherent nature. It serves to define American identity in relation to outsiders, to explain and vindicate America's unequalled economic and social expansion, and to provide a reassuring defence against the degenerate corruption of the old world. In short, American democracy conveys the idea that America is unique and that its democracy is not transferable.

This perspective is qualified by another, and equally traditional, interpretation of American democracy. In one sense, it can be used to support the proposition that American democracy is indeed exceptional. But this perspective carries quite different implications and can serve to inflate even further American pretensions to superlative uniqueness. It is the belief that American democracy is different in scope but not in kind, and that as a consequence it should be seen more as a model democracy capable of being copied elsewhere. The notion of America acting as a vanguard of social progress goes back to the late eighteenth century. In Peter Gay's words, "the American Revolution converted America from an importer of ideas into an exporter. What it exported was, of course, mainly itself, but that was a formidable commodity – the program of enlightenment in practice."

While the old world could only imagine and formulate sets of enlightened social proposals, it was the United States that enacted them. America, liberated from imperial rule and British orthodoxy, served to enhance an intellectual emancipation that in its turn led to a more secular and practical application of intelligence to human affairs. The belief in the systematic examination and appraisal of human nature and in the construction of political institutions on the basis of autonomous and collective experience was central to America's reputation for humane progress. America's professed contempt for history and established authority and its attachment to science and technology, practical utility, social progress and personal liberty stands not only as a general inspiration to the rest of the world but as a realizable objective for other countries. America's status as a democracy may have been special and unusual, but not unique. In the spirit of the Enlightenment, it can and has been seen as something universal – as an international example whose authenticity as a model of democracy is equated with its applicability to other nations and cultures.

It follows that the United States can conceive itself as either the embodiment of emancipation from the malaise of European traditions, or the exemplar of Western civilization and the living fulfilment of its social and democratic ideals. Both outlooks support the notion of American exceptionalism, but each possesses different implications for America's view of the world and its own society. What is clear is that liberal democratic values constitute both the agent and the object of America's national identity. The very conception of the world lying outside America is itself a product of the core conviction that the new world is separated from the old world by an ocean of democratic principles and ideas. It has often been observed that America is peculiarly dependent upon its sense of differentiation from anything else. To Daniel Campbell, for example, no state relies more upon the posited distinction between the "self" and the "other" for its imagined community:

> Arguably more than any other state, the imprecise process of imagination is what constitutes American identity. In this context, the practices of "foreign policy" come to have a special importance. If the identity of the "true national" remains intrinsically elusive and "inorganic", it can only be secured by the effective and continual ideological demarcation of those who are "false" to the defining ideals.

This has led even within an avowedly open society to the characteristically

American compulsion to equate outsiders with subversion, strangers with heresy and foreigners with the danger of un-American ideas. It is the alien world therefore that generates the deepest anxieties over the nation's identity and evokes the strongest reactions over the integrity and strength of its democracy. The beliefs in both the uniqueness and universality of American democracy serve to highlight the ambiguous nature of America's perspective of, and posture towards, the world – i.e. its mixed reactions, its fluctuating attitudes, and its inconsistencies over engagement and detachment. In fact, it is the unique and universal attributes of American democracy, together with the strong moral overtones invested in both constructions, which are central to the perennial question that afflicts America's international position – namely, whether the world provided a service or a disservice to the United States.

IV

American Democracy and the World: Cause and Effect

In one sense, the relationship between American democracy and the external world is seen as one of indigenous values and experiences being successfully applied to areas lying outside their immediate point of origin. According to this perspective, the world is a proving ground and a vindication of America's democratic integrity. Its democratic principles and obligations are not compromises so much as fulfilled by their outward movement. Indeed, the belief in the United State's exceptional status as the embodiment of democratic values is so strong that it has often led to the equally firm belief that such values cannot be confined to America but must inevitably find their expression on a world wide basis. With this outlook, any encounter between the United States and the international arena can be interpreted as a relationship in which America is necessarily the independent variable.

Originally, this notion of America as an improving template for the rest of humanity took the form of a moral example and a model for republican emulation. America was "a city upon a hill"; a social laboratory in which the feasibility of the republican ideal would be affirmed and acclaimed to a hopeful world. As the United States multiplied in size, its sense of passive example began to assume a more active dimension. The scale and speed of its acquisitions gave weight to the view that the United States possessed an inner virtue and a providential design. It also encouraged the view that America had a national mission to annex new lands, in order to maximise the spread of republican institutions of liberty to the furthest reaches of the continent.

American expansion in the nineteenth century bred a self-confidence both in its own social and political arrangements, and in the malleability of new lands and old societies to adapt to the American enlightenment. In one respect, physical expansion had always been central to American consciousness. The outreach of the original maritime colonies had been deepened, compounded and extended by the availability of vast tracts of western land. The founders of the American republic wove this natural resource into their conception of liberty and into the theoretical foundations of their systems of government. Republicanism became a geo-political construct in which expansion was directly related to the preservation of freedom. James Madison wrote,

> Extend the sphere and you take in a greater variety of parties and interests; you make it less probable that a majority of the whole will have a common motive to invade the rights of other citizens; or if such a common motive exists, it will be more difficult for all who feel it to discover their own strength and to act in unison with each other.

Even the libertarian, Thomas Jefferson, came round to the idea that where the American republic was concerned, it was a case of "the bigger, the better":

> I know that the acquisition of Louisiana has been disapproved by some, from a candid apprehension that the enlargement of our territory would endanger its union. But who can limit the extent to which the federative principle may operate effectively? The larger our association, the less will it be shaken by local passions; and in any view, is it not better that the opposite bank of the Mississippi should be settled by our own brethren and children, than by strangers of another family? With which shall we be most likely to live in harmony and friendly intercourse?

What had begun as a largely benign and speculative statement of intent by an apprehensive and defensive young republic had changed by the 1840s into a solid belief that the United States possessed a special role in the world. Its universal presumption received its classic enunciation by John O'Sullivan. The republic's ascribed role was "to overspread and to possess the whole continent which providence has given us for the development of the great experiment of liberty and federated self-government". The end result was now no longer in doubt. American expansion could only be explained by reference to a "manifest destiny" to become a continental power. To William Gilpin, it was evident that the United States was the centrepiece of a process "to establish a new order in human affairs ... to teach old nations a new civilization ... (and) to unite the world in one social family". Given the virtue of its strength and the strength of its virtue, the United States could not fail simply to prevail as the exemplar of the new world and, by implication, the proselytising model for the old world. To Ray Alan Billington, the American people in the middle of the nineteenth century

> ... sincerely believed their democratic institutions were of such magnificent perfection that no boundaries could contain them. Surely a benevolent Creator did not intend such blessings for the few; expansion was a divinely ordered means of extending enlightenment to despot-ridden masses in nearby countries! This was not imperialism, but enforced salvation.

Half a century later, America's position and its democratic presumption had simply been scaled up. It had become a world power but not one that was engaged in the process of international security management. It had entered World War I but claimed to have done so not as an ordinary nation involved in a conflict with other ordinary countries, but as an extraordinary intervention through selfless moral choice and sacrifice "to make the world safe for democracy". Woodrow Wilson made it quite clear in the peace process that the United States had no interest in the moribund arrangements of the old powers. He condemned balances of power, spheres of influence and imperial protectorates, and pressed for national self-determination, free trade and open diplomacy. He wished to invest the process of collective security with American principles of democracy, liberty, natural rights and the rule of law.

The rejection of the League of Nations, and therefore, of American progress, began the United States retreat into isolationism. The implacable and myopic nature of its political isolation in the 1930s was itself a testament to America's continuing belief in the uniqueness of its own position and status as a nation. Convinced that the European powers had failed to appreciate America's altruism or to respond to its visionary and progressive leadership, the United States engaged in one of its periodic reactions against what it believed to be the chronically regressive and illiberal nature of the old world. Even though the US speculated on whether Europe was beyond redemption, it nevertheless continued to expand its economic empire and, with it, to become ever more closely implicated in international markets, commerce and trade. Eventually, the irresistible force of America's growing presence in the international economy opened the way to the United States entry into World War II and, subsequently, to its pre-eminent position as a global superpower. Within ten years, the United States changed from being merely "the arsenal of democracy" to the "leader of the free world".

At the end of World War II, the United States was in the ascendancy. It was the supreme military power and the only country with access to nuclear weapons. In the highly unstable international environment following the war, American forces were often the only means of providing protection and order, in areas threatened with civil strife, subversion or invasion. The supremacy of the American military was matched by the American economy which, for similar reasons, had benefited by default from the devastation of its competitors. By 1950, the United States was responsible for over half of the world's foreign investment, half of the world's gross national product. The dollar provided the foundation to the post-war system of international exchange because it was the most dominant and reliable currency. The United States used its economic power to become the chief guarantor to a series of measures designed to rebuild Europe's shattered economies and to restore stability to its currencies and its investment and banking systems.

As the political and ideological impasse between the United States and the USSR intensified, America's confidence in its own guiding principles became dependent upon its capacity to impart those principles to as many countries as possible in the international arena. The defining Cold War position adopted by the United States was set out in *NSC 68: Objectives and Programs for National Security* (1950). The projection of American military and economic force was underpinned by the political conviction that the Soviet Union was a "slave state" set upon the "complete subversion and forcible destruction of the machinery of government and structure of society" in the free countries. In contrast to 1918, the end of World War II had witnessed a power vacuum in Europe and the Far East. To the United States, the devastation was analogous to the sort of *tabula rasa* on which US itself had been formed in the new world. America's belief in the spontaneity and universalism of the social dynamics supporting liberal democracy was affronted by the Soviet Union's rejection of the natural authenticity of the American way. To Americans, communism was a denial of America's own experience of nature and it, therefore, amounted to a perversion of nature itself. American freedom was simply taken to be genuine freedom.

The conflict between communism and the United States was defined in *NSC 68* as "momentous, involving the fulfillment or destruction not only of the Republic but of civilization itself". Given that the assault on free institutions was world-wide and that liberty was now conceived to be internationally indivisible, the confrontation with the Soviet Union "impose(d) on us, in our own interests, the responsibility of world leadership". The Cold War drew the United States decisively onto the world stage and into a host of alliances that would ensure its active engagement in international politics on a permanent basis. It was no longer enough that American democratic values were transferable to other countries. It was now strategically and ideologically imperative that they were actually transferred and established in as many nations as possible. The validity of America's democratic principles, and the sense of national purpose activated by these principles, had been given an international dimension. As *NSC 68* made clear,

> the assault on free institutions is worldwide now, and in the context of the present polarization of power a defeat of free institutions anywhere is a defeat everywhere. We must lead in building a successfully functioning political and economic system in the free world. It is only by practical affirmation, abroad as well as at home, of our essential values, that we can preserve our own integrity.

The Cold War succeeded in polarizing world politics and in creating an ideological dichotomy in which co-existence was interpreted as illegitimate and any victory for American liberal democracy was bought at the price of a more intense animus against the United States and its values in the "communist bloc". The scale and commitment of the cold war conflict ensured the US of an ideological security in the west, and especially so in America itself, where critical dissent was discouraged and tolerance was circumscribed for the greater good of America's war effort in the war of ideas. The United States has often been described as nothing other than the mobilization of liberal and democratic ideas. The cold war provided a mobilization that was different in scale but not in nature. The American disposition to regard "truths to be self-evident" was extended to American behaviour abroad to defend such truths. Democracy was equated not only with American democracy but with whatever American leaders and forces ascertained to be necessary to the American defence of the free world. As a consequence, American foreign policy decisions and actions overseas came to be explained and defended according to a set of permanent first principles of Cold War intentions and objectives.

This compulsion towards deductive rationalization combined American history and contemporary purpose in a highly enclosed and unified system of premises and conclusions. The Cold War was a distinctly American responsibility and one characterised by American notions of virtue and vice. It was also an extrapolation of America's past development, and of the moral purpose and benign mission served by the nature of its unprecedented growth. The international confrontation with communism, therefore, was not merely a test of American democracy's universality; it was also a means by which America might revive itself through an enhanced self- awareness of its unique democratic credentials. Even forty years after World War II, an American president found it was possible to sustain his public popularity for two terms of office by using the world outside to restore America's faith in its own democracy. Ronald Reagan exemplified the force of this cold war outlook in substantiating American claims to indigenous virtue and ancient destiny. Reagan wished to re-commemorate American democracy in the face of a renewed threat from a resurgent Soviet Union. To Reagan, the outside world made it clear that American was still a shining "city upon a hill". Even after two centuries, it was still a beacon, "still a magnet for all who must have freedom, for all the pilgrims from all the lost places who are hurtling through the darkness towards home."

America's sense of its remedial qualities was enhanced still further by the decline of communism and the disintegration of the Soviet Union. To President Bush, the end of the Cold War era represented "a victory for all humanity" and one which demonstrated that: "America's leadership is indispensable. Americans know that leadership brings burdens and sacrifices. But we also [know] why the hopes of humanity turn to us. We are Americans. We have a unique responsibility to do the hard work of freedom." President Clinton, the first post Cold War chief executive, showed little sign of deviating from the hallowed norm. In Clinton's view, American democracy remains "the envy of the world". As such, "clearly America must continue to lead the world we did so much to make ... our mission is timeless."

According to this perspective, the Old World may pose dangers to the United States, but it still provided the main contributory factor in America's democratic consciousness and the chief reason behind the society's self-assurance in seeking to enlighten and redeem the remainder of humanity without compromising its own principles.

V

The World and American Democracy: Cause and Effect

The alternative construction of the United States' relationship with the external world views the latter as the independent variable and the former as the dependent object. In this guise, the world reveals Americans to be just as worldly as everyone else – so much so in fact that it reduces the notion of one external world differentiated from the United States to something of a chimera. Whether America's contact with the international community is seen as having had a corruptive influence on the new world, or as simply demonstrating that the United States is not immune to original sin and human nature, the net effect has been to create a tension between America's professed ideals and the conduct and consequences of its foreign policy. Sometimes this tension is regarded as an inconsistency inherent in the United States position as a vanguard of social and moral improvement at work in a degenerate world. But on many other occasions, the United States is condemned for using the external world as a separate dimension of values and conduct in which its domestic principles are deliberately suspended for the sake of America's national interests and security. In this respect, the United States is only different to the extent that it seeks to conceal its motives and objectives by an enriched rhetoric of selfless devotion to human rights and the welfare of humanity. The net effect of this deception is an implicit denial of its own democracy and of the rationale of its cultural distinctiveness.

In contrast to the traditional conception of the United States having been reluctantly propelled by force of circumstances into acting as a lynchpin of global security, this more critical perspective of America's relationship with the international community places the emphasis on historical continuity and mundane social behaviour rather than on cultural exceptionalism. A different combination of uniqueness and universalism applies in this case. The United States may well have begun its development with a strong identity geared to spreading the democratic creed by force of example. Nevertheless, it can be claimed that this passive message of moral propagation was soon displaced by a pattern of presumption more reminiscent of imperialism than of an ideal republic. Mission was progressively superseded by the conviction that the United States possessed a manifest destiny to make the sub-continent American for the greater good of humanity.

The imprimatur of manifest destiny lent weight to the republic's increasingly aggressive foreign policy goals in the nineteenth century. It justified a *de facto* internal imperialism in which new lands were to be liberated by becoming American. This would be achieved either by coercion, or by the displacement of its people. The progressive and enlightened nature of America's indigenous democracy was now cast as the overriding rationale for the borders of the United States to be extended over and against the claims of either the moribund and corrupt powers of the old world (Spain, Britain), or the regressive and savage nature of inferior peoples like Mexicans and the American Indians. To Arthur Ekirch, manifest destiny represented a sea change in America's national consciousness. Whereas the concept of mission gave emphasis to the peaceful propagation of American ideas, manifest destiny implied a belligerent form of expansion:

> It turned the defensive and idealistic notions of isolationism and mission toward the course of a unilateral, nationalist, political and territorial expansion. And, in so doing it also transposed broader, more universal values of genuine international importance – the natural rights philosophy, for example – into a narrower doctrine of the special rights of Americans over and against other people.

It can be argued that the sheer magnitude of American expansion concealed the extent to which it was becoming an imperial power comparable in nature to the European empires. Manifest destiny wrapped America's enlargement in a circular analysis of justification. Since the United States growth was said to be motivated by virtue and progress, then the consequences of expansion necessarily increased the sum of virtue and progress on the continent and provided the justification for future growth. Democracy was a progression in both senses of the world. Virtue could be equated with a spatial dimension. Such expansion therefore was not imperial at all. It was the extended autonomy of free people – a self-made nation of self-made men and women whose values and motives know no bounds and who did not respect any artificial boundaries to enlightenment and emancipation. An empire by democratic means was by definition no empire at all.

The ethical myopia that accompanied America's internal imperialism began to break down towards the end of the nineteenth century. The comfortable licence of righteous and providential fulfillment became infused with more worldly ingredients – namely, America's own industrial and financial power, the Darwinian imperatives of competitive interaction between nations and the rise of a new imperialistic international order involving the global projection of force and the drive by each participant to co-opt as much available land as possible to prevent it from falling into the hands of others. As a consequence, American attitudes towards neighbouring and competing powers grew more belligerent.

Even by the beginning of the twentieth century, the United States was engaged in an Asian land war. As part of its effort to liberate Cuba from Spanish imperial control in the Spanish-American War of 1898, the United States had sent a naval force to destroy the Spanish fleet harboured at Manila in the Philippine Islands on the other side of the Pacific Ocean. Here as in Cuba there was a local insurrectionist movement dedicated to relieving Spain of its colonial possessions. Led by Emilio Aguinaldo, it was initially supported and armed by the United States. When an American invasion force was sent to capture Manila itself, it was assisted by Aguinaldo. But when President William McKinley forced the Spanish in the peace negotiations to cede control not just of Manila but of the whole Philippine archipelago, and when he subsequently issued the order to American troops to occupy the country, Aguinaldo's forces resisted the United States. The principle of national self-determination could not be allowed to withstand American's prerogative rights of defining the terms of Filipino emancipation and freedom. The Senate passed a treaty of annexation in 1899 and for the next three years United States forces were engaged in crushing the resistance to American liberation. Over 125,000 Americans fought in the war and 4,234 died as a result of it. Approximately 10,000 Filipinos died in battle; another 200,000 lost their lives in "reconcentration camps". An unknown number were killed in civilian massacres taken in reprisal for guerrilla attacks. By 1902, the United States had prevailed but had in the process destroyed Asia's first genuine experiment in democracy.

It is true that this sort of overt and crude imperialism did not become established American practice. American intervention has been too intermittent and, at times, startlingly episodic to rank alongside any conventional imperial power. Nonetheless, when American force had been applied it can, and has been, brutal in nature and aggressively self-serving in its righteousness. To many, the United States' relationships with the rest of the world reveal it to be simply another country given to self-interest and power politics. Just as references to the Wilsonian axiom that America is the only idealistic nation in existence are dismissed as delusions, so the idea that the American "empire" can be called an "empire by invitation" is seen as pure casuistry. The world either acts as a lens through which America's unexceptionalism is demonstrably refracted, or it constitutes the actual agency of corruption which turns American innocence into a state of mortal affliction.

On the one hand, it is possible to assert that America has always been an expansionary and imperialist power. Just as the pattern of its interior settlement was tantamount to a *de facto* internal imperialism, so its later pattern of influence over other countries (i.e., *de facto* external empire) was merely an extension of the same pre-existing set of dynamics. To William Appleman Williams, for example, both patterns of United States history reveal the same controlling impulse towards empire which ranks as the defining characteristic of the American experience. In this light, America serves to affirm the existence of the universal motives and impulses to acquire interests, exploit resources and increase power to the fullest possible extent. On the other hand, the same evidence can support the contention that America may have begun as a unique national entity and undergone an exceptional form of development, but was then shown to be as corruptible as any other social order once the United States had become massively engaged in the international system. In fact, given the United States' avowed commitment to a public philosophy of democracy, freedom, equality and natural rights, it could even be said that America had shown itself to be exceptionally corruptible – i.e., uniquely more mundane than ordinary nations in its failure to live up to the high ideals which characterise its historical traditions and which continue to inform its contemporary political rhetoric.

Whichever contention is adopted, American democracy stands condemned through its contact with the rest of the world. The record of American foreign policy can be made to show that in the furtherance of American welfare and security, the United States has not only compromised the rights of self-determination in other nations, but has actively intervened abroad to ensure that the shape and policy of overseas governments conform to the overriding interests of what Henry Kissinger termed the "master democracy". Contrary to its own revolutionary origins and the implicitly evolutionary principles of its declared national ethos, the United States has been a potent force for counter-revolution in the twentieth century. To Michael H. Hunt, America's record is clear and consistent. Since its inception, a single ideology has informed and motivated foreign policy. This ideology, which has been conspicuously prominent since World War II, is composed of three elements – namely, a conception of national mission, the classification of other peoples according to a racial hierarchy and an overt hostility towards social revolutions. This outlook had legitimated over forty military and covert interventions in the United States "sister republics" in Latin America since 1900. Very often they have been made on behalf of palpably undemocratic governments and forces. But to a critic like Noam Chomsky, American behaviour in Latin America is only part of a much larger pattern of malignant American policy around the world:

> We invaded South Vietnam, overthrew the democratic capitalist
> government of Guatemala in 1954 and have maintained the rule
> of murderous gangsters ever since, ran by far the most extensive

international terror operations in history against Cuba from the early 1960s and Nicaragua through the 1980s, sought to assassinate Lumumba and installed and maintained the brutal and corrupt Mobutu dictatorship, backed Trujillo, Somoza, Marcos, Duvalier, the generals of the southern cone, Suharto, the racist rulers of southern Africa, and a whole host of other major criminals and on, and on.

The embarrassment of American democracy by the world is not, however, limited to foreign lands. The United States itself is endangered by its own activities abroad, not just from the point of view of being morally compromised, but from the harmful effects that its foreign policy poses to its own democratic structures and processes. The huge military establishment and its central role in the American economy, the vast array of intelligence and security services, the enhancement of the executive's prerogative powers, and the use of secrecy as an instrument of government have all become permanent features of American society. The United States has found it difficult to reconcile these accoutrements of a national security state with the declared principles of its democratic government. The efforts to accommodate these devices within the US constitution have been far from straightforward and less than convincing in character.

In similar vein, the Cold War consensus for many years mobilised American society on a war footing for an international ideological confrontation. The consequent subordination of diversity and dissent in favour of a disciplined closure of ranks in the face of a common enemy fostered an atmosphere of domestic intolerance and the enactment of illiberal measures against minorities. Liberty at home was jeopardised by its defence abroad. To Michael Hunt, the paradox approached the territory of tragedy – i.e., that "liberty might be undermined by its very exercise". Certainly Max Lerner believed that in spite of America's "genius for equilibrium" it would be a hard task "to balance the struggle for world power with the moral sensitivity it would need to save its democratic soul". *NSC 68*, America's Cold War catechism, made it clear that liberty was to a large extent the freedom to mobilise and demonstrate American democracy's "unique degree of unity". According to *NSC 68*, the "democratic way is harder than the authoritarian way" because it demands that the individual "distinguish between the necessity of tolerance and the necessity for just suppression. A free society is vulnerable in that it is easy for people to lapse into excesses – the excess of a permanently open mind [and] the excess of tolerance degenerating into indulgence of conspiracy." In this way, the pressures of the world, and of America's role within it, served to endanger the democratic order of the United States, and with it, the very substance of America's example to other nations.

VI

American Foreign Policy and the Democratic Conscience

The position of the United States as a liberal, yet historically insular society that became a modern superpower, operating in the largely illiberal world of power politics, has led to a profusion of tensions surrounding American foreign policy. Nowhere are these instrumental and substantive strains more starkly revealed than in the response of America's political system to the varied requirements of international relations. According to de Tocqueville's classic dictum, democracies are "decidedly inferior to governments carried upon different principles where foreign relations are concerned. Foreign politics demand scarcely any of those qualities which a democracy possesses; they require, on the contrary, the perfect use of almost all those faculties in which it is deficient." The qualities he had in mind were secrecy, perseverance, patience, unity and speed of action. His conclusions on the generic inadequacies of democracy in these respects were drawn from the governing arrangements of the United States in the 1830s. Fortunately for the young republic, its early democratic development coincided with a diminished need for a foreign policy. It was only later that de Tocqueville's observations would come to haunt the United States.

As America rose to become a great power, anxieties multiplied over the extent to which a cogent foreign policy could be squared with the maintenance of an informed public, making choices through a fully representative and accountable government. The fragmentation of America's political system and its corollary of checks and balances, together with the cultural tradition of open government and the transmission of public opinion, appeared to fly directly in the face of the structural and substantive needs of foreign policy-making. So severe was the apparent disjunction between the disarray of American democracy and the order, reason and perseverance required of a foreign policy, that it repeatedly led to deep anxieties over whether American institutions were compatible with international *realpolitik*.

The main response to this conundrum came in the form of an expanded presidency. In the same way that the presidency came to symbolise the centralised provision of services in the positive state, so it came to rationalise the rise of a national security state. In both instances the presidency facilitated and signified the transformation of American government in response to recognised need. The presidency provided the focal point of political energy that made change not only possible but also legitimate. It was the very singularity of the presidential office which evoked the idea of the American nation being realized by central executive power. The conjunction of popular sovereignty, conveyed through a presidential election and the social solidarity and collective purpose suggested by an active president animating central government, fundamentally altered the relationship within government, and between the government and society. This was especially evident in the field of foreign relations.

The rise of the modern presidency coincided with the rise of the United States as a superpower. The two developments were not unconnected. The presidency was the main agent and the chief beneficiary of America's enhanced status in the international community. In many respects, the presidency became synonymous with the American nation. The state of the presidency came to be regarded as the state of the nation. A crisis in the presidency represented a crisis for the nation. This is not just because the president had become in Robert Hirschfield's phrase the "democratic symbol of national unity". It was because of the widespread recognition that the presidency was the only agency in American government with the functional capacity to respond decisively to international events. It is also the only part of the political system with the capability of evoking that level of national trust that would permit the constitution to be circumvented for the sake of America's security. Where foreign relations were concerned, the presidency was the necessary instrument of adaptive change in an international environment that did not operate according to the principles of the American constitution. America's successful evolution in these dangerous and even anarchic conditions, therefore, was attributable to the comparable evolution of its political system towards progressive executive power in the service of a higher obligation to save American democracy. For the presidency to be cast into doubt in these conditions was tantamount to endangering America's continued evolution and, ultimately, its very survival.

The implications of these brutal but compulsive realities were recognised by the Supreme Court as early as 1936. In the landmark decision of *U.S. v. Curtiss-Wright Export Corporation*, the guardians of American's Constitution all but excused the presidency from constitutional constraint in the area of international relations. The Court recognised that the presidency possessed not only powers implied in the constitution, but also powers inherent to the nature of the executive function. The president's position was not limited to constitutional provisions and Acts of Congress, but was drawn from historical precedent, forces of circumstance and the "nature of foreign negotiations". As a consequence, the president was afforded "a degree of discretion and freedom from statutory restriction which would not be admissible were domestic affairs alone involved". The Court's conclusion that the president possessed a "very delicate, plenary and exclusive power … as the sole organ of the federal government in the field of international relations" was driven by a realistic appraisal of the state of international security in the 1930s. The threats posed by such severe instability transformed sweeping executive prerogative into a simple necessity. The explosion of American interests in, and anxiety about, the world outside brought with it a commensurate implosion of internal powers towards the executive centre. The Court inferred that such powers were not simply a legitimate extension of external sovereignty but were in fact derived from sources outside the constitution and were, therefore, not limited by it. As Harold Koh concluded, "if the president actually possessed such extensive extra-constitutional powers, it is unclear why his actions in foreign affairs should ever be subjected to the consent of the governed."

It was only later that the full significance of the decision became clear. Following World War II, when the United States no longer had the option of isolation to resolve its international problems, and when it became committed to the ambitious global policy of "containment," it built up a very large military and national security establishment. The presidency's wartime position was not merely sustained in the ambiguous "peacetime" of the "Cold War". It was enhanced by the progressive institutionalization of central executive power, by the statutory obligation to manage and co-ordinate the national security bureaucracy (cf. National Security Act 1947) and by the ever-increasing need to centralise power further, in order to subject what was an ever-increasing military capability to full civilian control. "The militarization of the American government during the Cold War" was in Ernest May's view justified as "a creative response to a challenge".

With the loss of America's nuclear monopoly (1949) and the subsequent heightening of tension between the "communist bloc" and the "free world", the need for presidential dominance became even more evident. Given the potential precariousness of the international system, as well as the continuing strides made in the accuracy, speed and destructive force of ever more advanced weapon systems, it was regarded as simply a matter of course that America should have the most sensitive, informed and effective decision-making apparatus that its political system was capable of providing. It was a testament to the proven track record of the presidency in crisis condition that hardly anyone seriously contested the view that the ultimate life and death decisions concerning America's security (i.e., the most important choices for any democracy) should be made by the single occupant of the White House. He was to make them on behalf of the American people; in their absence; often without their knowledge or opinion; and probably even against their implicit wishes.

The problem of democracy and foreign policy-making during the Cold War was as a consequence largely resolved by dividing politics and the requisites of democracy into two. The governing principles and processes in domestic policy-making were simply regarded as separate from the governing principles and process in foreign policy-making. The former conformed to the norms of traditional American democracy, while the latter was recognised as necessarily subject to different principles for the sake of the former, and for the wider national interest of the United States. The bifurcation was most clearly expressed in Aaron Wildavsky's "two presidencies" thesis. This suggested that while presidents were weakened at home by an array of competitors for power, they were conspicuously devoid of such rivals in foreign policy. "Compared with domestic affairs, presidents engaged in world politics [were] immensely more concerned with meeting problems on their own terms." Foreign policy was conceived as a matter of stimulus and response – i.e., the best way of making the appropriate reaction to a set of forces external to indigenous control. Only the presidency was able to lay claim to the prerogative first of ascertaining what the response had to be, and then of providing it. While domestic policy-making centred upon options, alternatives, choices and differing objectives, foreign policy-making was generally assumed to be devoid of voluntarism and autonomy. In this realm, the normal processes were simply immaterial. As a consequence, Wildavsky writing in 1966 could conclude that in foreign policy there had "not been a single major issue" since World War II "on which Presidents, when they were serious and determined [had] failed".

The "two presidencies" conception provided an acceptable device not only for explaining the differences in presidential power between the domestic sector and the international arena, but also for giving legitimacy to the centralised structure of foreign policy decision-making. The "two presidencies" gave expression to the idea of two different political systems co-existing with one another on the basis of shared functions and responsibilities to a common citizenry. It was in essence an extrapolation of America's traditional notion of a federal democracy. The power of the foreign policy presidency signified the corporate identity and collective purpose of the United States as a nation in the dimension of international relations. The comparative weakness of the presidency in domestic policy reflected the intrinsically plural nature of American society and politics. The central force of the foreign policy presidency attended to matters of national security, in order to make America safe for American democracy. The very fact that the presidency could not muster the equivalent political resources at home was in itself both an affirmation of the continued vitality of American democracy, and a confirmation of the need to protect foreign policy-making from the conventional operations of such a democracy. Where "the world" was concerned, the presidency was different from normal because the world was abnormally different from America.

The rise of presidential government in this most important area of governmental responsibility raised a host of problems concerning the principles and practices of a functioning democracy. It prompted the creation of various "democratic dilemmas". For example, the president's position in foreign policy raised the question of the extent to which the office had neutralised the constitution's checks and balances in favour of a concentration of power in the executive branch. Presidential pre-eminence prompted concern over the existence of a foreign policy elite that could limit, and even preclude, broad democratic participation. It was possible to argue that open government and accountability were continually jeopardised by closed hierarchical decision-making, by executive secrecy and by covert actions. Even the rule of law itself might be compromised by the chief executive's prerogative powers and by the general emphasis upon reaction and realism over process and form. It was difficult to discern whether the foreign policy apparatus amounted to a legitimate derivative of American democratic government, or to a suspension of normal governing arrangements. Was it a genuinely democratic response to undemocratic conditions? Or was it simply a necessarily undemocratic reaction to the international system, but one which was leavened by democratic motivations and justified by public acquiescence? To Clinton Rossiter, it was simply a matter of democratic survival – "in time of crisis, a democratic, constitutional government must be temporarily altered to whatever degree is necessary to overcome the peril". If American democracy did not adapt, then it would cease to be anything – least of all a democracy. On the other hand if, as de Tocqueville believed, that democratic governments could not cope effectively with foreign policy, then it might be concluded that, to the extent that the United States had successfully adapted to the requirements of foreign policy-making, it had ceased to be a democracy.

Some of the questions concerning the effects of foreign policy on American democracy and in particular the democratic status of the Cold War presidency, were answered in the late 1960s and early 1970s when a severe reaction set in against executive government. The presidency was held directly accountable for the mistakes and mismanagement of the Vietnam War and for the social dislocation and civil disorder generated by it. With the disarray in the economy and the perceived "failures" of progressive and presidentially sponsored social programmes, the political consensus, which had supported presidential power for a generation, came under enormous strain. Now it was widely believed that the "imperial presidency" had not only usurped powers from other parts of the political system, but had misused and even abused them. The problems of America were compulsively reduced to the problems of concentrated and, therefore, excessive power in the executive branch. Presidents were accused of breaking the rationale of the two presidencies by directly exploiting their executive prerogatives in the foreign policy area to enlarge their powers, and to defend their position, in the field of domestic politics. The extension of such prerogative privileges in order to harass political opponents, or to spy on American citizens, or to evade political responsibility, were seen as unwarranted and quite out of proportion to the asserted threats of internal subversion. To Arthur M. Schlesinger,

> The all purpose invocation of "national security," the insistence on executive secrecy, the withholding of information from Congress … the attempted intimidation of the press, the use of the White House itself as a base for espionage and sabotage directed against the political opposition – all signified the extension of the imperial Presidency from foreign to, domestic affairs.

The outcry over the "Caesarism" of the presidency led to a general reaction against the ethos and scale of executive power, and to remarkable revival in the constitution's original principles of institutional dynamics and reciprocal controls. Running counter to the evolutionary direction of the presidency and against its purportedly irreversible development towards greater executive hegemony, critics and reformers set about containing what Ambrose Pierce had described as the "greased pig" of American politics within the ancient fences of checks and balances. Animated by a resurgent constitutional fundamentalism and a restored conviction in the plurality and democratic benevolence of balanced government, the Congress passed a raft of legislation designed to monitor, supervise and control the president. The most significant aspect of the restoration of constitutional mechanics was Congress's incursion into foreign policy making. For over a generation, Congress had been unwilling to press its constitutional claims in this area. It was thought to be functionally ill-equipped and politically incapacitated to serve as a co-equal branch of government. But through much of the 1970s, Congress sprawled all over American foreign policy. Fired with the Cold War heresy that foreign policy could, and should, be susceptible to more democratic methods and objectives, Congress passed an array of measures designed to publicise and constrain decision-making in such sensitive areas as arms sales, military intervention, human rights, weapons systems, nuclear strategy, arms limitation and war powers. Despite being previously regarded as congenitally unsuitable for the intrinsic authoritarian necessities of foreign policy, Congress proceeded on the assumption that foreign policy and national security decisions could be democratised by making them approximate more to the former mechanics of the constitution.

This faith in the interchangeability of the legislative and the executive, and, with the substitution of a closed hierarchical control with an open and more pluralistic form of management took Congress to the point of challenging the Central Intelligence Agency. Previously its supervision of the agency had been characterised by a deep reluctance even to acquire information about its activities. It appeared to appreciate that there was something in the very essence of a secret service which rendered it, by definition, inconsistent with the normal standards and procedures of democratic supervision. To many both inside and outside the intelligence community, the CIA, by the nature of the function it was expected to perform, was simply not amenable to the customary norms of democratic control and direction. Problems were further compounded by the fact that the CIA was formally under Presidential direction and represented one of the fullest expressions of his obligation to preserve, protect, and defend both the security and the interests of the United States. The existence of such an organization seemed to bear witness to the critical threat facing America and its western allies, and the need to resort to extraordinary, and even extra-constitutional, means to meet it. Whether it was possible to impose democratic standards of control and accountability on the CIA, therefore, became bound up with whether it was consistent with the national good even to attempt to do so. As Rhodri Jeffreys-Jones points out, "democracy depends upon the secret intelligence for its survival, yet the relationship between the two has always been controversial, and, at times, mutually harmful." The feasibility of control became obscured by the Cold War consensus that resolved all such problems in favour of allowing the CIA to evade external constraints and for the American public to place their trust in the self-restraint of honourable men.

By the mid-1970s, however, perceptions had changed. Jeffreys-Jones observed that the "public's often easy tolerance of presidential abuse of intelligence evaporated into open dissent." From being a heroic adjunct of national destiny and American purpose, the CIA was variously derided as the "action arm of the imperial Presidency" and as a "Frankenstein's monster". It stood accused of large-scale surveillance of US citizens, unauthorised domestic intelligence-gathering, drug experimentation, intelligence operations against political dissidents, wire-tapping, break-ins, mail opening, clandestine military engagements abroad, destabilising foreign governments, and, most controversially of all, attempting to assassinate or being implicated in the assassination of foreign political leaders. In the 1950s such matters might well have been viewed fatalistically as examples of "the ways of the world". But such equanimity was absent in the 1970s. The CIA's activities were seen as being motivated more by considerations of executive power at home than by the power of the country's adversaries – more on behalf of the presidency's interests than the long-term interests of the United States. As a consequence, Congress immediately introduced a range of measures designed to monitor and control the CIA. The working assumption was that by taking action which suggested a balance between Congress and the presidency, it would be possible to acquire a balance between democracy and secrecy.

Despite the fervent affirmations of a solution being secured through balanced government and restored democracy, it remains unclear whether either condition was ever achieved; and whether they were even necessarily related to one another. Serious doubts remained over what a congressional check consisted of in an area like intelligence and covert operations; whether such a check was operationally feasible; and how the effectiveness of a legislative check might be determined one way or the other. Scepticism over the plausibility of public restraint upon a secretive body was further compounded by uncertainty over the point at which constraint might lead to impotence and ineffectiveness in an agency like the CIA. By democratising the process of intelligence and undercover work, it was possible to strengthen the democratic credentials of national security policy-making but at the price of undermining its effectiveness in the external world – thereby weakening the US and jeopardising America's internal democracy.

Where the CIA was concerned, it was widely believed at the end of the 1970s that Congress's checks had been too effective and that as a consequence the CIA had become so disabled it had failed to predict the Soviet invasion of Afghanistan (1979) and the Islamic revolution in Iran (1979). Perception of American decline and of American foreign policy in disarray led to a re-evaluation of Congressional insurgency in international affairs. With the onset of the Reagan Presidency and with the rise of public pressure for a more aggressive posture abroad, Congress adopted a more expansive approach to the statutory limitations on the CIA. This was symptomatic of a general relaxation in Congress's foreign policy incursions. In did not rescind any of its measures, but neither did it enact any substantial additions. Its original restraints had always included qualifying clauses to preserve the president's discretion to respond to the exigencies of changing international situations. Now these saving devices of executive prerogative were given free rein. Congress still assumed a position of co-partnership but was more prepared to give the presidency the general responsibility for foreign policy while reserving the right to monitor and to intervene on a selective basis. Control was now more a matter of deterrence than sustained constraint. In spite of the spectacular advances made by Congress in the 1970s, and in spite of the allusions at the time to a clear foreign policy "revolution" and to a balance between democracy and foreign policy-making, the net effect had been to displace one form of ambiguity with another – i.e., formal measures of control that were brittle in construction and unpredictable in effect were replaced by more informal, imprecise and discretionary forms of negotiated limitation.

While the measures of the 1970s show that democratic insurgency can penetrate into foreign policy-making, the reactive *realpolitik* of the 1980s reaffirms that existence of the inherent cross-pressures of internal democracy and foreign policy-making. On no occasion was this more evident than during the Iran-Contra affair. This complex scandal centred upon the Reagan Administration's efforts to continue to support the Contra guerrillas in Nicaragua, despite Congress's varied attempts to prevent American involvement in the insurgency campaign against the revolutionary Sandinista government. The administration regarded Nicaragua as a test case in its crusade against communist expansion in Latin America. It devoted prodigious amounts of political capital into persuading the American public that the Sandinista regime was a client state of the Soviet Union and, thereby, a strategic threat to the United States. To the Administration, Nicaragua provided an example of how the spread of communism could be halted and, thereupon, reversed so long as the United States adopted a sufficiently aggressive posture.

As criminal proceedings followed top-level resignations, the Contras were effectively abandoned. Consequently, the Reagan Presidency collapsed in pubic esteem and American foreign policy was plunged into disarray. Attempts to exert internal democracy had prompted the executive into elaborate efforts at deep cover foreign policy which included a secretive White House unit designed explicitly to act independently from the conventional apparatus of foreign policy-making. The question posed by de Tocqueville concerning the compatibility of an operational democracy and a coherent foreign policy, therefore, not only remains unresolved but, in the light of America's recent experience, is confirmed as fundamentally insoluble. As Ernest Volkman and Blaine Baggett state,

> No one has yet been able to figure out a system where the Legislative and Executive branches can share responsibility for the conduct of foreign policy – and at the same time act with great speed in the event of a sudden crisis. It is one of democracy's central flaws. Still, democracy is a flawed process, and it may well be that this central question will remain a permanent source of tension, so long as there is a constitutional system.

Conclusion: Primacy versus Democracy

As the United States nears the end of the "American Century," the country remains deeply affected by the ambivalent relationship that exists between democracy and great power. The disjunctions between ideals and self-interest, principles and practice, intentions and consequences, and between the ethics of liberal morality and the morality of power and security all continue to play a part in America's consciousness of the world and of its role within it. It may be thought that the "collapse of communism" would have clarified America's international position. According to Francis Fukuyama, America should have no reason any more for apprehension. With the Cold War won and the dominance of liberal democracy and the free market assured, the United States and its values can be regarded as marking an "end to history". Despite its flaws, no other system of thought has survived the twentieth century. The United States, therefore, stands not only as the predominant single superpower but as the archetype of a society that can be represented as the culminating point of social and political evolution. The sentiments echoed by Fukuyama and others suggest that the United States might adopt a more consistent posture towards the rest of the world. In the words of Louis Hartz's classic maxim, Americans in the past seemed "to oscillate between fleeing from the rest of the world and embracing it with too ardent a passion. An absolute national morality is inspired either to withdraw from 'alien' things or to transform them: it cannot live in comfort constantly by their side."

It could be said that Fukuyama's view neutralises Hartz's duality. With America's democratic supremacy and cultural hegemony assured, the world is now no longer qualitatively different to the United States. There is no reason for America to retreat into its own democracy because it would now only be withdrawing from its own mirror image. By the same token, it is arguably more out in the world, and feels less restraint in intervening to punish aggression and to facilitate the release of societies into the norm of liberal democracy.

American military action in the Persian Gulf and in the Horn of Africa would seem to have affirmed a radical shift of focus. In April 1991, *Time* magazine speculated on whether the United States was assuming the role of a "Globo-Cop" on behalf of democracy and human rights. According to *The Washington Post*, "Countries that fail to care decently for their citizens dilute their claim to sovereignty and forfeit invulnerability to outside political military intervention." Simon Jenkins in *The Times* deplored such views. To him, the fighting in Somalia or in the former Yugoslavia were scandals, but not world scandals requiring international intervention. Should the United States defer to the sentiments expressed in *The Washington Post* and a host of other media outlets, it would amount to a "caring imperialism" going "far beyond the Cold War doctrines of Dulles, Kennedy, Nixon and Kissinger, that foreign intervention was justified only if invited to save a nation from communism. If the *Post* is right, three-quarters of the globe is now at risk of attack from America or its UN proxies."

On closer examination, however, the universalism of the United States remains more apparent than real. America objects to melting into the rest of the world as dangerous, unresponsive and costly. The United States commitment to the Gulf War, for example, was made strictly dependent on limited objectives and immediate disengagement. More important than the decision to leave for the Gulf War was the display of democratic autonomy in returning home on time. Although President Bush insisted that "we've kicked the Vietnam syndrome once and for all," America's premature departure demonstrated the reverse. Fear of becoming sucked into a larger and longer commitment ensured an outcome of victorious retreat. Contrary to expectations, Saddam Hussein remained in power and the defeated Iraqi army was strong enough to crush the popular uprisings against the regime. During the deadlock negotiations between the United States and Iraq prior to the war, Fred Greenstein commented that: "what we're dealing with here is a basic limitation on the capacity of leaders in a democracy to play a game of chicken." At first, Bush appeared to have won the game by invading Kuwait and Southern Iraq. But by correctly gambling on the United States' reluctance to press on to Baghdad, it might be said that the authoritarianism of Saddam Hussein ultimately prevailed in the international game of chicken with American democracy.

The second reason for Americans to object to the concept of one world is that they fear the direction of the process. They are concerned that the United States is simply becoming like the rest of the world instead of the other way around. Whether it is the spectre of economic decline, the drugs' problem, the breakdown of law and order, the alienation and destitution of the inner cities, or the multicultural fragmentations of American society, the fear is that harmful transnational trends are making parts of the United States into an equivalent of the third world. The presidential election of 1992 demonstrated the extent to which the American public wished to turn its back on a successful foreign policy president and on the rest of the world, in favour of giving markedly more attention to domestic problems. In a year which also witnessed the Los Angeles riots and the federal government in Washington deteriorating further into scandal, gridlock and stagnation, the emphasis turned to an agenda of American renewal through the exertion of democratic will to make the United States altogether less like an altogether more deplorable outside world.

The third reason behind America's objection to being cast as an ordinary nation is its instinctive insistence that it is, and must remain, a wholly extraordinary country. Uniqueness remains an axiomatic element of American identity. It is integral to America's exceptionally demonstrative nationalism and its fervent patriotism. This American need to feel unique is satisfied more than anything else by the importance of democracy to America's culture and identity. The United States can only ever feel different through what it considers to be its exceptionally democratic society – i.e., its only serious historical claim to uniqueness. The circularity of this view is far less important than its effect, which is to satisfy America's need to be different from the world and to fulfil its *raison d'etre* of having something to offer the world. In essence, America needs to be unique to be universal in an active, originating and controlled way.

As a consequence, the United States remains with essentially two dimensions of democracy. On the one hand is a cultural democracy which finds expression in displays of national consensus and patriotic zeal; on the other hand, is an instrumental democracy of critical public opinion, pluralistic division, and embattled institutions. In many respects, the cultural democracy of the Cold War allowed the United States to withstand the fissiparous effects of its instrumental democracy. But with the grandeur of the East-West challenge having dissipated and with the decline of the social discipline and solidarity that it once elicited the United States has now become much less predictable in foreign policy than it once used to be. It has always had a reputation for relative inconsistency because of its geographical isolation and its democratic impulses.

The growing interdependence of the world has reduced the former. At the same time, America's emancipation from the strictures of the Cold War has helped to compensate for this diminishment of American independence. There is now a greater perception of choice in foreign policy-making than there used to be in the bi-polar conditions of East-West confrontation.

The growing susceptibility of foreign policy issues to America's instrumental democracy means a much greater unpredictability as to what means and objectives will receive the assent of America's cultural democracy. The scale of the international mass media, for example, can now immediately and directly suck issues into American public opinion with the effect of derailing presidential agendas and prompting erratic American action. Harrowing television pictures of famine and lawlessness in Somalia, for example, led President Bush to extend America's ancient mission of democracy to the banditry and clan warfare of Mogadishu, Kismayu and Badera. In Bush's words, Operation Just Cause was a humanitarian obligation. "You are doing God's work," he told his troops. "We will not tolerate armed gangs ripping off their own people." Just as important as the divine nature of the intervention, however, were the emphatic assurances given by the president that the operation would not stretch further than the public's tolerance and would, therefore, be of very limited duration. American public opinion that would be served by lurching into a country would be equally served by lurching out of a country.

In the post-Cold War context, the possibilities of intervention or other forms of American action are huge. By the same token, the potential for inconsistency and unpredictability is also extensive. America's cultural democracy can still be harnessed to foreign commitments, but increasingly the causes to which the United States will subscribe are being determined on the basis of running battles for American public opinion. In the current climate, de Tocqueville has been turned on his head. The impoverishment of foreign policy-making in the United States is now taken to be not a vice so much as a redeeming virtue – a sign of democratic choice and autonomy in a complex and interdependent world. America's "instrumental democracy" is supporting instead of detracting from America's "cultural democracy". The possible disarray of American foreign policy is not seen especially as a problem to be overcome, but as proof of a functioning democracy that makes the United States satisfyingly different to other countries. With so much of the world actively engaged in attempts to court American public opinion, especially through television, it is understandable that the United States considers itself confirmed as being uniquely democratic in character and, thereby, universal in purpose.

POSTSCRIPT
(2003)

The coming crisis.

I

A Manifold Inheritance

If the Clinton years marked the "end of history," they also underlined the problem of what such a state of existence might represent and, more significantly, what agencies would determine the direction of such a protean development. Ostensibly, it appeared self-evident that the United States as the epicentre of liberal democracy was the victor and, therefore, was in a position to define the nature of the victory. In many respects, the Enlightenment project of material progress and human development was stripped down to a one-to-one symmetry with American experience, guidance, and know-how. During the 1990s, the United States was largely responsible for the contraction of the world in its own image. Integration proceeded exponentially through financial investments, overseas acquisitions, communications networks, and knowledge-based industries that were all centred upon America in origin and application. The surge towards democratization, trade liberalization, privatization and structural adjustment programmes bore the imprint of the United States. The "Washington Consensus" itself was made synonymous with the presumption of a global consensus upon the American ethos of the free market.

In this context, the uniqueness of American democracy could be construed as the original patent for an international system evolving by democratic progression into a form of liberated fusion. The United States had become the reference point of emulation. It was now able to define democracy exclusively in terms of itself. Flexible markets, freedom of choice and self-determination would allow others to engage with the United States as full participants in the international economy. The operating assumption was that emancipated reason and self-interest would release societies into a natural harmonization with western democracies in general and the United States in particular. The United States could remain rooted in exceptionalism because progress did not appear to require any choices, or adjustments, or forms of self-examination. American democracy had been vindicated by the end of the Cold War and distinguished by its cultural supremacy.

This was an era when the sheer scale of America's global force became evident. In terms of "hard power," the US military acquired a position in which it surpassed the size of the next ten national forces combined. The Pentagon's budget for technological research and development dwarfed that of any other power centre. Its capability in force projection was equally immense with permanent military bases straddling a host of strategic and energy sensitive areas in over 55 countries.

This was also a period when analysts could refer categorically to the "soft power" of America's cultural prestige, normative presence and international reputation. "Soft power" was as far reaching as "hard power" and, arguably, more rooted in the real nature of America's global leverage. If an empire existed, then it was not merely an "empire by invitation", but an empire of the mind. Both "hard power" and "soft power" were earthed in America's proprietorship of a difference that legitimated their pre-eminence with moral distinction. The United States was uniquely dominant because of its domineering uniqueness.

Ironically, the expansion of America's global reach in the 1990s brought in its wake an increase in interdependency. The United States could successfully exert pressure upon other societies to comply with international agreements on trade, transport, capital flows, labour practices, investment and intellectual property rights. By the same token, the United States found that integration and co-operation cut both ways. America became increasingly dependent upon other states for regulating capital transfers, monitoring the drugs trade, gathering intelligence on security threats, and promoting social and economic development. Moreover, the global economy and information revolution gave greater influence to non-state organizations, thereby requiring further efforts by the United States in developing structures of co-operation.

At the end of the century American pre-eminence was confirmed but this status was tightly bound to a multilateral international order. Joseph Nye depicted the condition as a paradox of power. American preponderance was evident yet it was emplaced in a "web of international institutions that allows others to participate in decisions and that acts as a sort of world constitution to limit the capriciousness of American power." "Hyperpower" now appeared to run concurrently with global governance; "unipolarity" with the ganglia of the international community. The purity of the democratic word risked being compromised by other democratic voices as the world's complexities retained their position in the terms of trade. The Clinton era was marked by the disarray evoked by the need to determine the character and limits of America's role in the post-Cold War world. The United States' universal status and its attachment to the democratization of other societies generated considerable disquiet over the shape of a new democratic order.

The Clinton Presidency was widely criticised for its apparent lack of strategic vision at a time of dislodged certainties and porous borders. America may have acquired a kind of empire but it had yet to find a distinctive role. The old anchorage points of the Cold War had given America social cohesion and international purpose. Now, greater autonomy and choice for the United States increased the likelihood of inconsistency and even eclecticism. Clinton's own temporising style served to compound the impression of an administration with an episodic approach to international problems. His presidency became associated with the exertion of America's economic power and with the build-up of the country's military capacity. Despite his conspicuous attachments to racial and gender equality, and to the defence of human rights, Clinton's record on UN peacekeeping and humanitarian military intervention was marked by confusion, indecision and delay. The disasters of omission in Rwanda and Bosnia were interleaved with the conflated ambiguities of American actions in Kosovo and the Middle East. Within such a matrix of new issues, themes and theatres, the administration often appeared to suffer from a lack of overall direction.

Whether it was the high expectations of the peace dividend, or the genuinely complex nature of the emergent post-Cold War order, the Clinton White House came under increasing assault for what was seen to be an opaque foreign policy that made America's position ambivalent within an increasingly melded world. Many complaints centred upon the loss of American identity and autonomy inside the multilateral architecture of collective security. The apparent diffusion of America's distinctiveness was equated with a sense of diminishing moral capital and, thereby, a decline in moral direction.

It is true that Clinton's Secretary of State, Madeleine Albright, would habitually express her moral outrage against repressive states and dictatorial leaders. Her repeatedly stated conviction was that the United States remained "the indispensable nation" whose power was a force for good in the world: "I also totally believe in the beacon of American democracy, and I don't buy into the claim that democracy is only a western value – it's a universal value." Albright's critics, however, believed that she was depleting America's moral strength by failing to distinguish between the vital from the merely desirable in policy objectives. She was questioned over whether the United States was losing focus by expending its diplomatic resources on labour issues, human rights, religious freedom and the AIDS crisis. Promoting democracy and free markets may have been a noble intention, but her detractors pointed out that such a policy offered little guidance over the action to be taken when societies had chosen a course away from such ideals. When doubts over Albright's conceptual authority and tactical awareness were combined with Clinton's personal flaws and the political disarray of his presidency, the net effect was to open up the competition for foreign policy to a more unilateralist strain in both American society and American elite opinion.

II
The Millennial Turn

The influence of the Republican Right, and especially the neo-conservative group of opinion leaders, has become part of the genealogy of the Bush administration. Figures such as Donald Rusted, Dick Cheney, and Paul Wolfowitz all had an extensive background in the visceral opposition to Clinton's foreign policy and in the campaign to redirect American priorities according to a more fixed set of reference points. These sceptics questioned the meaning and even the existence of an "international community"; they opposed the use of American forces in peacekeeping and nation-building activities; and they drew attention to what they believed was a disjunction between Clinton's declared idealism and the required understanding of international power politics to support it.

Such an oppositionist perspective could afford to claim that the Clinton administration had been too reactive and adaptive to the world. The argument was that in acquiescing to the apparent limits of world politics, Clinton had given them a material reality – thereby unnecessarily limiting himself and the United States. The neo-conservative view was that American power was not as limited as Clinton's actions and statements implied. Instead, power had been diverted, distracted and, most importantly of all, unasserted and unused. Here lay the urgency. For too long, the United States had engaged in a policy of democratic promotion and simple hope. Hope that a democratic harmonization of societies and a state of democratic peace would emerge, more or less, through a process of spontaneous conformity. The operating presumption was that American power would be recognised as benignly democratic. As a result, it would not stimulate the organization of coalitions and forces directed against its international dominance. As early as 1992, Paul Wolfowitz and Lewis Libby in a confidential Pentagon memorandum disputed the linkage between social democratization and international peace. In the document, they stated that the United States had to prevent any "hostile power from dominating regions" whose resources would allow it to acquire great power status. Moreover, they believed that the US should discourage attempts by any other advanced industrial nation to challenge American leadership or to upset the established political and economic order. In effect, the United States should take concerted action to prevent the emergence of any potential global competitor. A decade later, Paul Wolfowitz and Lewis Libby had become senior members of the Bush administration – respectively, Deputy Secretary of Defence and National Security Adviser to Vice-President Dick Cheney

Paul Wolfowitz also had the distinction of being one of the founding members of the Project for a New American Century think-tank (PNAC). This highly influential organization advocated a strong military, a foreign policy that "boldly and purposefully promotes American principles abroad," and a "national leadership that accepts the United States' global responsibilities." By the late 1990s, the United States was coming under increasing pressure over the reach of its economic and cultural influence. Globalisation was becoming widely interpreted as a facilitating device for American corporate interest. In this context, America's soft power was easily seen as simply an adjunct to its hard power. By the same token, Samuel Huntingdon's thesis of a "clash of civilizations" appeared less implausible as Islamic radicalism cultivated a doctrinal rejection of western values and a cultural abhorrence of the "great Satan". To the PNAC group and its allies, the world had become a more dangerous place because of Clinton's foreign policy: "There is no middle ground between a decline in US power, a rise in world chaos, and a dangerous 21st century, on the one hand, and a Reaganite reassertion of American power and moral leadership on the other."

This strand of radical dissent was influential in the origins of George W. Bush's campaign for the presidency and subsequently in the formation of his administration. The new president's negative positions on the Kyoto Protocol, the International Criminal Court and the retention of the Anti-Ballistic Missile treaty bore the hallmarks of this schismatic outlook. Although the neo-conservatives and their allies were an important element in the Bush coalition, they were constrained by other viewpoints, traditions and institutions. Bush himself was primarily a domestic politician with little interest in the entangling complexities of foreign policy engagements. The terrorist attacks on September 11th, however, transformed his presidency and the political agenda of Washington. The assaults upon the World Trade Center and the Pentagon could be construed as dramatically affirming the worldview and prescriptions of the neo-conservatives. As Bush was propelled into foreign policy, the presidency was in urgent need of a moral compass that would combine direction with decisiveness. As a consequence, American security became increasingly defined by reference to the need to take strategic action in the defence of American democracy and, therefore, in the name of global democracy.

The aftermath of 9/11 has been one of Manichean polarities fuelled by claims to moral certainties, moral imperatives and moral leadership. The established state-based order of collective security was challenged by new doctrines of pre-emptive war, regime change and a free market for "coalitions of the willing". To the Bush administration, the organic mix of terrorist organizations, rogue states and biological, chemical and nuclear technologies formed a threat that could neither be contained nor deterred by conventional means. As a consequence, the "national security state" was deepened and combined with a homeland-security society reaching deep into areas previously protected by civil liberties and constitutional constraints. President Bush has declared a long war on terrorism in which 9/11 has served to alert the American nation and to mobilise its resources against an elusive and amorphous threat. The war has generated a profusion of high impact measures from the invasions of Afghanistan and Iraq to a new diplomatic doctrines and raw challenges to the United Nations. It has also fostered a state of myopia over the drive to maximise security through the free propagation of surveillance measures and cross-referenced databases. Soft pre-emption is coupled with its hard equivalent.

The asymmetrical attack on the United States has brought in its wake an asymmetrical response that has exposed once again the ambiguities between uniqueness and universalism within American identity and the nation's posture towards the world. Democracy has been repeatedly invoked by President Bush as the method, the motive and the objective of American action during the emergency. Liberation is stated as a self-evident process of emancipation into democracy. Enemies are defined as rogue states which are necessarily undemocratic and, therefore, open to terrorist networks and to the trade in weapons of mass destruction. Just as the moral undertow follows the tidal forces of American democratic experience, so the Bush administration has had no inhibitions in summoning up the universal theme of America's historical destiny to release oppression into freedom and democracy. The President has sought to be reassuring in that the liberty which America prized should be seen not as "America's gift to the world" but as "God's gift to humanity". America's role, therefore, is one of abiding by the ministrations of history and making "sacrifice for the liberty of strangers". The President has claimed that it is both "our responsibility and our privilege to fight freedom's fight … In a single instant, we realized that this will be the decisive decade in the history of liberty, that we've been called to a unique role in human events." Within this vocational context, the United States has no choice but to consummate its epic.

The extreme nature of the 9/11 assaults and their consequences has thrown into high relief the United States' sense of exceptionalism and, with it, a conviction of global centrality. The security of uniqueness is deployed against the insecurity of the outside world, but at the cost of an American fundamentalism that locates the world in a different moral space to that of the United States. Unilateral action by America has led to its premises of exceptionalism being challenged by reversing the argument into accusations of egregious deviancy – ironically expressed in terms of the United States as the pre-eminent rogue nation. This argument over the ethical integrity of American universalism is part of a larger struggle over the international ownership of the democratic brand name, and over an indigenous crisis within the United States itself that will in time be recognised as a unique crisis for democracy.

Most of this essay is a revised version of a contribution to The United States in the Twentieth Century: Empire *(Hodder and Stoughton, for The Open University, 1994). The "Postscript" appears here for the first time.*

Michael Foley is Professor of International Relations at the University of Wales, Aberystwyth. His works include American Political Ideas: Traditions and Usages *(Manchester University Press, 1991) and* The Politics of the British Constitution *(Manchester University Press, 1999).*

POEM AND RADIO PLAY

Cathal Ó Searcaigh

DÁN MOLTA

do Twin Morys i ndiaidh dó cathaoir na filíochta
a bhaint amach as feabhas a dháin ag Eisteddfod na bliana 2003

A bhard na Breataine Bige

Is tusa an bradán feasa
i linn na héigse;
Is tusa carria na mbeann
ar bhuaic na tuigse;
Is tusa an cór ainglí a chuireann
rithimí diaga sna reanna neimhe;
Is tusa farraige na filíochta
ag teacht i dtír i gcuanta ár gcéadfaí;
Is tusa teanga na gcúig ndúl
a thugann urlabhra na mbeo
dá bhfuil ionainn anois agus go deo
den tinidh agus den talamh
den spéir den uisce agus den aer

A bhard na Breataine Bige

Is tusa teanga thús an tsaoil;
Is tusa teanga an tSolais a las an lom;
Is tusa an Briathar, an tAdamh bunaidh
a bheartaigh a bhfuil ann, a bheathóidh a mbeidh ann;
Is tusa an tÓm síoraí
a cheansaíonn croí na cruinne;
Is tusa an teanga ársa
a anáileann na cnoic na clocha na caoráin
i bpoblacht Cheilteach ár ndúchais;
Is tusa teanga bhéal an Earraigh
ag gríosadh dán na glaise as corp an Gheimhridh;

Is tusa teanga Dé a thugann
briathra beannaithe d'aislingí do dhaoine.

A bhard na Breataine Bige

Inniu tá baird uaibhreacha do chine
na glúnta agus na glúnta
de dhraoithe agus de shaoithe
ag caint linn go tomhasta
as béal binn do dháin.
Inniu is tusa an smaolach fonnmhar
ag portaíocht i sceacha mo shamhlaíochta;
Inniu is tusa an chuach aoibhnis
ag cuachaireacht i mínte fraoigh m'uaignis;
Inniu is tusa an bard beo
a chuireann gaoth an bhriathair
ag séideadh ina stoirm shiabtha
fríd dhomhan mo dháin …

PRAISE POEM

for Twin Morys on achieving the poetry chair for the excellence
of his poem at the 2003 Eisteddfod

Bard of Wales

You are the salmon of knowledge
in the pool of poetry;
You are the antlered stag
on the peak of wisdom;
You are the angelic choir that sends
sacred rhythms into the bodies of heaven;
You are the sea of poetry
coming to land in the harbours of our senses;
You are the tongue of the five elements
that brings the speech of the living
to all that is in us now and forever

of fire and of land
of sky of water and of air.

Bard of Wales

You are the tongue of the beginning of life;
You are the Word, the primary Atom
that contrived all that is, will nurture all that will be;
You are the eternal Ohm
that quietens the heart of the world;
You are the ancient language
that the hills the stones the moors breathe
in the Celtic republic of our own place;
You are the tongue of the mouth of Spring
driving the song of greenness from the corpse of Winter;
You are the tongue of God that brings
blessed words to the visions of your people.

Bard of Wales

Today the proud bards of your race
generations and generations
of druids and sages
are speaking to us in measured tones
from the sweet mouth of your poem.
Today you are the melodious thrush
lilting in the bushes of my imagination;
Today you are the cuckoo of delight
chattering in the heather pastures of my solitude;
Today you are the living bard
who sends the wind of the word
blowing a drifting storm
through the world of my poem …

AN CHÉAD MHÁIRT D'FHÓMHAR

Dráma Raidió

—

Cathal Ó Searcaigh

Cogadh le Gall.

Suíomh: An Somme
Am: Meán Fómhair 1916
Pearsana: Éamann (23 bliain d'aois), Peadar (27 bliain d'aois)

Scríobhadh an dráma seo ar choimisiún ó Raidió na Gaeltachta. Tá an t-údar an-bhuíoch d'Edel Ní Chuirreáin, stiúrthóir Raidió na Gaeltachta i nDoirí Beaga, i dTír Chonaill.

Mír 1

ÉAMANN Chuir mé mo cheann amach, a Pheadair, go bhfeicinn caidé mar atá an oíche. Tá gealach iontach bháite ar an aer anocht. Tá sí ina luí ar chúl a cinn thuas ansin. Bhéarfá mionna gur blaosc cloigne atá intí - caite i dtrinse dubh sa spéir.

PEADAR D'ardaigh tú do cheann os cionn an trinse agus solas gealaí ann? Bhal, breallán ceart atá ionatsa, a Éamainn. Nach bhfuil fhios agat go bhfuil súile seabhaic ag na snipers sin amuigh? Tchífeadh siad dearnait dhubh thuas i do thóin sa dorchadas.

ÉAMANN Bhí fonn orm bolgam beag d'aer na hoíche a bhlaiseadh ach tá an t-aer ramhar le boladh na gcorp.

PEADAR Caidé eile a mbeithfeá ag súil leis i ndiaidh marfach millteanach an lae inné? Chan sa bhaile i gCaiseal na gCorr atá tú anois ag baint pléisiúir as aer úr folláin an fhómhair. Ar casadh duine ar bith ort thuas ansin sa trinse?

ÉAMANN Is beag den trinse atá fágtha. Landáil ceann de na pléascáin sin a bhíthear a scaoileadh linn níos luaithe, istigh ann. Réab sé na bruaigh.

PEADAR Caithfidh sé gur scrios an t-ionsaí deireannach sin cuid mhór den trinse, thíos agus thuas. Tá an chosúlacht air go bhfuil muid gearrtha ar shiúl ar an taobh ó dheas fosta. Tá muid anseo linn féin, a Éamainn, i "no man's land" denár gcuid féin.

ÉAMANN   Thig linn fanacht anseo go dtig na horduithe chugainn … uainnféin. Dhéanfaidh muid an cogadh a phleanáil ó seo; seo na "headquarters" úra, a Pheadair. I am Sir Edward Douglas Haig Gallagher, British Commander in Chief on the Western Front, and you are (*Blas Sasanach ar a chuid cainte*)

PEADAR   (*Blas Francach*) I am Peter Joseph Joffre O'Donnell, Commander in Chief of the French Army.

ÉAMANN   (*Blas Sasanach*) Let's drink some champagne. I always like a sip of bubbly before dinner.

PEADAR   (*Blas Francach*) I have a special bottle of bubbly for you. In Paris, we call this champagne, "Mún na luchóg mór".

(*Go tobann ligeann Éamann scread as féin*)

ÉAMANN   Snámhaí salach de luchóg mhór! Bhí píosa cáise i dtaisce agam istigh i mo phóca. Caithfidh sé go bhfuair sí an boladh. Tá sí ar shiúl leis.

PEADAR   An bhitseach shalach.

ÉAMANN   Tá an diabhal é féin ina sheasamh istigh sna luchógaí móra atá anseo.

PEADAR   Cá háit a bhfuair tú giota cáise sa pholl ocrach seo?

ÉAMANN   I mála droma an German udaí a scaoil mé inné. An cuimhneach leat nuair a bhí muid ar an ionsaí thall ansiúd faoi na crainn, tháinig mé ar shaighdiúir óg istigh i bpoll clábair agus scaoil mé é? Níl fhios agam cá tuige nár ith mé an píosa cáise sin níos luaithe. Chan é nach raibh ocras orm. Bhí leisce orm, b'fhéidir, de bharr gur ghoid mé é as mála an té a bhí marbh. Tá mé buartha gur scaoil mé é.

PEADAR   Bheinnse níos buartha faoi leadhb cáise a chailleadh ná mar a bheinn faoi bhás an German.

ÉAMANN   Bíodh croí agat, a Pheadair. Cha raibh sa tsaighdiúir bhocht sin ach fear óg gan urchóid cosúil linn féin.

PEADAR   Cac spréite agus féasóg air! Bíodh ciall agat, a Éamainn, German a bhí ann.

ÉAMANN   Nach bhfuil fhios agam? Nach bhfuil fhios agam sin go rímhaith? Is cuma, chuaigh sé go dtí an croí ionam déanamh ar shiúl leis an tsaighdiúir óg udaí. Níl mé i gceart ó shin, agus ní bheidh go brách.

PEADAR   Tá mearadh dearg ortsa. Níl fhios agam ó thalamh an domhain cá háit a bhfuil do chuid cainte ag teacht as.

ÉAMANN   Tá fhios agamsa, a Pheadair, cá háit a bhfuil mo chuid cainte ag teacht as. Tá mo chuid cainte ag teacht as áit atá saor ó stair. Áit nach bhfuil lucht creidimh nó lucht polaitíochta ag brú a dtola tíoránta féin ar an phobal. Tá mé ag caint as Tír an tSolais.

PEADAR   Níl le déanamh agat ach seasamh taobh amuigh den trinse seo; do thóin a chocáil leis na Gerries agus geallaim duit go dtógfaidh siad glan ón talamh tú agus go séidfidh siad tú, saor in aisce, go dtí an áit mhire sin i do mheabhair.

(Cluintear pléascadh mór)

PEADAR   Shílfeá go bhfuil na Gerries ag iarraidh eagla a chur orainn.

ÉAMANN   Muna bhfuil siad ach ag iarraidh eagla a chur orainn … abair leo stopadh anois díreach. D'éirigh leo. Tá crith mhagairlí orm.

PEADAR   Tá eagla ortsa, a Éamainn? Shíl mé nach dtiocfadh eagla a chur ort.

ÉAMANN   Tá eagla orm romham féin. Nuair a scaoil mé an German sin inné phléasc rud inteacht istigh ionam. D'éirigh mé níos boige.

PEADAR   Caidé atá ag teacht ort? Coinnigh suas d'uchtach. Nach muidinne fir Chaiseal na gCorr? Cruaidh agus cnámhach? Lucht na ndoirne is na ndaondalán? Nach cuimhneach leat nuair a bhíodh muid ag troid le muintir Bhaile na Bó an dóigh aicseanta a bhí agat le smitín i mbun na cluaise a thabhairt d'fhear amháin acu agus sabhstar i mbéal an bhoilg d'fhear eile? Cha raibh do shárú le fáil, a Éamainn, nuair a bhí cic na bó bradaí sna magairlí le tabhairt do bhoc inteacht. Bhain tú an teaspach as an chuid is fearr acu. Chuir tú an cár siar ina gcraos. Eagla, a Éamainn!   Bhí am ann agus rachfá a throid le do scáile féin, dá sílfeá go raibh sé ag éirí rómhór dona chuid bróga.

ÉAMANN   Cha raibh ansin ar fad ach cur i gcéill. An stócach ag iarraidh fear mór a dhéanamh dó féin. Ar scor ar bith nach bhfuil cead agam eagla bheith orm. Mothaím an bás ag siúl liom. Cluinim tramp … tramp … tramp … a choiscéimeanna ag tarraingt ar mo chroí.

PEADAR   Char chuala mé an cineál sin cainte uait ariamh.

ÉAMANN   Char ghoill sé orm ariamh a ghabháil amach in éadan na bpiléar agus mo dhualgas saighdiúra a dhéanamh. Ach nuair a scaoil mé an German óg sin inné …

PEADAR   Stad! Stad! Drochbhreith ar an German gránna sin …

ÉAMANN   Cha raibh ball gránna ina chorp. Bhí sé chomh dea-chumhtha le haingeal. B'fhéidir gur aingeal a bhí ann a dtáinig seachrán sí air sna spéarthaí agus gur chaill sé a shlí arís chun na bhFlaitheas.

PEADAR   Dhia, a Éamainn, an stadfaidh tú den amaidí cainte sin atá ort? Chuirfeá duine gan dóigh le do chuid bundúin. Rachadh sé níos mó chun sochair dúinn dá seinnfeá tiúin bheag ar an fhidil fhrancach.

(Cluintear fidil fhrancach ag seinnt Coinleach Ghlas an Fhómhair)

PEADAR   Coinleach Ghlas an Fhómhair. Chuirfeadh sé cumhaidh ort.

ÉAMANN   Is dóiche go bhfuil an fómhar istigh acu sa bhaile faoi seo.

PEADAR   Má tá an aimsir a dhath cosúil le seo lobhfaidh an fodar sna cuibhrinn.

ÉAMANN   Anseo tá coirp ag lobhadh sna cuibhrinn. Na mílte fear óg ag déanamh leasú ar thalamh curaíochta na Fraince.

PEADAR   Nuair a bheas an cogadh thart beidh muintir na háite ábalta a rá "Tá cnámh maith sa talamh seo". Agus ní bheidh focal bréige sa méid sin.

ÉAMANN   Beidh sin ann. Cnámha na marbh. Beidh an áit seo beo le taibhsí san am atá le theacht.

PEADAR   Dá mbeinn thall in Éirinn an t-am seo bliana bheinn ag déanamh cruacha coirce.

ÉAMANN   Bhí lámh mhaith agat ar thógail cruaiche.

PEADAR   An cuimhneach leat achan bhliain bhíodh sé nó seacht de chruacha coirce tógtha agam istigh i nGarradh an Chuilinn …?

ÉAMANN   Ón dóigh a mbíodh siad ina suí thart agat i gciorcal bhéarfá mionna gur ag déanamh cúrsa damhsa a bhí siad.

PEADAR   Cor seachtair na gcruach.

ÉAMANN   Níl a dhath chomh deas leis na cruacha coirce sin agus dath an óir orthu tráthnóna buí fómhair.

PEADAR   Tá tú ag cur cumhaidh orm. Nár dheas a bheith sa bhaile anois ag amharc ar an ghealach os cionn na hEargaile?

ÉAMANN   An síleann tú go dtig linn a ghabháil na bhaile i ndiaidh a
         bhfuil feicthe againn anseo … an marfach agus an scrios
         éagsamhalta seo atá thart orainn achan lá?

PEADAR   Cá háit eile a dtig linn a ghabháil ach na bhaile chuig ár
         ndaoine féin; chuig an tsaol a d'fhág muid inár ndiaidh? Cha
         dtáinig athrú ar bith ar sin …

ÉAMANN   Orainne a tháinig an t-athrach, a Pheadair. I ndiaidh a bhfuil
         feicthe againne den bhás agus den anbhás; den tséideadh agus
         den phléascadh anseo ar bhruach an Somme, beidh sé doiligh
         againn socrú síos ar bhruach Abhainn an Átha. Beidh an
         Somme agus an Marne, an Meuse agus an Oise linn go deo
         inár gceann. Beidh aibhneacha seo na fola ag sníomh fríd ár
         gcuimhní i gcónaí. Beidh bailte millte, scriosta seo an
         chogaidh; Ginchy agus Guillemont; Mamet agus La Boisella,
         Thiepval agus Hamel; beidh na bailte seo le feiceáil againn
         agus muid ag siúl fríd ár mbailte beaga féin sa bhaile. Ní
         bheidh an baile go brách arís mar a bhí sé …

PEADAR   Tá do cheann lán d'amaidí ó na leabharthaí sin ar fad a léigh
         tú in Albain sular liostáil muid. Bhí fhios agam nach ndéanfadh
         siad maith ar bith duit. Bhí an chuid eile againn amuigh ag
         déanamh cuideachta i Haddington, in East Linton, agus i
         nDunbar agus tusa istigh sa bhotaí ag léamh leabharthaí.
         Rinne siad strainséir duit, a Éamainn, i measc do dhaoine féin.
         Chuir siad ar strae tú.

ÉAMANN   B'fhéidir go raibh mé coimhthíoch i gcónaí, a Pheadair, i ngan
         fhios daoibhse. Coimhthíoch agus corr. Nuair a bhí mé i mo
         thachrán ba ghnách liom badaí beaga a dhéanamh as slatacha
         saileoige agus iad a chur ag snámh sa tsruthán. Liginn orm
         féin go raibh mé ag imeacht sa tsruth; ag seoladh ar shiúl go
         tír i bhfad i gcéin. Tír nár leagadh cois uirthi ariamh.
         Shamhlaigh mé go mbeinn liom féin ansiúd i ríocht an
         uaignis, go mbeinn beo ar chnuasach na trá agus ar thoradh na
         gcraobh. Ansiúd i dTír an tSolais. Sin an t-ainm a bhaist mé ar
         mo thír féin.

PEADAR   Cha dtiocfadh liom a bheith beo gan daoine; a gcomhrá agus
         a gcuideachta, tá fhios agat. Caidé a dhéanfá gan bean?

ÉAMANN   Cha raibh mé ag smaointiú ar mhná an t-am sin. Cha raibh
         ionam ach stócach beag soineanta. An raibh tú i do luí le bean
         go fóill, a Pheadair?

PEADAR | Nach tú atá fiosrach! Cha chuirfeá an cheist sin ar an diabhal.
ÉAMANN | Sa bhaile tá leisce orainn a bheith foscailte lena chéile ar na gnoithí seo. Ach anseo thig leat an snaidhm a bhaint de do theangaidh. Ar shásaigh tú an fear ionat ariamh le bean, a Pheadair?
PEADAR | Níl sé furast, tá fhios agat, an scéal a chur chun tosaigh ar ghirseach. An raibh tusa i do luí le bean ariamh?
ÉAMANN | Sé mhí ó shin nuair a bhí cead scoir agam ar feadh dornán laethe thug mé cuairt ar Páras. Bhí tusa san ospidéal ag an am ag teacht chugat féin ón fliú. Níl inse béil, a Pheadair, ar cé chomh galánta agus atá Páras. Bhí aoibh an Aibreáin ar na sráideacha amhail is dá mbeadh cóta de shíoda buí óir caite thar iomlán na cathrach. Achan áit bhí na crainn silíní amuigh i mbláth. Bhí mé ag siúl thart ag baint lán na súl as iontaisí aosta na cathrach agus ag smaointiú ag an am chéanna an fada eile a bheinn beo. An bhfaighinn seans an saol a bhlaiseadh, an gcasfainn ar dhuine inteacht a chuirfeadh eiteogaí ar mo chroí.
PEADAR | Bhal, ar casadh bean ort?
ÉAMANN | Tráthnóna amháin bhí mé liom féin i gcaife ag ól fíona nuair a shuigh fear óg síos i mo chuideachta. Phillipe, an t-ainm a bhí air. Saighdiúir in arm na Fraince, bhí 'leave' seachtaine aige agus bhí sé á chaitheamh lena mhuintir i bPáras. Nuair a chuala sé gur ó Éirinn mé cha dtiocfadh leis fáilte go leor a chur romham. Bhí dáimh speisialta aige le tír s'againne siocair go raibh sé iontach mór le buachaill as Baile Átha Cliath. Casadh an péire acu ar a chéile i bPáras cúig bliana ó shin nuair nach raibh siad beirt ach sé bliana déag. Cha ndéanfadh a dhath maith dó ach go dtiocfainn leis na bhaile. Bhí 'hotel' beag ag a mhuintir i dtuaisceart na cathrach. Char dhiúltaigh mé an cuireadh. Bhí dóigh dheas aige. Cha raibh sé rómhór ach bhí sé teann téagartha ina dhéanamh. Thaitin sé liom. Bhí sé iontach dóighiúil.
PEADAR | Tá tú ag déanamh strambán millteanach den scéal. Is cuma sa diabhal liom cé acu an raibh sé dóighiúil nó gránna.
ÉAMANN | Tchím.
PEADAR | Ar casadh bean ort? An dteachaigh tú go Toraigh inti? mar a deir muid sa bhaile.

ÉAMANN	Is cosúil gur chuir bean de na cailíní freastail sa hotel bheag a bhí ag muintir Phillippe spéis ionam. An oíche sin tháinig sí chugam i mo sheomra leapa agus gan tointe éadaigh uirthi ach braillín a chas sí thart ar a corp.
PEADAR	An dteachaigh tú léithe?
ÉAMANN	Cha dteachaigh. Chuaigh sise liomsa. Bhfuil tú ag meas go ndéanfainn í a chur ó dhoras, a uascáin, agus í á caitheamh féin orm?
PEADAR	An dteachaigh tú an bealach ar fad léithe?
ÉAMANN	Thiocfadh leat a rá go dteachaigh mé go barr na hEargaile cupla uair i gcaitheamh na hoíche.
PEADAR	Caidé a bhí sé cosúil leis …?
ÉAMANN	Bhí sé go díreach cosúil le bheith ag gabháil suas ar an Eargail. Bhí mé amach as anáil ar an bhealach suas agus allasach go maith … ach shleamhnaigh mé anuas gan mórán moille.
PEADAR	Caithfidh mé a ghabháil go Páras am inteacht agus fanacht san hotel sin. B'fhéidir go dtiocfadh bean na braillíne chugamsa fosta. Ar a laghad, a Éamainn, bhí tusa sa diallait…
ÉAMANN	Dá n-inseochainn iomlán an scéil duit, a Pheadair, cha seasfá ansin agus do thóin liom.
PEADAR	Caidé an gháireach atá ort, a ghraoisín?
ÉAMANN	Tá mé go díreach ag cuimhneamh ar an oíche sin i bPáras. Nuair a d'fhoscail an doras udaí, d'athraigh mo shaol.
PEADAR	Tá an t-ádh ort cuimhní leapa mar sin a bheith agat.
ÉAMANN	Tá mé ag gabháil a shíneadh síos anseo ar feadh tamall beag. Mothaím néal codlata ag teacht orm.
PEADAR	Tusa an bóidheán ceart, a Éamainn. Tá tú ag gabháil a chodhladh sa dóigh go dtig leat a bheith ag brionglóidigh ar bhean na braillíne…

Mír 2

ÉAMANN	Bhfuil an lá ag gealadh go fóill, a Pheadair?
PEADAR	Tá tú muscailte?
ÉAMANN	Tá. Bhí mo chodladh corrach go maith.
PEADAR	Chan iontas ar bith é sin agus gunnaí móra ag réabadh na hoíche. Baineadh cupla croitheadh millteanach as an talamh. Shíl mé go séidfí muid go Paiteagó. Tá an t-ádh ortsa, a

        Éamainn, go dtig leat do chodladh a dhéanamh agus an racán mire seo thart ort.

ÉAMANN   Bhí mé i mo chodladh ach má bhí féin ní bhfuair mé bomaite faoisimh.

PEADAR   Ón tiontú agus ón tosáil a bhí ort, déarfainn go raibh tú ag baint sásaimh as bean na braillíne.

ÉAMANN   Bhí brionglóid agam a bhain croitheadh anama asam. B'fhacthas domh, a Pheadair, go raibh mé ag comhrá leis an tsaighdiúir óg sin ar steall mé an inchinn as inné. Mo dhálta féin, cha raibh sé ach trí bliana fichead. Bhí sé ag inse domh go bhfuair a mháthair bás agus é ina thachrán agus gurb é an t-athair a thóg é. Ba eisean an t-aon duine clainne a bhí aige. Anois, bheadh an t-athair fágtha leis féin ar an fheirm bheag sléibhe a bhí acu i ndeisceart na Gearmáine. Nuair a chuirfí tásc a bháis na bhaile, a dúirt sé liom, gheobhadh an t-athair bás le briseadh croí. Bhí an bheirt acu iontach geallmhar ar a chéile.

PEADAR   Anseo, téann muid a chodladh, le dearmad a dhéanamh den chogadh agus de chéasadh an tsaoil. Cha dtig leat a bheith a do sciúrsáil féin le haithreachas, a Éamainn.

ÉAMANN   Ach d'éirigh an Gearmánach óg sin ó mharbh, a Pheadair, agus labhair sé liom.

PEADAR   Ná bí ag cur an locht ort féin, a Éamainn. Achab é gur scaoil tusa an t-urchar sin bheadh do chnámhasa spréite amuigh ansiúd i gclábar an Somme agus na luchógaí móra ag ithe do phutógaí. Caidé eile a dhéanfá ach piléar a chur ann?

ÉAMANN   Póg a thabhairt dó.

PEADAR   Bhfuil tusa ag gabháil bog sa chloigeann, a stócaigh?

ÉAMANN   B'fhearr liom bheith bog sa chloigeann ná cruaidh sa chroí.

PEADAR   Cuir an German gránna sin as do cheann, a Éamainn, nó glacfaidh sé seilbh ort. Cha dtig linn ár gcuid marbh féin a chaoineadh chan amháin cuid na namhad.

ÉAMANN   Dá gcasfaí orm é áit ar bith eile ach amháin anseo i mbéal Ifrinn bheadh muid mór lena chéile. Ní léir domh go raibh naimhdeas ar bith ina shúile nuair a d'amharc sé orm sular scaoil mé é. Súile a bhí chomh gorm le huisce fómhair.

PEADAR   Bí cinnte nach dtabharfadh seisean ceathrú anama ar bith duitse. Chuir tú piléar ann sula raibh deis aigesean dic a dhéanamh duitse.

ÉAMANN	Bhí sé ag iarraidh é féin a tharraingt amach as poll domhain clábair faoi na crainn réabtha sin thall, áit a dteachaigh sé go dtína thóin in abar. Bhí sé ag streachailt amach as an tsalachar nuair a tháinig mise air. D'amharc sé aníos orm agus bhí miongháire beag soineanta ar a bhéal. Shamhalfá gur buachaill beag a bhí ann ar beireadh air ag déanamh rud inteacht as áit; rud inteacht contráilte. Bhí a aghaidh bheag thanaí chomh gnaíúil le girseach. D'amharc mé síos isteach i dtobar gorm a shúl. D'ól mé deoch d'fhíoruisce an chineáltais, a Pheadair, as an tobar daonna sin. D'aithin muid a chéile. Shíl sé, is dóiche, go ndéanfainn trócaire air, go mbéarfainn greim láimhe air agus go dtarraingeochainn amach as poll dubh an chlábair é …
PEADAR	Níl muid anseo le truaigh a dhéanamh daofa. Tá muid anseo le iad a thiomáint amach as an tír. Le iad a shéideadh chun na síoraíochta.
ÉAMANN	Tá a chorp caite ar an talamh idir eatartha sin amuigh agus gan duine ar bith lena tharrtháil. Tá a spiorad ar strae idir an saol agus an tsíoraíocht agus gan Dia ar bith lena thabhairt slán. Tá sé caillte, a Pheadair, i bpoll clábair idir an saol seo agus an saol eile.
PEADAR	Ar dtús, shíl mé nach raibh ort ach rámhaillí chodlata ach tá tú ag gabháil as do chiall. Tá contúirt sa chaint sin. Tá mé á rá sin leat anois amach díreach. Ní thig leat dáimh a bheith agat le duine de na Germans sin thall. Dá gcluinfí tú ag caint mar sin chuirfí cúirt airm ort.
ÉAMANN	Is cuma liom. Tá cúirt anama curtha agam orm féin. Tá sin i bhfad níos tíoránta ná aon chúirt airm.
PEADAR	Cá háit a bhfuil tú ag gabháil leis an spád sin?
ÉAMANN	Tá mé ag gabháil amach le corp an German a chur i dtalamh. Ní thig liom é a fhágáil ar maos i gclábar, amuigh ansin ar lom an donais.
PEADAR	Cha dtig leat a ghabháil amach ansin, a Éamainn. Cuirfear do chnámha san aer.
ÉAMANN	Ó scaoil mé an German sin mothaím go bhfuil mo ré reaite. Bhí mé ag caint le saighdiúir as Newcastle an tseachtain seo caite, dílleachtaí a bhí ann. Dúirt sé ós rud é nach raibh baile ar bith aige i measc na mbeo go mb'fhéidir go n-aimseodh sé baile i measc na marbh. Tuigim an méid sin …

PEADAR Bhal, cha dtuigimse sin, dubh, bán, nó riabhach. Tá do bhaile i gCaiseal na gCorr, an áit a bhfuil do bhunadh ina gcónaí.

ÉAMANN Tá mo bhaile, a Pheadair, i mbaclainn an German sin amuigh. Le chéile beidh muid iomlán. Eisean an chuid domh féin atá caillte. Tá sé in am againn a ghabháil i gceann a chéile.

PEADAR Tá mearadh ort, a Éamainn, agus níl fhios agamsa faoi Dhia caidé a dhéanfaidh mé leat.

ÉAMANN Fanóchaidh tú anseo. Tá mé ag gabháil a shleamhnú anonn sula dtiocfaidh ball bán ar an lá …

PEADAR Char chuala mé a leithéid seo ariamh. Thuigfinn dá mba fear marbh denár gcuid féin a bhí i gceist ach … German agus German nach raibh aithne ar bith agat air, beag nó mór.

ÉAMANN Nuair a d'amharc an saighdiúir sin idir an dá shúil orm bhí fhios agam go raibh seanaithne na díleann againn ar a chéile. Labhair muid lena chéile ón chroí. Cha dtáinig tír nó treabh nó teangaidh eadrainn le muid a choinneáil scartha óna chéile. Ag an bhomaite sin bhí fhios agam gurb eisean an té a bhí mé a lorg. Ba eisean an chuid díom féin a bhí in easnamh orm. B'fhéidir gur sin an fáth ar scaoil mé é, le déanamh cinnte nach gcaillfinn é.

PEADAR Cha dtig liom brí ar bith a bhaint as do chuid cainte. Caidé atá tú a rá liom?

ÉAMANN Go raibh mé, go bhfuil mé agus go mbeidh mé go deo na ndeor i ngrá leis an German sin amuigh.

PEADAR Íosa Críost na Glóire! Tá tú an dóigh udaí, a Éamainn. Caidé faoin bhean i bPáras …?

ÉAMANN D'inis mé bréag duit ar mhaithe le tú a shásamh, a Pheadair. Nuair a d'fhoscail doras mo sheomra an oíche udaí chan bean a tháinig chugam ach fear. Philippe. Luigh muid le chéile. Cha raibh a dhath domhain sa teangbháil sin. Cha raibh ann ach go dtug muid sásamh fiáin na feola dá chéile in uaigneas na hoíche. Ach nuair a d'amharc an German orm lena shúile solais bhí fhios agam gur seo an té a bhí i ndán domh. Bhí mo chleamhnas déanta.

PEADAR Cuireann tú náire orm, a Éamainn, náire agus gráin shaolta. Chuirfinn piléar ionat anois achab é go bhfuil meas agam ar do mhuintir.

ÉAMANN Tiocfaidh an lá, bíodh sin fada nó gairid agus beidh glacadh ag an phobal le mo leithéidí. Beidh fir óga, mo mhacasamhail

	féin agus lánchead acu titim i ngrá lena chéile. Beidh mo leithéidí le fáil i Mín a' Leá, i bFána Bhuí, ar an Bhealtaine …
PEADAR	Druid do bhéal, a Éamainn, nó cuirfidh mé mo dhorn siar i do chraos. Níl mé ag gabháil a sheasamh anseo ag éisteacht le piteog fir mar thusa; Síle shalach d'fhear, ag caitheamh masla agus salachair ar an bhaile.
ÉAMANN	Níl sé ionat, a Pheadair, a dhath a dhéanamh liomsa. Bainimse anois le ré úr, le ham eile, le haois na saoirse. Tá mise ag tabhairt m'aghaidh ar an am atá le theacht. Tá tusa sáite sa tseantsaol ach tá tú róbhómánta le sin a thuigbheáil.
PEADAR	Bhfuil tusa ag rá gur bómán atá ionamsa, a phiteacháin shalaigh?
ÉAMANN	Déarfainn go bhfuil níos mó sa cheann ag cráin muice ná mar atá i do chloigeannsa.
PEADAR	Tá go leor ráite agat.

(Tugann sé rúide ar Éamann, cluintear iad ag gabháil i ngleic lena chéile. Tormán troda — tá an bhua ag Éamann)

ÉAMANN	Nach cuimhne leat, a Pheadair, cé chomh haicseanta agus a bhí mé? Smitín i mbun na cluaise, sabhstar i mbéal an bhoilg agus cic na bó bradaí sna magairlí. Bhfuil do sháith buailte faighte agat anois ó phiteog fir, nó an gcaithfidh mé urchar gunna a chur suas i do thóin?
PEADAR	Dhia, a Éamainn, ná scaoil mé. Tá mé – tá mé buartha.
ÉAMANN	Tá tú buartha mar go bhfuil tú buailte. Thiocfadh liom déanamh ar shiúl leat anois agus ní bheadh fhios ag duine ar bith nach sniper a chuir urchar ionat.
PEADAR	Tá fhios agam nach bhfuil meas ar bith agat orm i ndiaidh an mhasla a thug mé duit … bhain tú siar asam, a Éamainn, le do chuid cainte Char casadh do leithéidse ariamh orm. Caidé a thiocfadh le fear garbh mar mé féin a dhéanamh ach lán a bhéil d'íde a thabhairt duit? B'fhéidir go dtiocfadh liom glacadh leis an dóigh a bhfuil tú ach … seans a fháil. Caithfidh tú foighid a bheith agat liom.
ÉAMANN	Beidh foighid na síoraíochta agam ar ball. Tá mé ag gabháil trasna anois.
PEADAR	Agat féin is fearr atá fhios caidé atá le do leas. Ádh mór ort agus coimirce Dé ort fosta.

ÉAMANN   Má thig tú amach as an chogadh seo beo, a Pheadair, inis an fhírinne daofa sa bhaile. Beidh sé cruaidh orthu, ach lá níos faide anonn rachaidh mo scéal chun sochair d'fhear óg inteacht i gCaiseal na gCorr, fear óg inteacht a bhfuil an claonadh céanna ann agus atá ionamsa.

(Tosaíonn sé a sheinnt ar an fhidil fhrancach agus é ag gabháil amach an mullach — An Chéad Mháirt d'Fhómhar.*)*

PEADAR   Tá tú ag gabháil a thabhairt d'aghaidh ar na Germans le ceol. Éamainn, seo do ghunna. Nach bhfuil tú ag gabháil a thabhairt do ghunna leat...? Tá tú ag gabháil a thrasnú an talaimh sin gan cosaint ar bith. Dhéanfaidh siad púdar de do chnámha

(Cluintear an ceol agus ansin an phléasc ... urchar ó ghunna nó cupla urchar ... cluintear scread ó Éamann)

PEADAR   Éamainn ... Éamainn ... go ndéanaidh Dia trócaire ort ... go ndéanaidh Dia trócaire ort a Éamainn Uí Ghallchóir ... *(Tá sé ag caoineadh)*

Críoch

Cathal Ó Searcaigh is the Irish Language Editor of this journal. His most recent volume of poetry is Ag Tnúth Leis an tSolas *(Clo Iar-Chonnachta, 2000).*

from HORSE LATITUDES

―

Paul Muldoon

Bannockburn

Though he was mounted on a cob
rather than a war-horse, the Bruce
still managed to side-step a spear
from Henry de Bohun and tax
de Bohun's poll with his broad-based pole-ax
and leave de Bohun's charger somewhat leer.
Her grandfather had yet to find a use
for the two-timing partisan
his grandfather brought man-to-man
against all those Ferdinandies
until he saw it might come in handy
for whacking the thingammybobs
off pine and fir, off pine and fir and spruce
and all such trees as volunteer.

Blackwater Fort

As I had held Carlotta close
that night we watched some Xenophon
embedded with the 5th Marines
in the old Sunni triangle
make a half-assed attempt to untangle
the ghastly from the price of gasoline.
There was a distant fanfaron
in the Nashville sky where the wind
had now drawn itself up and pinned
on her breast a Texaco star.
"Why," Carlotta wondered, "the House of *Tar*?
Might it have to do with the gross
imports of crude oil Bush will come clean on
only when the Tigris comes clean?"

Blenheim

Small birds were sounding the alert
as I followed her unladen
steed through a dell so dark and dank
she might have sported the waders
her grandfather had worn at the nadir
of his career, scouring the Outer Banks
for mummichog and menhaden.
Those weeks and months in the doldrums
coming back as he ran his thumb
along an old Veneitian blind
in the hope that something might come to mind,
that he might yet animadvert
the maiden name of that Iron Maiden
on which he was drawing a blank.

Badli-ke-Serai

Pork-barrels. *Pork*-butts. The Widescreen
Surround Sound of a massed attack
upon the thin red cellulose
by those dust- or fust- or must-cells
that cause the tears to well and well and well.
At which I see him turning up his nose
as if he'd bitten on a powder-pack
like yet another sad Sepoy
who won't fall for the British ploy
of greasing with ham the hammer
or smoothing over Carlotta's grammar:
"*On which* ... *On which* Bush will come clean."
Her grandfather a man who sees no lack
of manhood in the lachrymose.

Paul Muldoon grew up in The Moy, Co Armagh. His most recent volume of poems is Moy Sand and Gravel *(Faber, 2003). He is Professor of Poetry at Oxford University and the Director of the Program in Creative Writing, Princeton University.*

THE IRISH PERIODICAL

Malcolm Ballin

Jostling at the crossroads.

The Irish Scene

A recent *Writer's Handbook* lists eight current literary magazines from Ireland including one from Northern Ireland. The *Poetry Kit* website delivers another five, two from the North. Not all of these titles are easily obtainable; some may be already moribund; some do not even respond to offers of subscriptions. But they include old stalwarts, like *Poetry Ireland Review* going back to 1981 and even *The Honest Ulsterman,* now apparently no longer in production. Others are newer and well-established, easily obtainable from bookshops, like *Metre,* an example of a magazine doubly borne up by Arts Council support from both North and South. However, these listings exclude other current periodicals, such as the venerable *Studies* (founded by the Jesuits in 1912), *The Dublin Review,* a comparative newcomer but now at its eleventh issue, the broadsheet *Fortnight* from Belfast and more recent productions such as *The Black Mountain Review,* or *The Yoke.* They also leave out well-known more academic journals such as *The Irish Review, Irish University Review* or *Irish Studies Review.* Without much difficulty, then, we can count more than twenty contemporary Irish periodicals.

The literary magazine appears, then, at the very least, to be surviving in Ireland. Indeed I maintain that at least two of the major sub-genres of the periodical, as they have developed historically in Ireland, are still in existence and that they constitute a notable case of the persistence of historical literary forms. Despite the competition from other media the printed periodical is still the first point of departure for most new writers and the main focus for critical discussion about literature. The tradition of the Irish literary magazine since the eighteenth century has recently been documented in scholarly detail by Tom Clyde, in his new book about Irish literary magazines up to 1985 (*Irish Literary Magazines: An Outline History and Descriptive Bibliography,* 2002). He records a peak of production in the mid-twentieth century with a record number of new magazines starting in the three decades between 1953 and 1985. He associates this richness with the social and political upheavals of the period, and goes on to conclude that the period since 1985 represents something of a downturn. Clyde considers that two products of post-war intellectual consensus, namely the "twin pillars" of the expansion of higher education and the extension of state-funding for the arts, are both now under threat and that editors have yet to come up with a satisfactory response. The views of Tom Clyde, at one time the editor of *The Honest Ulsterman,* must carry a great deal of credibility in this area. Whilst there will not be space to discuss these important issues in depth, this article should cast some light on the effects of state subsidy (or the withholding of it) on magazines and also on the prospects for the creation of a continuing audience for literary productions of this kind.

First, however, let us consider some of the periodicals that are available at present on the Irish market. I have decided to confine myself to two main genres, the little magazine and the miscellany and to look at just two examples of each of these in some detail. This does mean, I fear, doing scant justice to other interesting periodicals that I shall barely have time to mention. But I hope the evidence will be sufficient to support the argument that these genres persist actively and effectively.

Little Magazines

Tom Clyde's bibliography includes such early publications as Yeats's *Beltaine, Samhain* and *The Arrow,* the first Irish little magazines. Yeats's magazines look back in their form to the aesthetic movement associated with *The Yellow Book* and forward to later modernist manifestos like Wyndham Lewis's *Blast.* Clyde itemises at least twenty clearly recognisable examples of the little magazine from the later twentieth-century. These include David Marcus's *Irish Writing* and his associated *Poetry Ireland* in the 1940s, John Ryan's *Envoy* (1949-51) and *Kavanagh's Weekly* (1952). He includes from the 1960s and 1970s, such various offerings as James Delahanty's *Kilkenny Magazine,* James Liddy and Michael Hartnett's *Arena* and *The Lace Curtain,* edited by Michael Smith and Trevor Joyce. In the North we have *Lagan* and *Rann* in the 1940s and 1950s, *Threshold* in the 1950s and 60s and, in the late 60s, *The Honest Ulsterman.* The essential characteristics of little magazines, as identified in Wolfgang Gortschachers' magisterial study of the genre (*Little Magazine Profiles: The Little Magazines in Great Britain,* 1993) are all present in these contemporary examples: physical slimness, a sense of experimentation, financial and operational difficulties in sustaining production without patronage or subsidy, a self-conscious appeal to an intellectual minority, editorial independence often to the point of intransigence, youthfulness, and intellectual defiance. As Douglas Dunn once put it, "a little magazine can survive on a coterie and a prayer."

The South of Ireland's wide range of contemporary little magazines, includes the well-established *Poetry Ireland Review, Cyphers* and *Metre* and newer and more experimental publications, such as *Riposte,* THE SHOp, and *The Yoke.* I have had the opportunity of discussing these publications with some of their editors. Many of them speak of common preoccupations: a special concern with poetry and short fiction, a sharp awareness of the importance of their own periodical's appearance and design, and some concern about their relationships with Arts Councils. Practical problems feature in these comments, especially the following: under-staffing; major difficulties with distribution – especially given the unwillingness of most bookshops to sell little magazines (Eason's being an honourable exception); shortage of advertisers; and the difficulties of managing web-sites, especially in arranging the administration of vital credit card subscriptions. *Poetry Ireland Review,* which sees itself as a journal of record enjoying a semi-official institutional status, has a rotating editorship, changing every year and including many senior figures from academia and the literary establishment. This is seen as protecting it from any "poetic *diktat,*" whether generated by editorial preference or gender prejudice. *Cyphers,* too, has been produced for more than twenty-eight years. Described as "an occasional publication on literature and the arts," it is a slim fifty pages mostly devoted to poetry and short fiction but also including reviews and criticism. Edited by four practising poets, this bilingual magazine has produced translations from twenty languages including special issues from Italian, French, Hungarian and Vietnamese and it has been especially influential in promoting the work of Paul Durcan. *Metre* is self-consciously international in outlook with offices in Prague as well as Dublin. *The Yoke,* a new and youthful production from Howth which has an enjoyably anarchic presence, claims a direct lineage from the angry tones of *Kavanagh's Weekly* (1952) and has messages of personal support from Peter Kavanagh. *Riposte,* while lacking Arts Council support, has a unique presentation, as a folded broad-sheet with a published list of subscribers and a special pride in giving opportunities to new and hitherto unpublished poets, most of whom are without any great literary pretensions.

I would like, however, to look in some more detail at one particular example of the contemporary little magazine from the South. THE SHOp: *A Magazine of Poetry,* edited from Cork by John and Hilary Wakeman, was launched in 1999 with a small grant from the Arts Council and some gifts from friends. John Wakeman had previously edited an English poetry magazine, *The*

Rialto. THE SHOp's advertising flyer carries encomia from writers such as Seamus Heaney, John Montague, Dermot Bolger and Brendan Kennelly. It has high production standards including, until very recently, a nominated designer (Joakim Säflund) who oversees beautifully designed covers, individually commissioned, together with numerous high-quality illustrations; the poems form an elegant rivulet of text flowing between wide margins. Now at its twelfth quarterly issue, it has increased its funding from the Arts Council, gained further financial support from Cork County Council and, according to the editor, is "inundated with poems from all over the world." This is clearly a success story.

THE SHOp takes its name from "the foul rag-and-bone shop of the heart" in the poem of Yeats, where he is impelled to "enumerate old themes". However, rather than confine itself to these "old themes," this little magazine has a cosmopolitan stance and English editors. At the same time it takes pains to emphasise its Irish location and origin. The editorials have little to say about critical standards or selection policy nor do they betray any strong ideological position. The odd quotation from Walter Benjamin suggests perhaps some radical inclination but the magazine is resolutely devoted to aesthetic rather than overtly political objectives. The editorial notes betray a particular interest in Irish language poetry, declaring the intention to publish Irish originals alongside translations. There is thoughtful recognition of the conflict between making poetry in Irish more accessible and doing undue obeisance to the cultural hegemony of English. Its competition for translations provides the last seven pages of the tenth issue, led by Deirdre Brennan's translation of her own moving poem, "Stillbirth". This commences:

> All during spring, anxious
> lest I lose a second of your life,
> I swelled with bulb and bud,
> the dizzy sap rising in me,
> your pulses echoing
> in every hollow and harbour of my body.
> I could hardly wait for you to lie in my arms.

This is admirably direct and heart-rendingly immediate. It is a small indication of the quality of much of the poetry carried elsewhere in the magazine. The lists of contributors contain some well-known names, Gerald Dawe, John Montague, Dermot Bolger among them, but are mainly formed from names that are new, at least to me. Since the early twentieth century, little magazines have been shown to be the first place of publication for the overwhelming majority of recognised poets and have often set a groundbreaking agenda for new cultural development. An early study by Hoffman, Allen and Ulrich in the States (*The Little Magazine; A History and Bibliography,* 1947) suggested that more than eighty percent of writers made their first appearance in little magazines. THE SHOp is going some way to continuing to fulfill this perennial need.

If we now turn to Northern Ireland we have *The Black Mountain Review* from Ballyclare, and, although now seemingly at its end, the *Honest Ulsterman* from Belfast. *HU* started in 1968, against the background of the Civil Rights Movement. Originally a monthly, *HU* has appeared irregularly since the 1980s and has recently appeared to fade from the scene altogether. What started as a little magazine, sub-titled "monthly handbook for a revolution," developed over time into the voice of a Northern literary establishment that it played a significant part in creating. The last issue of *HU,* appearing in 2001, was dominated by a special feature about Michael Longley, taking up sixty of its hundred and four pages. It also noted the death of its original editor, James Simmons, and promised a celebration of his life in a later issue (yet to appear after two years). *HU* worked its way through a trajectory rather typical of little magazines that are regularly subsidised by Arts Councils, moving from an initial sparky radicalism towards a rather more institutionalised maturity, finally losing much of its original energy.

The Black Mountain Review, on the other hand, is still relatively in its infancy. Founded in 1999, edited by Niall McGrath, it is a quarterly, devoted to poetry and short fiction but also publishing some short reviews. Its paratext reveals high production standards, using a professional designer, with individual covers and good quality paper, printed in a neat, small font. Niall McGrath sees it as consciously bidding to reflect a new balance, making a link between urban and rural cultures in Northern Ireland. The magazine is associated with a non-profit publishing venture, which attracts support from the Arts Council of Northern Ireland, and sometimes anthologises material from the magazine.

The Autumn 2002 issue runs to ninety-five pages. It groups together sets of individual poems by a range of writers, so that, for example, there are six consecutive poems by Nigel McLoughlin, typically with mythic invocations of a harsh country life in Ulster. Here is a flavour of one of them:

> Ours is legendary:
> A strange apple
> Harvest gathered in;
> A pot at the hearth
> That won't run dry
> Filled bitter for the tasting.

We are a people fleeced
For the thief to dress in sheepskin.
Lies like a coach and four
Are driven through
The loopholes of our history.

This sense of an outraged identity is still a frequent theme in Northern Irish poetry. There are five pieces of short fiction, some of them written in an intensely literary language, like Simon Howell's two-page "Meeting Beauty" about a small girl climbing a tree and encountering a jackdaw. New and established writers mingle together in this issue of *The Black Mountain Review*, providing an eclectic mix within which Northern Irish writers appear alongside Americans from Rhode Island, writers in residence from the English midlands, and hitherto unpublished poets from Glasgow.

The prevalent ideology in *The Black Mountain Review* tends to be radical and oppositional, but is marked by an abstention from direct political involvement. Issue 3 has an interview with Robert McLiam Wilson where he describes the main dynamic of his novel, *Ripley Bogle,* as being the leavening of poverty, homelessness and violence by a generous and democratic resource to humour. The writer here distances himself to a degree from the subversive discourse of the main character in his novel. The title of the interview characterises Wilson as "The prophet of the Pleochroic," i.e., as providing a prism that splits light into many colours. This seems to me characteristic of the *Black Mountain Review's* stance, and, indeed of many contemporary little magazines — luxuriating in the use of literary language, taking a generally liberal and cosmopolitan view while still, however, always privileging the aesthetic over the social.

Miscellanies

Little magazines have, in the past, formed a highly distinctive genre, strongly differentiated from the miscellany periodical or the review. As I look now at some examples of contemporary miscellanies I am drawn towards the provisional conclusion that this differentiation has become rather less sharp in today's Ireland. Miscellany periodicals have a long and turbulent history, stemming from early English examples like Edward Cave's *Gentleman's Magazine* (1731-1905) and carried into Ireland later in the eighteenth century. *The Hibernian Magazine or Compendium of Entertaining Knowledge* (1771-1811) blended elegant enlightenment discourse with support for the Protestant

Ascendancy; the deeply subversive *Watty Cox's Magazine* (1807-15) kept alive the memory of the 1798 rebellion with its vigorous and satirical articles and cartoons. Nineteenth-century miscellanies included Samuel Lover and Philip Dixon Hardy's *Dublin Literary Gazette* (1830) – which was quickly discontinued after publishing an article praising the atheist, Shelley – and the anonymous *The Citizen* (1839-41) which published a meld of liberal articles on social issues as well as realist fiction by William Carleton. Twentieth-century exemplars include such controversial and seminal publications as Standish O'Grady's *All Ireland Review*. Later in the century, we see influential models such as George Russell's *The Irish Statesman* (1923-30) and *The Bell* (1940-54), edited by Séan Ó Faoláin, which took on the task of opposing the illiberal values of the post-revolutionary establishment dominated by Eamon de Valera.

The common characteristics of all these miscellanies derive in my view from the dynamics of their form, which is, as Mikhail Bakhtin (*Speech Genres and Other Late Essays,* 1986) says of mixed genres, "deliberately multi-styled and hetero-voiced" with a starting point in the living present. Editors of miscellanies arrange articles, poems and stories in creative ways, often implicitly commenting on one another's messages. As Séan Ó Faoláin says of *The Bell,* such a periodical will engage with current dilemmas and will demonstrate "the merit of acute contemporaneity"; he says that "it comes from where the crowds jostle at the crossroads." This has often led miscellanies into a dissident stance, challenging the status quo, seeking new readerships, inspiring dialogue and debate. This has often had a social or political purpose. Some editors of contemporary miscellanies, as will appear, resist having their productions styled as miscellanies, perhaps believing that the term has connotations of a somewhat trivial approach. However, the examples cited from the tradition outlined above scarcely reflect this judgement.

Examples of miscellany journals published in Ireland today include *The Stinging Fly,* edited from Dublin by Declan Meade. A typical contents page mingles together interviews and poems, short stories, an extract from a play, and a chapter from a novel. It nods to its predecessors by carrying as a motto the same quotation from *The Last Days of Socrates* – about his city's need for stimulation from a stinging insect – that Ó Faoláin took for the banner headline of *The Bell* in the 1940s. It enjoys Arts Council support. Or there is *Imagine,* another quarterly, this time from Waterford, an offshoot of the Tallow Writers Group, with a similar mix of contents. *Imagine* wants to be inclusive, like many other earlier miscellanies, and "to cater for a diversity of interest in all forms of art." It is supported by the local Arts Council in Dungarvan, and it attracts contributions from Seamus Heaney and compliments from the Taoiseach. Both these magazines are handsomely produced on glossy paper with many photographs. Both mix literary modes in the characteristic miscellany manner. Unlike predecessors in the genre, however, neither magazine has any apparent political or social mission. They inhabit an uncharted territory situated somewhere between the insouciant stance of the little magazine and the more politicised world of the traditional Irish miscellany.

This intermediate territory is specifically claimed by the editor of *The Dublin Review*. Brendan Barrington wants his magazine, now approaching its twelfth issue, to embrace a wide variety of high quality materials, including essays, reviews, poetry, fiction, autobiography, and reportage. He distinguishes it from more academic publications (*Irish Review, Studies*) and also from the little poetry magazines. Despite the magazine's "Review" title, preferred by the editor, this is, it seems to me, a quintessential miscellany poise. *The Dublin Review* has a less glossy appearance than many of the magazines we have discussed earlier, but it still has differently coloured covers for each issue, is printed in a distinctive typeface, acknowledges financial assistance from the Arts Council and breathes its editor's concern with quality. If we take the Autumn 2002 issue as typical, it is clear that Barrington's objectives are reflected fully in the contents. He eschews any editorialising but the magazine nevertheless declares an individualist and liberal stance. There is an opening article, centred about immigration procedures at the railway station at Dundalk, which directly challenges the racism implied in the accepted practices in checking for compliance with immigration controls. This is followed immediately by a thoughtful essay about translating Joseph Roth, which touches again, in a more literary mode, on the difficulties of precise understanding of the alien. Other contributions in the same issue also deal with the dilemmas of mediation between some aspect of reality and its literary expression. This is a common theme of Caitríona O'Reilly's consideration of Eoin McNamee's novels based around factual events, of Molly McCloskey's article about the task of skim-reading and abstracting articles on an industrial scale and of Seamus Heaney's brilliant meditation on the act of poetic composition. This demonstrates the miscellany's ability to refract different elements of a theme by placing articles, consciously or otherwise, in a strategic relationship to one another. Once again we encounter in *The Dublin Review* an aversion to direct political intervention, a prioritisation of the literary and aesthetic, accompanied nonetheless by an unimpeachable liberal ethos.

The last publication I want to discuss, a new magazine from Belfast, *Irish Pages*, edited by Chris Agee and Cathal Ó Searcaigh, has some similar characteristics. We only have two issues to go on at present, but the opening number immediately proclaims itself by its exterior as a sober journal of high quality, seeking an international profile, running to a bulky two hundred and forty pages, and intended to be biannual. It is addressed to the "island of Ireland in a purely apolitical and geographic sense". This early disavowal of the sectarian or the overtly political echoes many of the earlier attitudes we have observed in other contemporary journals. Its initial editorial, though, betrays a sharp awareness of the political context in which it stands, referring to John Hewitt's concerns with the issues of nationalism and internationalism, and reflecting on the Troubles and the Ceasefires. The Editor invokes the name of Hubert Butler and republishes a major article by him aiming to situate Ireland in a broader international scene. The first production of the publishing arm of *Irish Pages* is *Unfinished Ireland: Essays on Hubert Butler* (2003). Butler famously planned an all-Ireland journal to be called *The Bridge* designed to follow on from *The Bell's* countering of cultural barriers within Ireland. Chris Agee is also personally conscious of his debts to *The Bell,* which is seen by him as the most relevant earlier Irish model. However, Agee is one of the editors who feels that the term "miscellany" has some negative associations; he prefers to think of *Irish Pages* as constituting a kind of open forum or *agora.*

The second issue ("The Justice Issue") is, like *The Bell,* immediately intent on engaging with the contemporary, albeit contextualised in a very broad view of history. It sets the Bush administration in the States against a background of the mission of Roman imperialism and its opening contributions from Wendell Berry represent a potent internal American critique of post-September 11 policies. The creative writing in this issue enhances the sense that the present is invaded by issues and themes that have been inherited from the past. Seamus Heaney sees these current events through the perspectives of Horace's Ode that evokes Jove and his thunderbolt. The Astronomer Royal (quite literally) takes a cosmic view of the universe within which present human concerns are being played out. The editorial positioning of excerpts from Ciaran Carson's new translation of Dante's *Inferno* against the introductory contributions is highly characteristic of the miscellany periodical's powerful ability to suggest parallels between widely different contributions within one set of covers. Following these articles later by Robin Fairlie's essay on the worldwide debate between environmentalists and the advocates of technology as the provider of answers to environmental problems ensures that, at the least, *Irish Pages* will not fail for lack of breadth of view or ambition. There may, indeed, be some prospect of the local being occluded by the global in the extensive view taken from the Linen Hall. But this issue also has its poems by Irish writers, its Irish language contributions and an extensive section, *From the Irish Archive* that reprints important articles, translations and essays from the twentieth century.

As noted earlier, *Irish Pages* has its own publishing venture and it has agreed a favourable distribution deal involving Eason's and Central Books. The first issue sold two impressions and the print-run of the second ran to about fourteen hundred, which is phenomenal for a publication of this order. The first issue of *Irish Pages* acknowledged the involvement of a wide range of cultural institutions, especially Imagine Belfast, The Orion Society in the United States, and The Linen Hall Library. The Arts Councils are not mentioned although I understand that the ACNI is giving some assistance for coming issues. *Irish Pages* critical reception has been outstanding, especially attracting plaudits for its blending of local and global perspectives. Chris Agee sees the magazine operating along the crucial intellectual intersections between the literary, the historical, the ethical and the social. Indeed, in a sense echoing Séan Ó Faoláin's perception of the role of *The Bell*, this contemporary periodical is still seen as coming from where people are jostling at the intellectual crossroads.

Irish Pages, then, illustrates many of the themes of this article. It shows how a periodical genre, in my view linked to the tradition of the miscellany journal, persists stubbornly while at the same time it mutates, taking account of contemporary pressures. The magazine also demonstrates some of the concern with self-presentation that is common to almost all the publications I have looked at. As we advance further into what Walter Benjamin called the age of mechanical reproduction, typewriter art and basic production standards are no longer acceptable. It also reflects the internationalism that is felt as an essential part of the development of contemporary Irish culture and marks out a degree of emancipation from the preoccupation with identity politics that is seen in earlier Irish journals. Catering for a more international audience also helps to compensate for the restrictions of the limited market available within Ireland itself.

Irish Pages has sought to address at an early stage many of the root problems of circulation, distribution and finance that continually beset its contemporaries. The highly ambivalent relationship with the Arts Councils experienced by many editors has also been short-circuited here, at least at the early stages of the magazine's life. Nicholas Spice in his sensitive and thorough review of the funding of literary magazines in Scotland (*The Funding Of Literary Magazines by the Scottish Arts Council, 2002*) has looked at the funding situation facing editors in Wales and Ireland as well as in Scotland itself. He points out that the Arts Councils in general display a lower concern for editors than for writers. Their needs to earn a reasonable living from their editing are usually effectively ignored. He also recognises that there is a sense in which long-term funding can seem like a "kiss of death" to some little magazine editors, depriving them of their undisciplined firefly quality, the essential provisionality that energises their production. The dilemma for these editors, as he demonstrates forcibly, is that it is very difficult for such a publication to survive economically today without some subsidy of this kind. This is implicitly accepted by both the Arts Councils in Ireland. Their strict policy rules lead them, however, to discriminate in favour of professional and against amateur publications and the same rules also ensure that they decline to subsidise anything which is overtly political. The Southern Irish Arts Council especially wishes to encourage more critical discourse in the literary field, directed at the general reader rather than towards academia, perceiving this as a current area of lack.

One consequence of this is that many contemporary Irish magazines avoid too much overt political involvement, both in the interests of retaining their appeal to a wider international audience and also so as to enhance their chances of being supported by funding bodies. Whether consciously or otherwise this seems a common theme among many of the examples I have examined. Funding bodies, administering public money, may also look more kindly on well-produced internationalist publications without too heavy an investment in ideology. There is also a canny perception at some level that the most faithful modern audience for literary magazines is concerned with the aesthetic and the cultural as much as it is with the social or the political. The future belongs to those periodical publications that manage to live most successfully at the busy crossroads of human communications.

This is a revised version of an article first presented to a conference on Contemporary Irish Literature at the University of Central Lancaster, England, in April 2003.

Malcolm Ballin teaches English at Cardiff University, Wales.

SIGNAL IN A SEA OF NOISE

Sven Birkerts

On the art of editing.

The following is the editorial prefacing the first issue of Agni *(No 57) under the editorship of Sven Birkerts.* Agni *was founded in 1973 and is now based at Boston University.*

My early literary life was powered by fantasies, most of them the standard "grandiose" thing having to do with landing brilliant pieces in glamorous places and winning the esteem of famous and beautiful people. But there were a few that were humbler, and of these one was the fantasy of editing a literary magazine, which, if I scratch away at it, was really much more about being in the thick of literary life than it was about doing the work of taste-making.

I knew nothing, and I still know nothing, except, self-reflexively, the all-important truth that is the first part of this sentence. I certainly didn't imagine that fairly suddenly, at the age of fifty – in the middle of the cliché-ridden period of male self-reckoning – I would find myself emerging from the keyed-up isolation that is writing to take on, all thumbs-feeling, the keyed-up quasi-public life that is editing. Here I am, though, dazedly emerged, and full of thoughts about what has felt like a dauntingly steep learning curve.

To begin with, I was more or less ignorant when I took the *Agni* helm from my predecessor, Askold Melnyczuk, of what was meant by editing. I had allowed the word to become a kind of synonym for "putting together," as in "Let's put together a literary magazine." Wrong. Assemblage, I discovered, is a late-game activity. It took only a few days on site (and taking instruction from the maestro, Managing Editor Eric Grunwald) to see that a magazine is, figuratively speaking, a receiving dock for the products of our collective dream-life – those "pure products" that Williams invoked – and that editing is, before readying manuscripts for publications, very much a business of cutting away the less essential in order to expose the more essential. I mean this both in practical and philosophical terms. Editing, I have found, is the search for signal in a sea of noise.

The winnowing of inessentials would seem to presuppose that one has a clear sense of what the essential is, and here the business gets interesting. I discovered quickly (and self-contradictorily) that I both do and don't have such a sense. I certainly could not, for love or money, set out anything like a firm prescriptive aesthetic: that is what the best writing ought to be; this is what *Agni* will promote. No, my allegiances, both formally and in terms of content, are too widely flung – I have no *jihad* to prosecute. But I have come to see that I do have a very acute set of preferences.

I almost wrote "personal preferences" but checked myself. If I believed they were *merely* personal I would not have taken on the position. I discovered long ago as a critic and reviewer, and now again in the throes of my self-interrogation, that I have preferences I feel are worth fighting for, worth promoting, and that if they don't add up to a clearly defined aesthetic, they nonetheless do describe a bias. It is on behalf of this bias – and because of the beliefs and assumptions that underlie it – that I decided to try my hand at editing *Agni*.

But this is far too abstract, and the editor here needs to edit himself. What I am trying to say is that I am, at root, moved and heartened when I find what strike me as the best words in the best order, never mind the ostensible subject. Language used with high artistic consciousness. Words arranged in a way that declares: here is a living mind; here is a spirit. A good sentence describing piece of gummy candy can telegraph this as certainly as any high-flown rhetoric on the soul or the fate of nations. Reading literature attends as much to the saying as to the said.

What's more, when I read language that connects me to the world, I react, and my reaction has an outward fling: I want to carry the news to others. Before, I have done this by writing essays and reviews, and I'm sure that will continue. But the special attraction of editing a magazine is that rather than waiting for others to package the news for me to evaluate, I have a chance – neat reversal – to evaluate and put out the news myself. Is this vanity or public service? Probably both.

There's no getting around it: putting out a journal asks me to believe that my opinion stands for more than itself, that it has reach, that other people feel enough the same – or can be made to feel enough the same – about life. In other words, I have to trust that many of us go about in search of the quickening word, the phrase that can break through the fatigue of inundation, and the work that repositions the self, however slightly – as almost every good book did when we were younger.

I start out, then with the belief that my longings, if not universal, are at least not *just* mine, and that if I can identify the work that honestly reaches me, then the broader dissemination of that work may have some value, creating a needed intensification where it counts, in the self of the reader. Askold's thirty-year experiment showed me that this could happen in larger political and social ways as well. I only hope I can grow my biases outward with the same confidence he did.

Whatever I may have imagined and projected when I set out to edit my first issue, the fact is that as I write this I have the contents of my debut issue more or less in place. Instead of thinking in terms of what I would *like* to do, then, I can ask myself what I have already done, where my readerly instincts have taken me. Looking over the contents of this first issue, I will confess I am confounded. Squint at the list how I will, I cannot find – stylistically or thematically – anything that looks like the figure in the carpet. If I had less faith in my responses – if I doubted that they were somehow organic and integral – I would be more nervous.

But then the answer, the justification, comes: I see that what I need in this inspection is a change in the frame of reference. I have been looking for commonality in too narrowly defined a sense. So when my associate fiction editor, Jenna Blum, asked me these same questions yesterday, I answered, almost abruptly, "Each of these pieces is completely unique, completely unlike any other." As soon as I said that, it felt right. Difference – uniqueness – as a basis of commonality, I like that. At least enough to make it this moment's platform.

And now, with my own space running out, I will only add that I hope you agree and that you take the time to ponder how it is that so many universes can be collected in such a small place.

Sven Birkerts is an essayist and critic. His books include The Gutenberg Elegies: The Fate of Reading in an Electronic Age *(Faber, 1996) and* My Sky Blue Trades: Growing Up Counter in a Contrary Age *(Penguin, 2003).*